# LaTeX

*A Document Preparation System*

*User's Guide and Reference Manual*

## Leslie Lamport

Digital Equipment Corporation

Illustrations by Duane Bibby

### ADDISON–WESLEY

Boston • San Francisco • New York • Toronto • Montreal
London • Munich • Paris • Madrid
Capetown • Sidney • Tokyo • Singapore • Mexico City

The publisher offers discounts on this book when ordered in quantity for special sales. For more information, please contact:

Pearson Education Corporate Sales Division
201 W. 103rd Street
Indianapolis, IN 46290
(800) 428-5331
corpsales@pearsoned.com

Visit AW on the Web: www.awl.com/cseng/

*Library of Congress Cataloging-in-Publication Data*
Lamport, Leslie.
    LaTeX : a document preparation system / Leslie Lamport.—2nd ed.
       p. cm.
    Includes bibliographical references and index.
    ISBN 0-201-52983-1
    1. LaTeX (Computer file)  2. Computerized typesetting.  I. Title.
    Z253.4.L38L35 1994
    682.2′2544536—dc20                       93–39691
                                                             CIP

This documentation was prepared with LaTeX and reproduced by Addison-Wesley from camera-ready copy supplied by the author.

This book describes LaTeX2$_\varepsilon$, the second widely released version of LaTeX.

Text printed on recycled and acid-free paper.
ISBN  0201529831
13 1415161718 CRW  04 03 02 01
13th Printing    November 2001

*To Ellen*

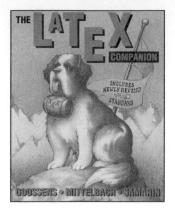  

*The LATEX Companion*

Michel Goossens, Frank Mittelbach, and Alexander Samarin

An in-depth guide to LATEX based on the current LATEX $2_\varepsilon$ standard. Packed with descriptions of over 150 packages, and techniques for defining new commands and environments.

*"The LATEX Companion* is the place to look if you can't find what you need in my book."
– Leslie Lamport

*The LATEX Graphics Companion*

Michel Goossens, Sebastian Rahtz, and Frank Mittelbach

Everything you need to know about incorporating graphics files into a LATEX document. Provides the first full description of the standard LATEX color and graphics packages, and shows how you can combine TEX and PostScript capabilities to produce beautifully illustrated pages.

*The LATEX Web Companion*

Michel Goossens and Sebastian Rahtz

This book shows how you can publish LATEX documents on the Web. HTML and today's Web browsers deal inadequately with the nontextual components of scientific documents. This book, describes tools and techniques for transforming LATEX sources into Web formats for electronic publication, and for transforming Web sources into LATEX documents for optimal printing.

---

# Look for forthcoming books in the Addison-Wesley Series on Tools and Techniques for Computer Typesetting

Frank Mittelbach, Series Editor

## http://www.awl.com/cseng

# Contents

**Preface**                                                                    **xv**

**1  Getting Acquainted**                                                        **1**
   1.1   How to Avoid Reading This Book . . . . . . . . . . . . . .      2
   1.2   How to Read This Book . . . . . . . . . . . . . . . . . .      3
   1.3   The Game of the Name . . . . . . . . . . . . . . . . . .      5
   1.4   Turning Typing into Typography . . . . . . . . . . . . . .      5
   1.5   Why LaTeX? . . . . . . . . . . . . . . . . . . . . . . . .      7
   1.6   Turning Ideas into Input . . . . . . . . . . . . . . . . .      8
   1.7   Trying It Out . . . . . . . . . . . . . . . . . . . . . . .      8

**2  Getting Started**                                                          **11**
   2.1   Preparing an Input File . . . . . . . . . . . . . . . . . .     12
   2.2   The Input . . . . . . . . . . . . . . . . . . . . . . . . .     13
         2.2.1   Sentences and Paragraphs . . . . . . . . . . . . .     13
                 Quotation Marks . . . . . . . . . . . . . . . . .     13
                 Dashes . . . . . . . . . . . . . . . . . . . . . .     14
                 Space After a Period . . . . . . . . . . . . . . .     14
                 Special Symbols . . . . . . . . . . . . . . . . . .     15
                 Simple Text-Generating Commands . . . . . . . . .     15
                 Emphasizing Text . . . . . . . . . . . . . . . . .     16
                 Preventing Line Breaks . . . . . . . . . . . . . .     17
                 Footnotes . . . . . . . . . . . . . . . . . . . . .     17
                 Formulas . . . . . . . . . . . . . . . . . . . . .     18
                 Ignorable Input . . . . . . . . . . . . . . . . . .     19
         2.2.2   The Document . . . . . . . . . . . . . . . . . . .     19
                 The Document Class . . . . . . . . . . . . . . . .     19
                 The Title "Page" . . . . . . . . . . . . . . . . .     20
         2.2.3   Sectioning . . . . . . . . . . . . . . . . . . . .     21
         2.2.4   Displayed Material . . . . . . . . . . . . . . . .     23
                 Quotations . . . . . . . . . . . . . . . . . . . .     24
                 Lists . . . . . . . . . . . . . . . . . . . . . . .     24

Poetry . . . . . . . . . . . . . . . . . . . . . . 25
Displayed Formulas . . . . . . . . . . . . . . . 26
2.2.5  Declarations . . . . . . . . . . . . . . . . . . . . . 27
2.3  Running LaTeX . . . . . . . . . . . . . . . . . . . . . . . 28
2.4  Helpful Hints . . . . . . . . . . . . . . . . . . . . . . . . 31
2.5  Summary . . . . . . . . . . . . . . . . . . . . . . . . . 32

**3  Carrying On**                                         **35**
3.1  Changing the Type Style . . . . . . . . . . . . . . . . . 36
3.2  Symbols from Other Languages . . . . . . . . . . . . . . 38
3.2.1  Accents . . . . . . . . . . . . . . . . . . . . . . . . 38
3.2.2  Symbols . . . . . . . . . . . . . . . . . . . . . . . . 38
3.3  Mathematical Formulas . . . . . . . . . . . . . . . . . . 39
3.3.1  Some Common Structures . . . . . . . . . . . . . . 40
Subscripts and Superscripts . . . . . . . . . . . 40
Fractions . . . . . . . . . . . . . . . . . . . . . . 40
Roots . . . . . . . . . . . . . . . . . . . . . . . . 40
Ellipsis . . . . . . . . . . . . . . . . . . . . . . . 40
3.3.2  Mathematical Symbols . . . . . . . . . . . . . . . . 41
Greek Letters . . . . . . . . . . . . . . . . . . . 41
Calligraphic Letters . . . . . . . . . . . . . . . . 42
A Menagerie of Mathematical Symbols . . . . . . . 42
Log-like Functions . . . . . . . . . . . . . . . . . 44
3.3.3  Arrays . . . . . . . . . . . . . . . . . . . . . . . . . 45
The **array** Environment . . . . . . . . . . . . . . 45
Vertical Alignment . . . . . . . . . . . . . . . . . 46
More Complex Arrays . . . . . . . . . . . . . . . 46
3.3.4  Delimiters . . . . . . . . . . . . . . . . . . . . . . . 46
3.3.5  Multiline Formulas . . . . . . . . . . . . . . . . . . 47
3.3.6  Putting One Thing Above Another . . . . . . . . . . 49
Over- and Underlining . . . . . . . . . . . . . . . 49
Accents . . . . . . . . . . . . . . . . . . . . . . . 49
Stacking Symbols . . . . . . . . . . . . . . . . . 50
3.3.7  Spacing in Math Mode . . . . . . . . . . . . . . . . 50
3.3.8  Changing Style in Math Mode . . . . . . . . . . . . 51
Type Style . . . . . . . . . . . . . . . . . . . . . 51
Math Style . . . . . . . . . . . . . . . . . . . . . 52
3.3.9  When All Else Fails . . . . . . . . . . . . . . . . . . 52
3.4  Defining Commands and Environments . . . . . . . . . . 53
3.4.1  Defining Commands . . . . . . . . . . . . . . . . . 53
3.4.2  Defining Environments . . . . . . . . . . . . . . . . 55
3.4.3  Theorems and Such . . . . . . . . . . . . . . . . . 56
3.5  Figures and Other Floating Bodies . . . . . . . . . . . . 58

     3.5.1   Figures and Tables . . . . . . . . . . . . . . . . . 58
     3.5.2   Marginal Notes . . . . . . . . . . . . . . . . . . 59
  3.6  Lining It Up in Columns . . . . . . . . . . . . . . . . . 60
     3.6.1   The tabbing Environment . . . . . . . . . . . . 60
     3.6.2   The tabular Environment . . . . . . . . . . . . 62
  3.7  Simulating Typed Text . . . . . . . . . . . . . . . . . 63

**4  Moving Information Around         65**
  4.1  The Table of Contents . . . . . . . . . . . . . . . . . 66
  4.2  Cross-References . . . . . . . . . . . . . . . . . . . . 67
  4.3  Bibliography and Citation . . . . . . . . . . . . . . . 69
     4.3.1   Using BibTeX . . . . . . . . . . . . . . . . . . 70
     4.3.2   Doing It Yourself . . . . . . . . . . . . . . . . 71
  4.4  Splitting Your Input . . . . . . . . . . . . . . . . . . 72
  4.5  Making an Index or Glossary . . . . . . . . . . . . . 74
     4.5.1   Compiling the Entries . . . . . . . . . . . . . 74
     4.5.2   Producing an Index or Glossary by Yourself . . . . . . . 75
  4.6  Keyboard Input and Screen Output . . . . . . . . . . 76
  4.7  Sending Your Document . . . . . . . . . . . . . . . . 77

**5  Other Document Classes         79**
  5.1  Books . . . . . . . . . . . . . . . . . . . . . . . . . . 80
  5.2  Slides . . . . . . . . . . . . . . . . . . . . . . . . . . 80
     5.2.1   Slides and Overlays . . . . . . . . . . . . . . 81
     5.2.2   Notes . . . . . . . . . . . . . . . . . . . . . . 83
     5.2.3   Printing Only Some Slides and Notes . . . . . . . . . 83
     5.2.4   Other Text . . . . . . . . . . . . . . . . . . . 84
  5.3  Letters . . . . . . . . . . . . . . . . . . . . . . . . . 84

**6  Designing It Yourself         87**
  6.1  Document and Page Styles . . . . . . . . . . . . . . . 88
     6.1.1   Document-Class Options . . . . . . . . . . . . 88
     6.1.2   Page Styles . . . . . . . . . . . . . . . . . . . 89
     6.1.3   The Title Page and Abstract . . . . . . . . . . 90
     6.1.4   Customizing the Style . . . . . . . . . . . . . 91
  6.2  Line and Page Breaking . . . . . . . . . . . . . . . . 93
     6.2.1   Line Breaking . . . . . . . . . . . . . . . . . 93
     6.2.2   Page Breaking . . . . . . . . . . . . . . . . . 96
  6.3  Numbering . . . . . . . . . . . . . . . . . . . . . . . 97
  6.4  Length, Spaces, and Boxes . . . . . . . . . . . . . . . 99
     6.4.1   Length . . . . . . . . . . . . . . . . . . . . . 99
     6.4.2   Spaces . . . . . . . . . . . . . . . . . . . . . 101
     6.4.3   Boxes . . . . . . . . . . . . . . . . . . . . . . 103
          LR Boxes . . . . . . . . . . . . . . . . . . . 104

| | | | |
|---|---|---|---|
| | | Parboxes | 104 |
| | | Rule Boxes | 106 |
| | | Raising and Lowering Boxes | 107 |
| | | Saving Boxes | 107 |
| | 6.4.4 | Formatting with Boxes | 108 |
| 6.5 | | Centering and "Flushing" | 111 |
| 6.6 | | List-Making Environments | 112 |
| | 6.6.1 | The list Environment | 112 |
| | 6.6.2 | The trivlist Environment | 115 |
| 6.7 | | Fonts | 115 |
| | 6.7.1 | Changing Type Size | 115 |
| | 6.7.2 | Special Symbols | 116 |

**7 Pictures and Colors** — **117**

| | | | |
|---|---|---|---|
| 7.1 | | Pictures | 118 |
| | 7.1.1 | The picture Environment | 119 |
| | 7.1.2 | Picture Objects | 120 |
| | | Text | 120 |
| | | Boxes | 120 |
| | | Straight Lines | 122 |
| | | Arrows | 123 |
| | | Stacks | 123 |
| | | Circles | 124 |
| | | Ovals and Rounded Corners | 124 |
| | | Framing | 125 |
| | 7.1.3 | Curves | 125 |
| | 7.1.4 | Grids | 126 |
| | 7.1.5 | Reusing Objects | 127 |
| | 7.1.6 | Repeated Patterns | 127 |
| | 7.1.7 | Some Hints on Drawing Pictures | 128 |
| 7.2 | | The graphics Package | 129 |
| 7.3 | | Color | 131 |

**8 Errors** — **133**

| | | |
|---|---|---|
| 8.1 | Finding the Error | 134 |
| 8.2 | LaTeX's Error Messages | 136 |
| 8.3 | TeX's Error Messages | 140 |
| 8.4 | LaTeX Warnings | 145 |
| 8.5 | TeX Warnings | 147 |

**A Using *MakeIndex*** — **149**

| | | | |
|---|---|---|---|
| A.1 | | How to Use *MakeIndex* | 150 |
| A.2 | | How to Generate Index Entries | 150 |
| | A.2.1 | When, Why, What, and How to Index | 150 |

    A.2.2  The Basics . . . . . . . . . . . . . . . . 151

    A.2.3  The Fine Print . . . . . . . . . . . . . . 153

  A.3  Error Messages . . . . . . . . . . . . . . . . . 154

**B  The Bibliography Database        155**

  B.1  The Format of the `bib` File . . . . . . . . . . . 156

    B.1.1  The Entry Format . . . . . . . . . . . . 156

    B.1.2  The Text of a Field . . . . . . . . . . . . 157

        Names . . . . . . . . . . . . . . . . . . 157

        Titles . . . . . . . . . . . . . . . . . . 158

    B.1.3  Abbreviations . . . . . . . . . . . . . . 158

    B.1.4  Cross-References . . . . . . . . . . . . . 159

  B.2  The Entries . . . . . . . . . . . . . . . . . . . 160

    B.2.1  Entry Types . . . . . . . . . . . . . . . 160

    B.2.2  Fields . . . . . . . . . . . . . . . . . . 162

**C  Reference Manual        165**

  C.1  Commands and Environments . . . . . . . . . . 166

    C.1.1  Command Names and Arguments . . . . . 166

    C.1.2  Environments . . . . . . . . . . . . . . 167

    C.1.3  Fragile Commands . . . . . . . . . . . . 167

    C.1.4  Declarations . . . . . . . . . . . . . . . 168

    C.1.5  Invisible Commands and Environments . . . . 169

    C.1.6  The \\ Command . . . . . . . . . . . . 169

  C.2  The Structure of the Document . . . . . . . . . 170

  C.3  Sentences and Paragraphs . . . . . . . . . . . . 170

    C.3.1  Making Sentences . . . . . . . . . . . . 170

    C.3.2  Making Paragraphs . . . . . . . . . . . . 171

    C.3.3  Footnotes . . . . . . . . . . . . . . . . 172

    C.3.4  Accents and Special Symbols . . . . . . . 173

  C.4  Sectioning and Table of Contents . . . . . . . . . . 174

    C.4.1  Sectioning Commands . . . . . . . . . . 174

    C.4.2  The Appendix . . . . . . . . . . . . . . 175

    C.4.3  Table of Contents . . . . . . . . . . . . 175

    C.4.4  Style Parameters . . . . . . . . . . . . . 176

  C.5  Classes, Packages, and Page Styles . . . . . . . . 176

    C.5.1  Document Class . . . . . . . . . . . . . 176

    C.5.2  Packages . . . . . . . . . . . . . . . . . 178

    C.5.3  Page Styles . . . . . . . . . . . . . . . 179

    C.5.4  The Title Page and Abstract . . . . . . . 181

  C.6  Displayed Paragraphs . . . . . . . . . . . . . . 183

    C.6.1  Quotations and Verse . . . . . . . . . . 184

    C.6.2  List-Making Environments . . . . . . . . 184

|  | C.6.3 | The `list` and `trivlist` Environments | 185 |
|  | C.6.4 | Verbatim | 186 |
| C.7 | | Mathematical Formulas | 187 |
|  | C.7.1 | Math Mode Environments | 187 |
|  | C.7.2 | Common Structures | 189 |
|  | C.7.3 | Mathematical Symbols | 189 |
|  | C.7.4 | Arrays | 190 |
|  | C.7.5 | Delimiters | 190 |
|  | C.7.6 | Putting One Thing Above Another | 190 |
|  | C.7.7 | Spacing | 191 |
|  | C.7.8 | Changing Style | 191 |
| C.8 | | Definitions, Numbering, and Programming | 192 |
|  | C.8.1 | Defining Commands | 192 |
|  | C.8.2 | Defining Environments | 192 |
|  | C.8.3 | Theorem-like Environments | 193 |
|  | C.8.4 | Numbering | 194 |
|  | C.8.5 | The `ifthen` Package | 195 |
| C.9 | | Figures and Other Floating Bodies | 197 |
|  | C.9.1 | Figures and Tables | 197 |
|  | C.9.2 | Marginal Notes | 200 |
| C.10 | | Lining It Up in Columns | 201 |
|  | C.10.1 | The `tabbing` Environment | 201 |
|  | C.10.2 | The `array` and `tabular` Environments | 204 |
| C.11 | | Moving Information Around | 207 |
|  | C.11.1 | Files | 207 |
|  | C.11.2 | Cross-References | 209 |
|  | C.11.3 | Bibliography and Citation | 209 |
|  | C.11.4 | Splitting the Input | 210 |
|  | C.11.5 | Index and Glossary | 211 |
|  |  | Producing an Index | 211 |
|  |  | Compiling the Entries | 212 |
|  | C.11.6 | Terminal Input and Output | 212 |
| C.12 | | Line and Page Breaking | 213 |
|  | C.12.1 | Line Breaking | 213 |
|  | C.12.2 | Page Breaking | 214 |
| C.13 | | Lengths, Spaces, and Boxes | 215 |
|  | C.13.1 | Length | 215 |
|  | C.13.2 | Space | 216 |
|  | C.13.3 | Boxes | 217 |
| C.14 | | Pictures and Color | 219 |
|  | C.14.1 | The `picture` Environment | 219 |
|  |  | Picture-Mode Commands | 220 |
|  |  | Picture Objects | 221 |

Picture Declarations . . . . . . . . . . . . . . . . . . . 223
C.14.2 The graphics Package . . . . . . . . . . . . . . . . . 223
C.14.3 The color Package . . . . . . . . . . . . . . . . . . . 224
C.15 Font Selection . . . . . . . . . . . . . . . . . . . . . . . 225
C.15.1 Changing the Type Style . . . . . . . . . . . . . . . 225
C.15.2 Changing the Type Size . . . . . . . . . . . . . . . . 226
C.15.3 Special Symbols . . . . . . . . . . . . . . . . . . . 226

D  What's New                                               227

E  Using Plain TₑX Commands                                 231

Bibliography                                               235

Index                                                      237

# List of Tables

3.1   Accents. . . . . . . . . . . . . . . . . . . . . . . . .   38
3.2   Non-English Symbols. . . . . . . . . . . . . . . . . .   39
3.3   Greek Letters. . . . . . . . . . . . . . . . . . . . .   41
3.4   Binary Operation Symbols. . . . . . . . . . . . . . .   42
3.5   Relation Symbols. . . . . . . . . . . . . . . . . . .   43
3.6   Arrow Symbols . . . . . . . . . . . . . . . . . . . .   43
3.7   Miscellaneous Symbols. . . . . . . . . . . . . . . . .   43
3.8   Variable-sized Symbols. . . . . . . . . . . . . . . .   44
3.9   Log-like Functions. . . . . . . . . . . . . . . . . .   44
3.10  Delimiters. . . . . . . . . . . . . . . . . . . . . .   47
3.11  Math Mode Accents. . . . . . . . . . . . . . . . . . .   50

# List of Figures

6.1   Boxes and how TeX puts them together. . . . . . . . .   103
6.2   The complete definition of the \face command. . . . . .   110
6.3   The format of a list. . . . . . . . . . . . . . . . .   113

7.1   Points and their coordinates. . . . . . . . . . . . .   119
7.2   \put (1.4,2.6){\line(3,-1){4.8}} . . . . . . . . . . .   122

C.1   Making footnotes without the \footnote command. . . . .   173
C.2   Sectioning and table of contents commands. . . . . . .   174
C.3   Page style parameters. . . . . . . . . . . . . . . . .   182
C.4   An example title. . . . . . . . . . . . . . . . . . .   183
C.5   Writing programs with the ifthen package's commands. . . . .   196
C.6   A tabbing environment example. . . . . . . . . . . . .   202
C.7   Examples of the tabular and tabular* environments. . . . . .   204
C.8   A sample picture environment. . . . . . . . . . . . .   220

# Preface

The first edition of this book appeared in 1985. It described LATEX 2.09, the first widely used version of LATEX. Since then, LATEX has become extremely popular, with many thousands of users around the world. Its functionality has grown through the efforts of many people. The time has come for a new version, LATEX $2_\varepsilon$, which is described in this edition. LATEX $2_\varepsilon$ includes many of the enhancements that were made to LATEX 2.09, as well as some new ones.

I implemented most of LATEX 2.09 myself. LATEX $2_\varepsilon$ was implemented by a group led by Frank Mittelbach, which included Johannes Braams, David Carlisle, Michael Downes, Alan Jeffrey, Sebastian Rahtz, Chris Rowley, and Rainer Schöpf. They were assisted by many testers of the new version, and by the following organizations: the American Mathematical Society, the Open University (UK), and the Zentrum für Datenverarbeitung der Universität Mainz. Lyle Ramshaw helped with the implementation of Bezier curves. My thanks to all of these people—especially Frank and Chris, with whom I have spent many enjoyable hours arguing about LATEX.

LATEX has been made more useful by two programs: BIBTEX, written by Oren Patashnik, and *MakeIndex*, written by Pehong Chen and modified by Nelson Beebe.

Many people helped me write this book—often without knowing it. Advice given to me over the years by Cynthia Hibbard and Mary-Claire van Leunen has found its way onto a number of these pages. Andrei Broder was my local informant for Romanian. Helen Goldstein assisted with research on matters ranging from art to zoology.

This edition was improved by the corrections and suggestions of Marc Brown, Michel Goossens, and the implementers of LATEX $2_\varepsilon$. Stephen Harrison helped produce the final output. Errors and infelicities in the first printing were found by Rosemary Bailey, Malcolm Clark, and Ellen Gilkerson. The following people found errors in, or suggested improvements to, the previous edition: Martín Abadi, Helmer Aslaksen, Barbara Beeton, Rick Clark, John DeTreville, Mathieu Federspiel, Michael Fischer, Stephen Gildea, Andy Hisgen, Joseph Hurler, Louis E. Janus, Dave Johnson, Charles Karney, Nori Kawasaki, Steve Kelem, Mark Kent, William LeFebvre, Jerry Leichter, Hank Lewis, Stephen Peckham,

Hal Perkins, Flavio Rose, Scott Simpson, David Sullivan, Matthew Swift, Walter Taylor, Joe Weening, Sam Whidden, Edgar Whipple, Chris Wilson, David Wise, and Rusty Wright. I also received helpful comments and complaints about preliminary versions of LaTeX and of the first edition of this book from Todd Allen, Robert Amsler, David Bacon, Stephen Barnard, Per Bothner, David Braunegg, Daniel Brotsky, Chuck Buckley, Pavel Curtis, Russell Greiner, Andrew Hanson, Michael Harrison, B. J. Herbison, Calvin W. Jackson, David Kosower, Kenneth Laws, Tim Morgan, Mark Moriconi, Stuart Reges, A. Wayne Slawson, David Smith, Michael Spivak, Mark Stickel, Gary Swanson, Mike Urban, Mark Wadsworth, and Gio Wiederhold. Assistance in the development of LaTeX 2.09 was provided by David Fuchs, Richard Furuta, Marshall Henrichs, Lynn Ruggles, Richard Southall, Chris Torek, Howard Trickey, and SRI International.

Since the introduction of version 2.09, my work on LaTeX has been supported by Digital Equipment Corporation. I want to thank Robert Taylor and all the other members of Digital's Systems Research Center for making it a fun place to work.

Finally, I want to express my special thanks to two men who made this book possible. Donald Knuth created TeX, the program on which LaTeX is based. He also answered all my questions, even the stupid ones, and was always willing to explain TeX's mysteries. Peter Gordon persuaded me to write the first edition, despite my doubts that anyone would buy a book about a typesetting system. Over the years, he has provided advice, fine dining, and friendship.

L. L.

Palo Alto, California
September 1994

# CHAPTER 1
# Getting Acquainted

LaTeX is a system for typesetting documents. Its first widely available version, mysteriously numbered 2.09, appeared in 1985. LaTeX is now extremely popular in the scientific and academic communities, and it is used extensively in industry. It has become a *lingua franca* of the scientific world; scientists send their papers electronically to colleagues around the world in the form of LaTeX input.

Over the years, various nonstandard enhancements were made to LaTeX 2.09 to overcome some of its limitations. LaTeX input that made use of these enhancements would not work properly at all sites. A new version of LaTeX was needed to keep a Tower of Babel from rising. The current version of LaTeX, with the somewhat less mysterious number $2_\varepsilon$, was released in 1994. LaTeX $2_\varepsilon$ contains an improved method for handling different styles of type, commands for including graphics and producing colors, and many other new features.

Almost all standard LaTeX 2.09 input files will work with LaTeX $2_\varepsilon$. However, to take advantage of the new features, users must learn a few new LaTeX $2_\varepsilon$ conventions. LaTeX 2.09 users should read Appendix D to find out what has changed. The rest of this book is about LaTeX, which, until a newer version appears, means LaTeX $2_\varepsilon$.

LaTeX is available for just about any computer made today. The versions that run on these different systems are essentially the same; an input file created according to the directions in this book should produce the same output with any of them. However, how you actually run LaTeX depends upon the computer system. Moreover, some new features may not be available on all systems when LaTeX $2_\varepsilon$ is first released. For each computer system, there is a short companion to this book, titled something like *Local Guide to LaTeX for the McKludge PC*, containing information specific to that system. I will call it simply the *Local Guide*. It is distributed with the LaTeX software.

There is another companion to this book, *The LaTeX Companion* by Goossens, Mittelbach, and Samarin [3]. This companion is an in-depth guide to LaTeX and to its *packages*—standard enhancements that can be used at any site to provide additional features. The LaTeX *Companion* is the place to look if you can't find what you need in this book. It describes more than a hundred packages.

## 1.1   How to Avoid Reading This Book

Many people would rather learn about a program at their computer than by reading a book. There is a small sample LaTeX input file named `small2e.tex` that shows how to prepare your own input files for typesetting simple documents. Before reading any further, you might want to examine `small2e.tex` with a text editor and modify it to make an input file for a document of your own, then run LaTeX on this file and see what it produces. The *Local Guide* will tell you how to find `small2e.tex` and run LaTeX on your computer; it may also contain information about text editors. Be careful not to destroy the original version of `small2e.tex`; you'll probably want to look at it again.

The file `small2e.tex` is only forty lines long, and it shows how to produce only very simple documents. There is a longer file named `sample2e.tex` that contains more information. If `small2e.tex` doesn't tell you how to do something, you can try looking at `sample2e.tex`.

If you prefer to learn more about a program before you use it, read on Almost everything in the sample input files is explained in the first two chapters of this book.

## 1.2   How to Read This Book

While `sample2e.tex` illustrates many of LaTeX's features, it is still only about two hundred lines long, and there is a lot that it doesn't explain. Eventually, you will want to typeset a document that requires more sophisticated formatting than you can obtain by imitating the two sample input files. You will then have to look in this book for the necessary information. You can read the section containing the information you need without having to read everything that precedes it. However, all the later chapters assume you have read Chapters 1 and 2. For example, suppose you want to set one paragraph of a document in small type. Looking up "type size" in the index or browsing through the table of contents will lead you to Section 6.7.1, which talks about "declarations" and their "scope"—simple concepts that are explained in Chapter 2. It will take just a minute or two to learn what to do if you've already read Chapter 2; it could be quite frustrating if you haven't. So, it's best to read the first two chapters now, before you need them.

LaTeX's input is a file containing the document's text together with commands that describe the document's structure; its output is a file of typesetting instructions. Another program must be run to convert these instructions into printed output. With a high-resolution printer, LaTeX can generate book-quality typesetting.

This book tells you how to prepare a LaTeX input file. The current chapter discusses the philosophy underlying LaTeX; here is a brief sketch of what's in the remaining chapters and appendices:

**Chapter 2** explains what you should know to handle most simple documents and to read the rest of the book. Section 2.5 contains a summary of everything in the chapter; it serves as a short reference manual.

**Chapter 3** describes logical structures for handling a variety of formatting problems. Section 3.4 explains how to define your own commands, which can save typing when you write the document and retyping when you change it. It's a good idea to read the introduction—up to the beginning of Section 3.1—before reading any other part of the chapter.

**Chapter 4** contains features especially useful for large documents, including automatic cross-referencing and commands for splitting a large file into smaller pieces. Section 4.7 discusses sending your document electronically.

**Chapter 5** is about making books, slides, and letters (the kind you send by post).

**Chapter 6** describes the visual formatting of the text. It has information about changing the style of your document, explains how to correct bad line and page breaks, and tells how to do your own formatting of structures not explicitly handled by LaTeX.

**Chapter 7** discusses pictures—drawing them yourself and inserting ones prepared with other programs—and color.

**Chapter 8** explains how to deal with errors. This is where you should look when LaTeX prints an error message that you don't understand.

**Appendix A** describes how to use the *MakeIndex* program to make an index.

**Appendix B** describes how to make a bibliographic database for use with BibTeX, a separate program that provides an automatic bibliography feature for LaTeX.

**Appendix C** is a reference manual that compactly describes all LaTeX's features, including many advanced ones not described in the main text. If a command introduced in the earlier chapters seems to lack some necessary capabilities, check its description here to see if it has them. This appendix is a convenient place to refresh your memory of how something works.

**Appendix D** describes the differences between the current version of LaTeX and the original version, LaTeX 2.09.

**Appendix E** is for the reader who knows TeX, the program on which LaTeX is built, and wants to use TeX commands that are not described in this book.

When you face a formatting problem, the best place to look for a solution is in the table of contents. Browsing through it will give you a good idea of what LaTeX has to offer. If the table of contents doesn't work, look in the index; I have tried to make it friendly and informative.

Each section of Chapters 3–7 is reasonably self-contained, assuming only that you have read Chapter 2. Where additional knowledge is required, explicit cross-references are given. Appendix C is also self-contained, but a command's description may be hard to understand without first reading the corresponding description in the earlier chapters.

The descriptions of most LaTeX commands include examples of their use. In this book, examples are formatted in two columns, as follows:

The left column shows the printed output; the right column contains the input that produced it.

```
The left column shows the printed output;
the right column contains the input that
produced it.
```

Note the special typewriter type style in the right column. It indicates what you type—either text that you put in the input file or something like a file name that you type as part of a command to the computer.

Since the sample output is printed in a narrower column, and with smaller type, than LaTeX normally uses, it won't look exactly like the output you'd get from that input. The convention of the output appearing to the left of the corresponding input is generally also used when commands and their output are listed in tables.

## 1.3    The Game of the Name

The TeX in LaTeX refers to Donald Knuth's TeX typesetting system. The LaTeX program is a special version of TeX that understands LaTeX commands. Think of LaTeX as a house built with the lumber and nails provided by TeX. You don't need lumber and nails to live in a house, but they are handy for adding an extra room. Most LaTeX users never need to know any more about TeX than they can learn from this book. However, the lower-level TeX commands described in *The TeXbook* [4] can be very useful when creating a new package for LaTeX.

I will use the term "TeX" when describing standard TeX features and "LaTeX" when describing features unique to LaTeX, but the distinction will be of interest mainly to readers already familiar with TeX. You may ignore it and use the two names interchangeably.

One of the hardest things about using LaTeX is deciding how to pronounce it. This is also one of the few things I'm not going to tell you about LaTeX, since pronunciation is best determined by usage, not fiat. TeX is usually pronounced *teck*, making *lah*-teck, lah-*teck*, and *lay*-teck the logical choices; but language is not always logical, so *lay*-tecks is also possible.

The written word carries more legal complications than the spoken, and the need to distinguish TeX and LaTeX from similarly spelled products restricts how you may write them. The best way to refer to these programs is by their logos, which can be generated with simple LaTeX commands. When this is impossible, as in an e-mail message, you should write them as `TeX` and `LaTeX`, where the unusual capitalization identifies these computer programs.

## 1.4    Turning Typing into Typography

Traditionally, an author provides a publisher with a typed manuscript. The publisher's typographic designer decides how the manuscript is to be formatted, specifying the length of the printed line, what style of type to use, how much

space to leave above and below section headings, and many other things that
determine the printed document's appearance. The designer writes a series of
instructions to the typesetter, who uses them to decide where on the page to put
each of the author's words and symbols. In the old days, typesetters produced
a matrix of metal type for each page; today they produce computer files. In
either case, their output is used to control the machine that does the actual
typesetting.

LaTeX is your typographic designer, and TeX is its typesetter. The LaTeX
commands that you type are translated into lower-level TeX typesetting commands. Being a modern typesetter, TeX produces a computer file, called the
*device-independent* or `dvi` file. The *Local Guide* explains how to use this file
to generate a printed document with your computer. It also explains how to
view your document on your computer, using a screen previewer. Unless your
document is very short, you will want to see the typeset version as you're writing
it. Use a previewer instead of laying waste to our planet's dwindling forests by
printing lots of intermediate versions. In fact, unless you want to take a copy
with you on a wilderness expedition, you may never have to print it at all. It
is easier and faster to distribute your document electronically than by mailing
paper copies.

A human typographic designer knows what the manuscript is generally about
and uses this knowledge in deciding how to format it. Consider the following
typewritten manuscript:

```
The German mathematician Kronecker, sitting
quietly at his desk, wrote:
    God created the whole numbers; all
    the rest is man's work.
Seated in front of the terminal, with Basic
hanging on my every keystroke, I typed:
    for i = 1 to infinity
    let number[i] = i
```

A human designer knows that the first indented paragraph (`God created` ...)
is a quotation and the second is a computer program, so the two should be
formatted differently. He would probably set the quotation in ordinary roman
type and the computer program in a typewriter type style. LaTeX is only a
computer program and can't understand English, so it can't figure all this out
by itself. It needs more help from you than a human designer would.

The function of typographic design is to help the reader understand the author's ideas. For a document to be easy to read, its visual structure must reflect
its logical structure. Quotations and computer programs, being logically distinct
structural elements, should be distinguished visually from one another. The designer should therefore understand the document's logical structure. Since LaTeX
can't understand your prose, you must explicitly indicate the logical structure
by typing special commands. The primary function of almost all the LaTeX

commands that you type should be to describe the logical structure of your document. As you are writing your document, you should be concerned with its logical structure, not its visual appearance. The LaTeX approach to typesetting can therefore be characterized as *logical design*.

## 1.5   Why LaTeX?

When LaTeX was introduced in 1985, few authors had the facilities for typesetting their own documents. Today, desktop publishing is commonplace. You can buy a "WYSIWYG" (what you see is what you get) program that lets you see exactly what your document will look like as you type it. WYSIWYG programs are very appealing. They make it easy to put text wherever you want in whatever size and style of type you want. Why use LaTeX, which requires you to tell it that a piece of text is a quotation or a computer program, when a WYSIWYG program allows you to format the text just the way you want it?

WYSIWYG programs replace LaTeX's logical design with *visual design*. Visual design is fine for short, simple documents like letters and memos. It is not good for more complex documents such as scientific papers. WYSIWYG has been characterized as "what you see is all you've got".[1] To illustrate the advantage of logical over visual design, I will consider a simple example from the file `sample2e.tex`.

Near the top of the second page of the document is the mathematical term $(A, B)$. With a WYSIWYG program, this term is entered by typing `(A,B)`. You could type it the same way in the LaTeX input. However, the term represents a mathematical structure—the inner product of $A$ and $B$. An experienced LaTeX user will define a command to express this structure. The file `sample2e.tex` defines the command `\ip` so that `\ip{A}{B}` produces $(A, B)$. The term $(\Gamma, \psi')$ near the end of the document is also an inner product and is produced with the `\ip` command.

Suppose you decide that there should be a little more space after the comma in an inner product. Just changing the definition of the `\ip` command will change $(A, B)$ to $(A,\ B)$ and $(\Gamma, \psi')$ to $(\Gamma,\ \psi')$. With a WYSIWYG program, you would have to insert the space by hand in each formula—not a problem for a short document with two such terms, but a mathematical paper could contain dozens and a book could contain hundreds. You would probably produce inconsistent formatting by missing some formulas or forgetting to add the space when entering new ones. With LaTeX, you don't have to worry about formatting while writing your document. Formatting decisions can be made and changed at any time.

The advantage of logical design becomes even more obvious if you decide that you prefer the notation $\langle A|B \rangle$ for the inner product of $A$ and $B$. The

---

[1] Brian Reid attributes this phrase to himself and/or Brian Kernighan.

file `sample2e.tex` contains an alternate definition of `\ip` that produces this notation.

Typing `\ip{A}{B}` is just a little more work than typing `(A,B)` (though it's a lot easier than entering $\langle A|B\rangle$ if the symbols "$\langle$" and "$\rangle$" must be chosen with a mouse from a pull-down menu). But this small effort is rewarded by the benefits of maintaining the logical structure of your document instead of just its visual appearance.

One advantage of WYSIWYG programs is that you can see the formatted version of your document while writing it. Writing requires reading what you have already written. Although you want LaTeX to know that the term is an inner product, you would like to read $(A, B)$ or $\langle A|B\rangle$, not `\ip{A}{B}`. The speed of modern computers has eliminated much of this advantage. I now type a couple of keystrokes and, a few seconds later, a typeset version of the section I am working on appears on my screen. As computers get faster, those few seconds will turn into a fraction of a second.

## 1.6  Turning Ideas into Input

The purpose of writing is to present your ideas to the reader. This should always be your primary concern. It is easy to become so engrossed with form that you neglect content. Formatting is no substitute for writing. Good ideas couched in good prose will be read and understood, regardless of how badly the document is formatted. LaTeX was designed to free you from formatting concerns, allowing you to concentrate on writing. If you spend a lot of time worrying about form, you are misusing LaTeX.

Even if your ideas are good, you can probably learn to express them better. The classic introduction to writing English prose is Strunk and White's brief *Elements of Style* [6]. A more complete guide to using language properly is Theodore Bernstein's *The Careful Writer* [1]. These two books discuss general writing style. Writers of scholarly or technical prose need additional information. Mary-Claire van Leunen's *Handbook for Scholars* [7] is a delightful guide to academic and scholarly writing. The booklet titled *How to Write Mathematics* [5] can help scientists and engineers as well as mathematicians. It's also useful to have a weightier reference book at hand; *Words into Type* [8] and the *Chicago Manual of Style* [2] are two good ones.

## 1.7  Trying It Out

You may already have run LaTeX with input based on the sample files. If not, this is a good time to learn how. The section in the *Local Guide* titled *Running a Sample File* explains how to obtain a copy of the file `sample2e.tex` and run LaTeX with it as input. Follow the directions and see what LaTeX can do.

After printing the document generated in this way, try changing the document's format. Using a text editor, examine the file `sample2e.tex`. A few lines down from the beginning of the file is a line that reads

```
\documentclass{article}
```

Change that line to

```
\documentclass[twocolumn]{article}
```

Save the changed file under the name `chgsam.tex`, and use this file to print a new version of the document. To generate the new version, do exactly what you did the last time, except type `chgsam` wherever you had typed `sample2e`. Comparing the two printed versions shows how radically the appearance of the document can be altered by a simple change to a command. To try still another format, change `chgsam.tex` so the line above reads

```
\documentclass[12pt]{article}
```

and use the changed file to print a third version of the document.

From now on, I will usually ignore the process of going from the LaTeX input file to the printed output and will write something like: "Typing --- produces a long dash." What this really means is that putting the three characters --- in your input file will, when that file is processed by LaTeX and the device-independent file printed, produce a long dash in the printed output.

# CHAPTER 2
# Getting Started

## 2.1   Preparing an Input File

The input to LaTeX is a text file. I assume that you know how to use a text editor to create such a file, so I will tell you only what should go into your input file, not how to get it there. A good text editor can be customized by the user to make it easier to prepare LaTeX input files. Consult the *Local Guide* to find out how to customize the text editors on your computer.

On most computers, file names have two parts separated by a period, like `sample2e.tex`. I will call the first part its *first name* and the second part its *extension*, so `sample2e` is the first name of `sample2e.tex`, and `tex` is its extension. Your input file's first name can be any name allowed by your computer system, but its extension should be `tex`.

Let's examine the characters that can appear in your input file. First, there are the upper- and lowercase letters and the ten digits 0 ... 9. Don't confuse the uppercase letter O (oh) with the digit 0 (zero), or the letter l (the lowercase *el*) with the digit 1 (one). Next, there are the following sixteen punctuation characters:

$$. \; : \; ; \; , \; ? \; ! \; ` \; ' \; ( \; ) \; [ \; ] \; - \; / \; * \; @$$

Note that there are two different quote symbols: ` and '. You may think of ' as an ordinary "single quote" and ` as a funny symbol, perhaps displayed like ` on your screen. The *Local Guide* should tell where to find ` and ' on your keyboard, if they're not obvious. The characters ( and ) are ordinary parentheses, while [ and ] are called *square brackets*, or simply *brackets*.

The ten special characters

$$\# \; \$ \; \% \; \& \; \~{} \; \_ \; \^{} \; \backslash \; \{ \; \}$$

are used only in LaTeX commands. Check the *Local Guide* for help in finding them on your keyboard. The character \ is called *backslash*, and should not be confused with the more familiar /, as in 1/2. Most LaTeX commands begin with a \ character, so you will soon become very familiar with it. The { and } characters are called *curly braces* or simply *braces*.

The five characters

$$+ \; = \; | \; < \; >$$

are used mainly in mathematical formulas, although + and = can be used in ordinary text. The character " (double quote) is hardly ever used.

Unless your *Local Guide* tells you otherwise, these are the only characters that you should see when you look at a LaTeX input file. However, there are other "invisible" characters in your file: space characters, such as the one you usually enter by pressing the *space* bar, and special characters that indicate the end of a line, usually entered by pressing the *return* key (sometimes labeled *enter*). These invisible characters are all considered the same by TeX, and I will treat them as if they were a single character called *space*, which I will sometimes denote by ␣. Any sequence of space characters is handled the same as a single one, so it doesn't matter if the space between two words is formed by one space character or several of them. However, a blank line—one containing nothing but space characters—is interpreted by TeX as the end of a paragraph. Some text editors organize a file into pages. TeX acts as if there were a blank line between the pages of such a file.

## 2.2  The Input

Most LaTeX commands describe the logical structure of the document. To understand these commands, you must know how LaTeX perceives that logical structure. A document contains logical structures of different sizes, from chapters down through individual letters. We start by considering the very familiar intermediate-sized structures: sentences and paragraphs.

### 2.2.1  Sentences and Paragraphs

Describing simple sentences and paragraphs to LaTeX poses no problem; you pretty much type what comes naturally.

The ends of words and sentences are marked by spaces. It doesn't matter how many spaces you type; one is as good as 100.

One or more blank lines denote the end of a paragraph.

```
The ends  of words and sentences are marked
   by   spaces. It  doesn't matter how many
spaces    you type; one is as good as 100.

One   or more  blank lines denote the  end
of  a paragraph.
```

TeX ignores the way the input is formatted, paying attention only to the logical concepts end-of-word, end-of-sentence, and end-of-paragraph.

That's all you have to know for typing most of your text. The remainder of this book is about how to type the rest, starting with some other things that occur fairly frequently in ordinary sentences and paragraphs.

#### Quotation Marks

Typewritten text uses only two quotation-mark symbols: a double quote " and single quote ', the latter serving also as an apostrophe. Printed text, however, uses a left and a right version of each, making four different symbols. TeX interprets the character ' as a single left quote, and the character ' as a single right quote. To get a double quote, just type two single quotes.

'Convention' dictates that punctuation go inside quotes, like "this," but I think it's better to do "this".

```
'Convention' dictates that punctuation go
inside quotes, like ''this,'' but I think
it's better to do ''this''.
```

Remember that the right-quote character ' is the one you're used to thinking of as a single quote, and the left-quote character ' is the one you're probably unfamiliar with. An apostrophe is produced with the usual ' character.

Typing a double quote followed by a single quote, or vice versa, poses a problem because something like ' ' ' would be ambiguous. The solution is to type the command \, (a \ character followed by a comma) between the two quotation marks.

"'Fi' or 'fum?'" he asked.                                     `''\,'Fi'  or  'fum?'\,''  he asked.`

The \, is a typesetting command that causes TeX to insert a small amount of space. Don't leave any space in the input file before or after the \, command.

## Dashes

You can produce three different sizes of dash by typing one, two, or three "-" characters:

An intra-word dash or hyphen, as in X-ray.           `An intra-word dash or hyphen, as in X-ray.`
A medium dash for number ranges, like 1–2.          `A medium dash for number ranges, like 1--2.`
A punctuation dash—like this.                             `A punctuation dash---like this.`

There is usually no space before or after a dash. Minus signs are not dashes; they should appear only in mathematical formulas, which are discussed below.

## Space After a Period

Typesetters often put a little extra space after a sentence-ending period. This is easy for a human typesetter, but not for a program like TeX that has trouble deciding which periods end sentences. Instead of trying to be clever, TeX simply assumes that a period ends a sentence unless it follows an uppercase letter. This works most of the time, but not always—abbreviations like "etc." being the most common exception. You tell TeX that a period doesn't end a sentence by using a \␣ command (a \ character followed by a space or the end of a line) to make the space after the period.

Tinker et al. made the double play.                        `Tinker et al.\  made the double play.`

It doesn't matter how many spaces you leave after the \ character, but don't leave any space between the period and the backslash. The \␣ command produces an ordinary interword space, which can also be useful in other situations.

On the rare occasions that a sentence-ending period follows an uppercase letter, you will have to tell TeX that the period ends the sentence. You do this by preceding the period with a \@ command.

The Romans wrote I + I = II. Really!                    `The Romans wrote I + I = II\@.  Really!`

If a sentence-ending period is followed by a right parenthesis or a right quote (single or double), then the period's extra space goes after the parenthesis or quote. In these cases too, TeX will need a hand if its assumption that a period ends a sentence unless it follows an uppercase letter is wrong.

"Beans (lima, etc.) have vitamin B."                 ``Beans (lima, etc.)\  have vitamin B\@.''

Extra space is also added after a question mark (?), exclamation point (!), or colon (:) just as for a period—that is, unless it follows an uppercase letter. The \␣ and \@ commands are used the same way with each of these punctuation characters.

## Special Symbols

Remember those ten special characters, mentioned on page 12, that you type only as part of LaTeX commands? Some of them, like $, represent symbols that you might very well want in your document. Seven of those symbols can be produced by typing a \ in front of the corresponding character.

$ & % # _ { } are easy to produce.              \$ \& \% \# \_ \{ \} are easy to produce.

The other three special characters (~, ^, and \) usually appear only in simulated keyboard input, which is produced with the commands described in Section 3.7.

   You can get LaTeX to produce any symbol that you're likely to want, and many more besides, such as: § £ $\psi$ $\star$ $\otimes$ $\approx$ $\bowtie$ $\Leftarrow$ $\flat$ ♣. Sections 3.2 and 3.3.2 tell how.

## Simple Text-Generating Commands

Part of a sentence may be produced by a text-generating command. For example, the TeX and LaTeX logos are produced by the commands \TeX and \LaTeX, respectively.

Some people use plain TeX, but I prefer LaTeX.       Some people use plain \TeX, but I
                                                     prefer \LaTeX.

A useful text-generating command is \today, which produces the current date.

This page was produced on October 14, 1996.       This page was produced on \today.

Another useful text-generating command is \ldots, which produces an *ellipsis*—the sequence of three dots used to denote omitted material. (Simply typing three periods doesn't produce the right spacing between the dots.)

If nominated ... , I will not serve.              If nominated \ldots, I will not serve.

Most of the command names you've seen so far have consisted of a \ (backslash) followed by a single nonletter. From now on, most commands you will encounter have names consisting of a \ followed by one or more letters. In reading the input file, TeX knows it has come to the end of such a command name when it finds a nonletter: a digit like "7", a punctuation character like ";", a special character like "\", a space, or the end of a line. The most common way to end this kind of command name is with a space or end of line, so TeX ignores all spaces following it. If you want a space after the logo produced by the \LaTeX command, you can't just leave a space after the command name; all such spaces are ignored. You must tell TeX to put in the space by typing a \␣ command.

This page of the LaTeX manual was produced on May 18, 1994.

```
This page of the \LaTeX\ manual was
produced on \today .
```

Note how TeX ignored the space after the \today command in the input and did not produce any space after the date in the output.

The case of letters matters in a command name; typing \Today produces an error, because the correct command name is \today. Most command names have only lowercase letters.

### Emphasizing Text

Emphasized text is usually <u>underlined</u> in a typewritten manuscript and *italicized* in a printed document. Underlining and italics are visual concepts; when typing your document, you should be concerned only with the logical concept of emphasis. The \emph command tells LaTeX that text is to be emphasized.

Here is some silly *emphasized text*.

```
Here is some silly \emph{emphasized text}.
```

In the \emph{emphasized text} command, \emph is the command name and emphasized text is its *argument*. Most commands have either no arguments, like \today, or a single argument, like \emph. However, there are a few with multiple arguments, each of which is enclosed in braces. Spaces are ignored between the arguments, and between the command name and its first argument.

Commands like \emph can be nested within one another in the obvious way. Most styles use ordinary roman type for emphasized text that appears inside emphasized text.

You can have *emphasized text* within *emphasized text* too.

```
You can have \emph{emphasized text
\emph{within} emphasized text} too.
```

Emphasis should be used sparingly. Like raising your voice, it is an effective way to get attention, but an annoying distraction if done too often.

### Preventing Line Breaks

In putting text onto paper, a paragraph must be broken into lines of print. Text becomes hard to read if a single logical unit is split across lines in an arbitrary fashion, so typesetters break lines between words when possible and split words only between syllables (inserting a hyphen at the break). Sometimes a line should not be broken between or within certain words. Human typesetters recognize these situations, but TeX must be told about some of them.

Line breaking should be prevented at certain interword spaces. For example, the expression "Chapter 3" looks strange if the "Chapter" ends one line and the "3" begins the next. Typing ~ (a tilde character) produces an ordinary interword space at which TeX will never break a line. Below are some examples indicating when a ~ should be used.

```
Mr.~Jones        Figure~7        (1)~gnats
U.~S.~Grant      from 1 to~10
```

It is best not to break a line within certain words. For example, you should try to avoid splitting a name (especially your own). The \mbox command tells TeX to print its entire argument on the same line. In the following example, TeX will never split "Lamport" across lines.

Doctor Lamport, I presume?                    `Doctor \mbox{Lamport}, I presume?`

Most line breaks separate logically related units, and it would be nice if they could be avoided. However, unless you print your document on a mile-long strip of paper tape, line breaking is a necessary evil. Using too many ~ and \mbox commands leaves too few places to break lines. Inhibit line breaking only where necessary.

### Footnotes

Footnotes are produced with a \footnote command having the text of the footnote as its argument.

Gnus[1] can be quite a gnusance.              `Gnus\footnote{A gnu is a big animal.} can be quite a gnusance.`

⋮

---

[1] A gnu is a big animal.

There is no space between the Gnus and the \footnote in this example; adding space would have put an unwanted space between the text and the footnote marker (the [1]).

A \footnote command cannot be used in the argument of most commands; for example, it can't appear in the argument of an \mbox command. Section C.3.3 explains how to footnote text that appears in a command argument.

### Formulas

If you're writing a technical document, it's likely to contain mathematical formulas. A formula appearing in the middle of a sentence is enclosed by \( and \) commands.

The formula $x - 3y = 7$ is easy to type.

```
The formula \( x-3y = 7 \) is easy to type.
```

Any spaces that you type in the formula are ignored.

Does $x + y$ always equal $y + x$?

```
Does \(  x  +  y  \)  always equal \(y+x\)?
```

TEX regards a formula as a word, which may be broken across lines at certain points, and space before the \( or after the \) is treated as an ordinary interword separation.

Subscripts are produced by the _ command and superscripts by the ^ command.

$a_1 > x^{2n}/y^{2n}$

```
\( a_{1} > x^{2n} / y^{2n} \)
```

These two commands can be used only inside a mathematical formula.

When used in a formula, the right-quote character ' produces a prime ($'$), two in a row produce a double prime, and so on.

This proves that $x' < x'' - y'_3 < 10x'''z$.

```
  ...   \( x' < x'' - y'_{3} < 10 x''' z \).
```

Mathematical formulas can get very complex; Section 3.3 describes many additional commands for producing them. Here, I consider the use of formulas in the text. A formula is a grammatical unit; it should be treated as such in the sentence structure.

The formula $a < 7$ is a noun in this sentence. It is sometimes used as a clause by writing that $a < 7$.

```
The formula \( a<7 \) is a noun in this
sentence.  It is sometimes used ...
```

Beginning a sentence with a formula makes it hard to find the start of the sentence; don't do it. It is best to use a formula as a noun; it should certainly never appear as a complete sentence in the running text.

A variable like $x$ is a formula. To save you some typing, LATEX treats $...$ the same as \(...\).

Let $x$ be a prime such that $y > 2x$.

```
Let $x$ be a prime such that $y>2x$.
```

Use $...$ only for a short formula, such as a single variable. It's easy to forget one of the $ characters that surrounds a long formula. You can also type

```
\begin{math}   ...   \end{math}
```

instead of \(...\). You might want to use this form for very long formulas.

### Ignorable Input

When TEX encounters a % character in the input, it ignores the % and all characters following it on that line—including the space character that ends the line.
TEX also ignores spaces at the beginning of the next line.

| | |
|---|---|
| Gnus and armadillos are generally tolerant of one another and seldom quarrel. | `Gnus and armadi%   More  @_#!$^{&  gnus?`<br>`llos are generally ...` |

The % has two uses: ending a line without producing any space in the output[1]
and putting a comment (a note to yourself) in the input file.

## 2.2.2   The Document

We now jump from the document's intermediate-sized logical units to its largest
one: the entire document itself. The text of every document starts with a
\begin{document} command and ends with an \end{document} command.
LATEX ignores anything that follows the \end{document}. The part of the input
file preceding the \begin{document} command is called the *preamble*.

### The Document Class

The preamble begins[2] with a \documentclass command whose argument is
one of the predefined classes of document that LATEX knows about. The file
sample2e.tex begins with

        \documentclass{article}

which selects the **article** class. The other standard LATEX class used for ordinary documents is the **report** class. The **article** class is generally used for
shorter documents than the **report** class. Other standard classes are described
in Chapter 5.

In addition to choosing the class, you can also select from among certain
document-class options. The options for the **article** and **report** classes include
the following:

**11pt** Specifies a size of type known as *eleven point*, which is ten percent larger
than the ten-point type normally used.

**12pt** Specifies a twelve-point type size, which is twenty percent larger than ten
point.

**twoside** Formats the output for printing on both sides of the page. (LATEX has
no control over the actual printing.)

---

[1] However, you can't split a command name across two lines.

[2] As explained in Section 4.7, the \documentclass command may actually be preceded by
prepended files.

`twocolumn` Produces two-column output.

Other options are described elsewhere in this book; all the standard ones are listed in Section C.5.1. Your *Local Guide* tells what others are available on your computer.

You specify a document-class option by enclosing it in square brackets immediately after the "\documentclass", as in

```
\documentclass [twoside]{report}
```

Multiple options are separated by commas.

```
\documentclass [twocolumn,12pt]{article}
```

Don't leave any space inside the square brackets.

The `\documentclass` command can be used either with or without the option-choosing part. The options, enclosed in square brackets, are an *optional argument* of the command. It is a LaTeX convention that optional arguments are enclosed in square brackets, while mandatory arguments are enclosed in curly braces. TeX ignores spaces after a command name like `\documentclass` and between command arguments.

The document class defines the commands for specifying LaTeX's standard logical structures. Additional structures are defined by *packages*, which are loaded by the `\usepackage` command. For example, the command

```
\usepackage{latexsym}
```

loads the `latexsym` package, which defines commands to produce certain special math symbols. (See Section 3.3.2.) A package can have options, specified by an optional argument of `\usepackage` just like the one for `\documentclass`.

You will probably want to define some new commands for the special structures used in your particular document. For example, if you're writing a cookbook you will probably define your own commands for formatting recipes, as explained in Section 3.4. These definitions should go in the preamble, after the `\documentclass` and `\usepackage` commands. The preamble can also contain commands to change some aspects of the formatting. If you have commands or format changes that you use in several documents, you may want to define your own package, as described in Section 6.1.4.

## The Title "Page"

A document usually has a title "page" listing its title, one or more authors, and a date. I write "page" in quotes because, for a short document, this information may be listed on the first page of text rather than on its own page. The title information consists of the title itself, the author(s), and the date; it is specified by the three declarations `\title`, `\author`, and `\date`. The actual title "page" is generated by a `\maketitle` command.

Gnus of the World

R. Dather   J. Pennings   B. Talkmore

4 July 1997

```
\title{Gnus of the World}
\author{R. Dather \and J. Pennings
    \and B. Talkmore}
\date{4 July 1997}
    ...
\maketitle
```

Note how multiple authors are separated by \and commands.

The \maketitle command comes after the \begin{document}, usually before any other text. The \title, \author, and \date commands can come anywhere before the \maketitle. The \date is optional; LaTeX supplies the current date if the declaration is omitted, but the \title and \author must appear if a \maketitle command is used. Commands for adding other information, such as the author's address and an acknowledgment of support, are described in Section C.5.4.

### 2.2.3   Sectioning

Sentences are organized into paragraphs, and paragraphs are in turn organized into a hierarchical *section structure*. You are currently reading Subsection 2.2.3, titled *Sectioning*, which is part of Section 2.2, titled *The Input*, which in turn is part of Chapter 2, titled *Getting Started*. I will use the term *sectional units* for things like chapters, sections, and subsections.

A sectional unit is begun by a sectioning command with the unit's title as its argument.

**4.7  A Sectioning Command**

LaTeX automatically generates the section number. Blank lines before or after a sectioning command have no effect.

```
\subsection{A Sectioning Command}

\LaTeX\ automatically generates the section
number.  Blank lines before or after a ...
```

The document class determines what sectioning commands are provided, the standard classes have the following ones:[3]

| | | |
|---|---|---|
| \part | \subsection | \paragraph |
| \chapter | \subsubsection | \subparagraph |
| \section | | |

The article document class does not contain the \chapter command, which makes it easy to include an "article" as a chapter of a "report". The example above, like most others in this book, assumes the article document class, the 4.7 indicating that this is the seventh subsection of Section 4. In the report class, this subsection might be numbered 5.4.7, with "5" being the chapter number.

---

[3]The names \paragraph and \subparagraph are unfortunate, since they denote units that are often composed of several paragraphs; they have been retained for historical reasons.

The sectional unit denoted by each of these commands must appear as a subunit of the one denoted by the preceding command, except that the use of \part is optional. A subsection must be part of a section, which, in the report class, must be part of a chapter.

The \part command is used for major divisions of long documents; it does not affect the numbering of smaller units—in the article class, if the last section of Part 1 is Section 5, then the first section of Part 2 is Section 6.

If there is an appendix, it is begun with an \appendix command and uses the same sectioning commands as the main part of the document. The \appendix command does not produce any text; it simply causes sectional units to be numbered properly for an appendix.

The document class determines the appearance of the section title, including whether or not it is numbered. Declarations to control section numbering are described in Section C.4, which also tells you how to make a table of contents.

The argument of a sectioning command may be used for more than just producing the section title; it can generate a table of contents entry and a running head at the top of the page. (Running heads are discussed in Section 6.1.2.) When carried from where it appears in the input file to the other places it is used, the argument of a sectioning command is shaken up quite a bit. Some LaTeX commands are *fragile* and can break when they appear in an argument that is shaken in this way. Fragile commands are rarely used in the argument of a sectioning command. Of the commands introduced so far, the only fragile ones are \(, \), \begin, \end, and \footnote—none of which you're likely to need in a section title.[4] On the rare occasions when you have to put a fragile command in a section title, you simply protect it with a \protect command. The \protect command goes right before every fragile command's name, as in:

```
\subsection {Is  \protect\(   x+y  \protect\)  Prime?}
```

This is actually a silly example because $ is not a fragile command, so you can instead type

```
\subsection {Is $x + y$ Prime?}
```

but, because the problem is so rare, it's hard to find a good example using the commands described in this chapter.

An argument in which fragile commands need \protect will be called a *moving* argument. Commands that are not fragile will be called *robust*. For any command that one might reasonably expect to use in a moving argument, I will indicate whether it is robust or fragile. Except in special cases mentioned in Chapter 6 and Appendix C, a \protect command can't hurt, so it is almost always safe to use one when you're not sure if it's necessary.

---

[4]Section C.3.3 tells you how to footnote a section title.

### 2.2.4   Displayed Material

We return now to the level of the individual sentence. A sentence like

> He turned and said to me, "My answer is no!", and then he left.

contains a complete sentence quoted within it. An entire paragraph can even appear inside a sentence, as in

> He turned and said to me: "I've done all I'm going to. I refuse to have any further part in it. My answer is no!", and then he left.

It's hard to understand this sentence the way it is written. However, there's no problem if you read it aloud using a different tone of voice for the quotation. The typographic analog of changing your tone of voice is setting text off by indentation, also called *displaying*. The sentence above is much easier to read when typeset as follows:

> He turned and said to me:
>> I've done all I'm going to. I refuse to have any further part in it. My answer is no!
>
> and then he left.

Displayed material functions logically as a lower-level unit than a sentence, though grammatically it may consist of part of a sentence, a whole sentence, or even several paragraphs. To decide whether a portion of text should be a display or a separate sectional unit, you must determine if it is logically subordinate to the surrounding text or functions as an equal unit.

Quotations are often displayed.

The following is an example of a short displayed quotation.

> ... it's a good idea to make your input file as easy to read as possible.

It is indented at both margins.

```
... example of a short displayed quotation.
\begin{quote}
   \ldots\ it's a good idea to make your
   input file as easy to read as possible.
\end{quote}
It is indented at both margins.
```

This example illustrates a type of LaTeX construction called an *environment*, which is typed

> \begin{*name*} ... \end{*name*}

where *name* is the name of the environment. The quote environment produces a display suitable for a short quotation. You've already encountered two other examples of environments: the math environment and the document environment.

The standard LaTeX document classes provide environments for producing several different kinds of displays. Blank lines before or after the environment mark a new paragraph. Thus, a blank line after the \end command means that the following text starts a new paragraph. Blank lines before and after the environment mean that it is a complete paragraph. It's a bad idea to start a paragraph with displayed material, so you should not have a blank line before a display environment without a blank line after it. Blank lines immediately following a display environment's \begin command and immediately preceding its \end command are ignored.

### Quotations

LaTeX provides two different environments for displaying quotations. The quote environment is used for either a short quotation or a sequence of short quotations separated by blank lines.

| | |
|---|---|
| Our presidents have been known for their pithy remarks. | `Our presidents ... pithy remarks.` |
|     The buck stops here. *Harry Truman* | `\begin{quote}` |
|     I am not a crook. *Richard Nixon* | `  The buck stops here.  \emph{Harry Truman}` |
|     It's no exaggeration to say the undecideds could go one way or another. *George Bush* | `  I am not a crook.  \emph{Richard Nixon}` |
| | `  It's no exaggeration ...\emph{George Bush}` |
| | `\end{quote}` |

The quotation environment is used for quotations of more than one paragraph; as usual, the paragraphs are separated by blank lines.

| | |
|---|---|
| Here is some advice to remember when you are using LaTeX: | `Here is some advice to remember when you` |
| | `are using \LaTeX:` |
|     Environments for making quotations can be used for other things as well. | `\begin{quotation}` |
| | `    Environments for making quotations` |
|     Many problems can be solved by novel applications of existing environments. | `    ... other things as well.` |
| | `  Many ...  existing  environments.` |
| | `\end{quotation}` |

### Lists

LaTeX provides three list-making environments: itemize, enumerate, and description. In all three, each new list item is begun with an \item command. Itemized lists are made with the itemize environment and enumerated lists with the enumerate environment.

- Each list item is marked with a *label*. The labels in this itemized list are bullets.
- Lists can be nested within one another.
  1. The item labels in an enumerated list are numerals or letters.
  2. A list should have at least two items.

  LaTeX permits at least four levels of nested lists, which is more than enough.
- Blank lines before an item have no effect.

```
\begin{itemize}
  \item Each list item is ...  bullets.
  \item Lists can be ... one another.
    \begin{enumerate}
       \item The item labels ... letters
       \item A list should  ...  two items.
    \end{enumerate}
  \LaTeX\ permits ... more than enough.

  \item  Blank lines ... have no effect.
\end{itemize}
```

In the `description` environment, you specify the item labels with an optional argument to the \item command, enclosed in brackets. (Although the argument is optional, the item will look funny if you omit it.)

Three animals you should know about are:

**gnat**  A small animal, found in the North Woods, that causes no end of trouble.

**gnu**  A large animal, found in crossword puzzles, that causes no end of trouble.

**armadillo**  A medium-sized animal, named after a medium-sized Texas city.

```
Three animals you should know about are:
\begin{description}
  \item[gnat] A small animal ...
  \item [gnu] A large animal ....
  \item [armadillo] A medium-sized ...
\end{description}
```

The characters [ and ] are used both to delimit an optional argument and to produce square brackets in the output. This can cause some confusion if the text of an item begins with a [ or if an \item command's optional argument contains a square bracket. Section C.1.1 explains what to do in these uncommon situations. All commands that have an optional argument are fragile.

### Poetry

Poetry is displayed with the `verse` environment. A new stanza is begun with one or more blank lines; lines within a stanza are separated by a \\ command.

There is an environment for verse
Whose features some poets will curse.

For instead of making
Them do *all* line breaking,
It allows them to put too many words
  on a line when they'd rather be
  forced to be terse.

```
\begin{verse}
  There is an environment for verse \\
  Whose features some poets will curse.

  For instead of making\\
  Them do \emph{all} line breaking, \\
  It allows them  ...  to be terse.
\end{verse}
```

The \\* command is the same as \\ except that it prevents LaTeX from starting a new page at that point. It can be used to prevent a poem from being broken across pages in a distracting way. The commands \\ and \\* are used in all environments in which you tell LaTeX where to break lines; several such environments are described in the next chapter. The \\* command is called the *-form of the \\ command. Several other commands also have *-forms—versions of the command that are slightly different from the ordinary one—that are obtained by typing * after the command name.

The \\ and \\* commands have a little-used optional argument described in Section C.1.6, so putting a [ after them presents the same problem as for the \item command. Moreover, the * in the \\* command is somewhat like an optional argument for the \\ command, so following a \\ with a * in the text poses a similar problem. See Section C.1.1 for the solutions to these unlikely problems. Almost every command that has a *-form is fragile, and its *-form is also fragile.

### Displayed Formulas

A mathematical formula is displayed when either it is too long to fit comfortably in the running text, it is so important that you want it to stand out, or it is to be numbered for future reference. LaTeX provides the displaymath and equation environments for displaying formulas; they are the same except that equation numbers the formula and displaymath doesn't. Because displayed equations are used so frequently in mathematics, LaTeX allows you to type \[...\] instead of

```
\begin{displaymath}  ...  \end{displaymath}
```

Here is an example of an unnumbered displayed equation:
$$x' + y^2 = z_i^2$$
and here is the same equation numbered:
$$x' + y^2 = z_i^2 \qquad (8)$$

```
Here is an example of an unnumbered
displayed equation:
   \[ x' + y^{2} = z_{i}^{2} \]
and here is the same equation numbered:
   \begin{equation}
      x' + y^{2} = z_{i}^{2}
   \end{equation}
```

The document class determines how equations are numbered. Section 4.2 describes how LaTeX can automatically handle references to equation numbers so you don't have to keep track of the numbers.

A displayed formula, like any displayed text, should not begin a paragraph. Moreover, it should not form a complete paragraph by itself. These two observations are summed up in a simple rule: in the input, never leave a blank line before a displayed formula.

TeX will not break the formula in a displaymath or equation environment across lines. See Section 3.3.5 for commands to create a single multiple-line formula or a sequence of displayed formulas.

## 2.2.5   Declarations

You may want to emphasize a large piece of text, such as a quotation. You can do this with the \emph command, but that makes the input file hard to read because you have to search for the closing right brace to see where the argument ends. Moreover, it's easy accidentally to delete the closing brace when you edit the text. Instead, you can use the \em command, which tells TeX to start emphasizing text.

This prose is very dull.

    Wait! *Here is an exciting quote.*

Aren't you glad all that excitement is over?

```
This prose is very dull.
  \begin{quote}
  Wait!  \em  Here is an exciting quote.
  \end{quote}
Aren't you glad ...
```

As explained below, the \end{quote} caused TeX to stop emphasizing text.

    Unlike other commands you've encountered so far, \em produces neither text nor space; instead, it affects the way LaTeX prints the text that follows it. Such a command is called a *declaration*. Most aspects of the way LaTeX formats a document—the type style, how wide the margins are, and so on—are determined by declarations. The \em declaration instructs LaTeX to change the type style to the appropriate one for indicating emphasis. The *scope* of a declaration is ended by an \end command or a right brace. In the input, braces and \begin and \end commands must come in matched pairs. The scope of a declaration is ended by the first \end or } whose matching \begin or { precedes the declaration. The following example shows only the braces, \begin and \end commands (without their arguments and argument-enclosing braces), and an \em declaration from some input text; matching braces and matching \begin and \end commands have the same numbers. The shaded region is the scope of the \em declaration.

$\text{\begin}_1 \quad \{_2 \quad \}_2 \quad \{_3 \quad \text{\em} \quad \boxed{\text{\begin}_4 \quad \{_5 \quad \}_5 \quad \text{\end}_4} \quad \}_3 \quad \text{\end}_1$

The braces can be the ones that surround a command argument or ones that are inserted just to delimit the scope of a declaration, as in the first emphasized *that* of[5]

That *that* that *that* thatcher thought thrilling ...      `That {\em that} that \emph{that} ...`

The \{ and \} commands do not count for purposes of brace matching and delimiting the scope of declarations. Also, as explained in Section 3.4, argument braces for commands you define yourself do not act as scope delimiters.

    Every declaration has a corresponding environment of the same name (minus the \ character). Typing

---

[5]You should use the \emph command rather than the \em declaration for emphasizing small pieces of text because it produces better spacing.

```
\begin{em}  ...  \end{em}
```

is equivalent to typing {\em ... }. (If a declaration has arguments, they become additional arguments of the corresponding environment's \begin command.) Using the environment form of a declaration instead of delimiting its scope with braces can make your input file easier to read.

## 2.3   Running LaTeX

If you followed the directions in Section 1.7, you now know how to run LaTeX on an input file. If not, consult the *Local Guide* to find out. When you use your own input file for the first time, things are unlikely to go as smoothly as they did for `sample2e.tex`. There will probably be a number of errors in your file—most of them simple typing mistakes. Chapter 8 gives detailed help in diagnosing errors. Here I will tell you how to apply first aid from the keyboard while LaTeX is still running.

When you start LaTeX, it will probably be running in one of several windows on your computer's screen. For historical reasons, I will call that window the *terminal*. (If LaTeX runs by itself and takes up the entire screen, then your whole computer is the terminal.) What you type directly to LaTeX, and what it types back at you, are called terminal input and output.

With your text editor, produce a new file named `errsam.tex` by making the following four changes to `sample2e.tex`:

- Line 174 of the file contains an \end{enumerate} command. Delete the t to produce \end{enumerae}, simulating a typical typing error.

- Four lines below is an \item command. Turn it into \itemt, another typical typo.

- The sixth line down from there begins with the word Whose. Add a pair of brackets to change that word to [W]hose.

- About a dozen lines further down in the file is a line consisting of the single word is. Add a space followed by gnomonly to the end of that line.

Now run LaTeX with `errsam.tex` as input and see what error messages it produces. You needn't write them down because everything TeX writes on your screen is also written in a file called the *log* file.[6] For the input file `errsam.tex`, the log file is named `errsam.log` on most computers, but it may have a different extension on yours; check your *Local Guide*.

LaTeX begins by typing pretty much what it did when you ran it on the `sample2e.tex` file, but then writes the following message on your screen and stops.

---

[6]The log file also has some things that don't appear on your screen, including blank lines inserted in strange places.

```
! LaTeX Error: \begin{enumerate} on input line 167 ended by \end{enumerae}.

See the LaTeX manual or LaTeX Companion for explanation.
Type  H <return>  for immediate help.
 ...

l.174            \end{enumerae}

?
```

LaTeX translates a command like \end, which describes the document's logical
structure, into TeX's typesetting commands. Some errors are caught by LaTeX;
others cause it to generate typesetting commands containing errors that TeX
finds. The first line of this message, called the *error indicator*, tells us that the
error was found by LaTeX rather than TeX. Like all error messages, this one
begins with an exclamation point.

The error indicator tells what the problem is. Chapter 8 explains the meaning
of the error indicators for most LaTeX-detected errors and for the most common
errors that TeX finds. Here, LaTeX is complaining that the \end command that
matches the \begin{enumerate} is not an \end{enumerate}, as it should be.
The line beginning with l.174 is the *error locator*, telling you where in your
input file the error was discovered. In this case, it was on line 174, after TeX
read the \end{enumerae} command. The ? that ends the message indicates
that LaTeX has stopped and is waiting for you to type something.

Just pass over the error by pressing the *return* key, which instructs LaTeX to
continue processing the input. LaTeX now writes

```
! Undefined control sequence.
l.178   \itemt
                This is the third item of the list.
?
```

The absence of the LaTeX Error at the beginning of the message tells you that
this error was detected by TeX rather than LaTeX. TeX knows nothing about
LaTeX commands, so you can't expect much help from the error indicator. The
error locator indicates that the error was detected on line 178 of the input file,
after reading \itemt and before reading This. (The error locator line is broken
at the point where TeX stopped reading input.) Of course, this error is caused
by \itemt, which is a command name TeX has never heard of.

Continue past this error by pressing *return*. LaTeX next writes

```
! Missing number, treated as zero.
<to be read again>
                W
l.184   [W]
            hose features some poets % within a stanza.
?
```

This error was found by TeX not LaTeX, and the error indicator isn't very helpful. TeX has just read the [W], which looks all right, so the error must have been caused by something that came before it. Right before the [W] in the input file is a \\ command. Do you now see what the error is? If not, look in the index under "\\, [ after".

Press *return* to continue. You immediately get another error message very similar to the preceding one, with the same error locator. TeX has discovered a second error in the low-level typesetting commands generated by the \\ command. Type *return* again to get past this problem.

When you find the first error, it's tempting to stop the program, correct it, and start over again. However, if you've made one error, you've probably made more. It's a good idea to find several errors at once, rather than running LaTeX over and over to find one mistake at a time. Keep typing *return* and try to get as far as you can. You may reach an impasse. A single mistake can cause TeX to produce hundreds of error messages, or to keep generating the same message over and over again forever. You can stop LaTeX before it's finished by typing X followed by *return* in response to an error message.

TeX may write a * and stop without any error message. This is probably due to a missing \end{document} command, but other errors can also cause it. If it happens, type \stop followed by *return*. If that doesn't work, you'll have to use your computer's standard method for halting recalcitrant programs, which is described in the *Local Guide*.

Instead of sitting at your keyboard waiting for errors, you can let LaTeX run unattended and find out what happened later by reading the log file. A \batchmode command at the very beginning of the input file causes TeX to process the file without stopping—much as if you were to type *return* in response to every error message, except the messages are not actually written on your screen. This is a convenient way to run LaTeX while you go out to lunch, but you could return to find that a small error resulted in a very long list of error messages in the log file.

Meanwhile, LaTeX has finished processing your input file errsam.tex. After the last error message, it wrote

```
Overfull \hbox (10.51814pt too wide) in paragraph at lines 195--200
[]\OT1/cmr/m/n/10 Mathematical for-mu-las may also be dis-played. A dis-played
for-mula is gnomonly
```

This is a *warning* message; LaTeX did not stop (it didn't print a ?), but continued to the end of the input file without further incident. TeX generated the warning because it does not know how to hyphenate the word *gnomonly*, so it couldn't find a good place to break the line. If you look at the output, you'll find *gnomonly* extending beyond the right margin. This is not a serious problem; Section 6.2.1 describes how to correct it.

When you process your input file for the first time, LaTeX is likely to produce lots of error messages and warnings that you may not understand right away.

The most important thing to remember is, DON'T PANIC. Instead, turn to Chapter 8 to find out what to do.

## 2.4   Helpful Hints

The descriptions of individual LaTeX features include suggestions about their use. Here are a few general recommendations that can make your life easier.

As soon as you have some experience with LaTeX, read Section 3.4 to learn how to define your own commands and environments. When I write a paper, I change my notation much more than I change my concepts. Defining commands to express concepts allows me to change notation by simply modifying the command definitions, without having to change every occurrence in the text. This saves a lot of work.

To avoid errors and simplify making changes, keep your input file as easy to read as possible. Spacing and indentation can help. Use comments, especially to explain your command definitions. TeX doesn't care how the input file is formatted, but you should.

As you write your document, you will be continually running LaTeX on it so you can view the latest version. As the document gets longer, LaTeX takes longer to process it. When you make some changes to Section 7, don't run LaTeX on Sections 1–6 just to find errors in the new material. Find those errors fast by running LaTeX only on Section 7. Process the entire document only when you're pretty sure Section 7 has no more errors.

There are two ways to run LaTeX only on what's changed. The first is to create a new file containing just the preamble, a \begin{document} command, the new material, and an \end{document} command. This is easy to do with a good text editor. I have programmed my editor so, at the stroke of a couple of keys, it will create this file, run LaTeX on it, and display the output with a screen previewer—while I keep editing my document. The second way to run LaTeX just on what has changed is to keep your input in several files, using the commands of Section 4.4 to process one part at a time. Experiment to find out what method works best for you.

Perhaps the most annoying aspect of a computer program is the way it reacts to your errors. As with most programs, LaTeX's train of thought is derailed by simple errors that any person would easily correct. The best way to avoid this problem is to avoid those simple errors. Here are some common ones that are easy to eliminate by being careful:

- A misspelled command or environment name.

- Improperly matching braces.

- Trying to use one of the ten special characters # $ % & _ { } ~ ^ \ as an ordinary printing symbol.

- Improperly matching formula delimiters—for example, a \( command without the matching \).

- The use in ordinary text of a command like ^ that can appear only in a mathematical formula.

- A missing \end command.

- A missing command argument.

A good text editor can detect or help prevent some of these errors.

Because of a bit of fossilized stupidity, e-mail programs on the Unix operating system often add a > character to the beginning of every line that begins with the five characters From␣. The input >From causes TeX to produce the output "¿From". It's a good idea to search all LaTeX files received by e-mail for >From , and to add a space to the beginning of every line that starts with From in all files that you send by e-mail.

## 2.5   Summary

This chapter has explained everything you have to know to prepare a simple document. There is quite a bit to remember. Here is a summary to refresh your memory.

### Input Characters

The input file may contain the following characters: upper- and lowercase letters, the ten digits, the sixteen punctuation characters

$$. : ; , ? ! ` ' ( ) [ ] - / * @$$

the ten special characters

$$\# \$ \% \& \_ \{ \} \sim \char`\^ \backslash$$

(the first seven are printed by the commands \#, \$, etc.), and the five characters + = | < > used mainly in mathematical formulas. There are also invisible characters, which are all denoted by ␣, that produce spaces in the input file.

### Commands and Environments

Command names consist of either a single special character like ~, a \ followed by a single nonletter (as in \@), or a \ followed by a string of letters. Spaces and a single end-of-line following the latter kind of command name are ignored; use a \␣ command to put an interword space after such a command. The case of letters in command names counts; most LaTeX command names contain only lowercase letters. A few commands have a *-form, a variant obtained by typing * after the command name.

Command arguments are enclosed in curly braces { and }, except for optional arguments, which are enclosed in square brackets [ and ]. See Section C.1.1 if an optional argument has a square bracket or if a [ in the text could be confused with the start of an optional argument. Do not leave any extra space within an argument; use a % to end a line without introducing space.

Some commands have *moving arguments*. The name of a fragile command must be preceded by a \protect command when it appears in a moving argument. Fragile commands include \(, \), \[, \], \begin, \end, \\, \item, and \footnote. A \protect command seldom hurts; when in doubt use one.

A declaration is a command that directs LaTeX to change the way it is formatting the document. The scope of a declaration is delimited by enclosing it within curly braces or within an environment.

An environment has the form

> \begin{*name*} ... \end{*name*}

To every declaration corresponds an environment whose name is the same as the declaration's name without the \.

## Sentences and Paragraphs

Sentences and paragraphs are typed pretty much as expected. TeX ignores the formatting of the input file. A blank line indicates a new paragraph.

Quotes are typed with the ' and ' characters, used in pairs for double quotes. The \, command separates multiple quotation marks, as in ''\,'Fum'\,''.

Dashes of various sizes are produced with one, two, or three "-" characters.

A period, question mark, or exclamation point is considered to end a sentence unless it follows an uppercase letter. A \@ command before the punctuation character forces TeX to treat it as the end of a sentence, while a \␣ command placed after it produces an interword space.

The TeX and LaTeX logos are produced by the \TeX and \LaTeX commands. The \today command produces the current date, and \ldots produces an ellipsis (...).

Text is emphasized with the \emph command.

The ~ command produces an interword space at which TeX will not start a new line. The \mbox command prevents TeX from breaking its argument across lines.

Footnotes are typed with the \footnote command, whose argument is the text of the footnote.

In-line mathematical formulas are enclosed by \( ... \) or $ ... $. Subscripts and superscripts are made with the _ and ^ commands. The ' character produces a prime symbol ($'$).

## Larger Structures

The document begins with the preamble. The preamble begins (after any prepended files—see Section 4.7) with a \documentclass command, which may be followed by one or more \usepackage commands. The rest of the preamble may contain command definitions and special style declarations for the document. The actual text is contained in a document environment.

A title is produced by using the \title, \author, and \date commands to declare the necessary information, and the \maketitle command to generate the title. Multiple authors are separated by \and commands in the argument of \author.

A sectional unit is begun with one of the following sectioning commands

| | | |
|---|---|---|
| \part | \subsection | \paragraph |
| \chapter | \subsubsection | \subparagraph |
| \section | | |

whose argument produces the unit's heading and is a moving argument.

## Displayed Material

Short quotations are displayed with the quote environment and long quotations with the quotation environment.

LaTeX provides three list-making environments: itemize for itemized lists, enumerate for enumerated lists, and description for lists with user-specified labels. Each item is begun with an \item command whose optional argument provides the item labels in the description environment.

The verse environment is used for poetry. A blank line begins a new stanza, and a line that does not end a stanza is followed by a \\ command—use \\* instead of \\ to prevent a page break after the line. (See Section C.1.1 if a * follows an ordinary \\ command.)

Displayed mathematical formulas are produced with the displaymath environment or the equivalent \[ ... \] construction. The equation environment produces numbered displayed formulas.

# CHAPTER 3
# Carrying On

Chapter 2 described commands for simple documents. Sooner or later, you'll write something that requires more sophisticated formatting. The commands and environments described in this chapter will handle most of those situations. Before getting to them, you should know a little more about how TeX operates.

As TeX processes your input text, it is always in one of three *modes*: paragraph mode, math mode, or left-to-right mode (called LR mode for short).[1] Paragraph mode is TeX's normal mode—the one it's in when processing ordinary text. In paragraph mode, TeX regards your input as a sequence of words and sentences to be broken into lines, paragraphs, and pages.

TeX is in math mode when it's generating a mathematical formula. More precisely, it enters math mode upon encountering a command like $ or \( or \[ or \begin{equation} that begins a mathematical formula, and it leaves math mode after finding the corresponding command like \) that ends the formula. When TeX is in math mode, it considers letters in the input file to be mathematical symbols, treating `is` as the product of $i$ and $s$, and ignores any space characters between them.

In LR mode, as in paragraph mode, TeX considers your input to be a string of words with spaces between them. However, unlike paragraph mode, TeX produces output that keeps going from left to right; it never starts a new line in LR mode. The \mbox command (Section 2.2.1) causes TeX to process its argument in LR mode, which is what prevents the argument from being broken across lines.

Different modes can be nested within one another. If you put an \mbox command inside a mathematical formula, TeX is in LR mode when processing that command's argument, not in math mode. In the example

$y > z$ if $x^2$ real.

> \( y > z \mbox{ if $x^{2}$ real} \).

TeX is in math mode when processing ␣y␣>␣z␣, in LR mode when processing ␣if␣ and ␣real, and in math mode when processing x^{2}. The space between "$z$" and "if" is produced by the first ␣ in the \mbox command's argument, since space characters in the input produce space in the output when TeX is in LR mode. The ␣ in real}␣\) is processed in math mode, so it produces no space between "real" and "." in the output.

## 3.1   Changing the Type Style

Type style is used to indicate logical structure. In this book, emphasized text appears in *italic* style type and LaTeX input in `typewriter` style. In LaTeX, a type style is specified by three components: shape, series, and family.

---

[1]Paragraph mode corresponds to the vertical and ordinary horizontal modes in *The TeXbook*, and LR mode is called restricted horizontal mode there. LaTeX also has a restricted form of LR mode called *picture* mode that is described in Section 7.1.

| | |
|---|---|
| Upright shape. Usually the default. | `\textup{Upright shape...}` |
| *Italic shape. Often used for emphasized text.* | `\textit{Italic shape...}` |
| *Slanted shape. A bit different from italic.* | `\textsl{Slanted shape...}` |
| SMALL CAPS SHAPE. USE SPARINGLY. | `\textsc{Small caps shape...}` |
| Medium series. Usually the default. | `\textmd{Medium series...}` |
| **Boldface series. Often used for headings.** | `\textbf{Boldface series...}` |
| Roman family. Usually the default. | `\textrm{Roman family...}` |
| Sans serif family. Often used in ads. | `\textsf{Sans serif family...}` |
| Typewriter family.   Popular with hackers. | `\texttt{Typewriter family...}` |

These commands can be combined in a logical fashion to produce a wide variety of type styles.

| | |
|---|---|
| **Who** on **Earth** is *ever* going to use a boldface sans serif or an italic typewriter type style? | `\textsf{\textbf{Who \textmd{on} Earth}} is`  `\textit{\texttt{ever}} ...` |

Some type styles may be unavailable on your computer. If you specify a style that isn't available, LaTeX will write a warning message and substitute a style that it thinks is similar. (You may think otherwise.)

Each of the text-style commands described above has a corresponding declaration. Boldface text can be obtained with either the `\textbf` text-producing command or the `\bfseries` declaration.

| | |
|---|---|
| **More** and **more** armadillos are crossing the road. | `\textbf{More} and {\bfseries more} ...` |

The declarations corresponding to the text-producing command are:

| cmd | decl | cmd | decl | cmd | decl |
|---|---|---|---|---|---|
| `\textup` | `\upshape` | `\textsc` | `\scshape` | `\textrm` | `\rmfamily` |
| `\textit` | `\itshape` | `\textmd` | `\mdseries` | `\textsf` | `\sffamily` |
| `\textsl` | `\slshape` | `\textbf` | `\bfseries` | `\texttt` | `\ttfamily` |

These text-producing commands can be used in math mode to put ordinary text in a formula. (Their arguments are then processed in LR mode.) The declarations cannot be used in math mode. Section 3.3.8 explains how to change the type style of a formula's math-mode symbols.

Type style is a visual property. Commands to specify visual properties belong not in the text, but in the definitions of commands that describe logical structure. LaTeX provides the `\emph` command for emphasized text; Section 3.4 explains how to define your own commands for the logical structures in your document. For example, suppose you want the names of genera to appear in italic in your book on African mammals. Don't use `\textit` throughout the text; instead, define a `\genus` command and write

| | |
|---|---|
| *Connochaetes* seems to pop up everywhere. | `\genus{Connochaetes} seems to pop up ...` |

Then, if you decide that *Connochaetes* and all other genera should appear in slanted rather than italic type, you just have to change the definition of `\genus`.

## 3.2    Symbols from Other Languages

Languages other than English have a variety of accents and special symbols. This section tells you how to generate the ones used in most Western languages. These accents and symbols are not available in the typewriter family of type styles. All the commands introduced in this section are robust.

Commands to produce accents and symbols from other languages allow you to put small pieces of non-English text in an English document. They are not adequate for writing a complete document in another language. The `babel` package allows you to produce documents in languages other than English, as well as multilanguage documents. Consult the LaTeX *Companion* for details.

### 3.2.1    Accents

Table 3.1 shows how to make a wide variety of accents. In this and all similar tables, the TeX output is followed by the input that produces it, the first entry in Table 3.1 showing that you produce ò by typing `\`{o}`. The letter o appears in this table, but the commands can accent any letter.

El señor está bien, garçon.                                    `El se\~{n}or est\'{a} bien, gar\c{c}on.`

The letters *i* and *j* need special treatment because they should lose their dots when accented. The commands `\i` and `\j` produce a dotless *i* and *j*, respectively.

Él está aquí.                                    `\'{E}l est\'{a} aqu\'{\i}.`

The commands in Table 3.1 can be used only in paragraph and LR modes. Accents in math mode, which produce accented symbols in mathematical formulas, are made with commands described in Section 3.3.6.

### 3.2.2    Symbols

Table 3.2 shows how to make some symbols from non-English languages. Note that the symbols ¿ and ¡ are produced by typing a pair of punctuation characters, in much the same way that a medium-length dash is produced by typing two - characters. The commands in Table 3.2 can appear only in paragraph and LR modes; use an `\mbox` command to put one inside a mathematical formula.

| | | | |
|---|---|---|---|
| ò `\`{o}` | õ `\~{o}` | ǒ `\v{o}` | o̧ `\c{o}` |
| ó `\'{o}` | ō `\={o}` | ő `\H{o}` | ọ `\d{o}` |
| ô `\^{o}` | ȯ `\.{o}` | o͡o `\t{oo}` | o̲ `\b{o}` |
| ö `\"{o}` | ŏ `\u{o}` | | |

Table 3.1: Accents.

| œ | \oe | å | \aa | ł | \l | ¿ | ?` |
|---|-----|---|-----|---|-----|---|-----|
| Œ | \OE | Å | \AA | Ł | \L | ¡ | !` |
| æ | \ae | ø | \o | ß | \ss | | |
| Æ | \AE | Ø | \O | | | | |

Table 3.2: Non-English Symbols.

The following six special punctuation symbols can be used in paragraph and LR modes:

| † | \dag | § | \S | © | \copyright |
|---|------|---|-----|---|-----------|
| ‡ | \ddag | ¶ | \P | £ | \pounds |

The commands \dag, \ddag, \S, and \P can also be used in math mode. Remember also that the seven symbols # $ % & _ { } are produced by the seven commands \# \$ \% \& \_ \{ \}.

In addition to the symbol-making commands described here, there are many others that can be used only in math mode. They are described in Section 3.3.2.

## 3.3  Mathematical Formulas

A formula that appears in the running text, called an *in-text* formula, is produced by the math environment. This environment can be invoked with either of the two short forms \(...\) or $...$, as well as by the usual \begin ... \end construction. The displaymath environment, which has the short form \[...\], produces an unnumbered displayed formula. The short forms $...$, \(...\), and \[...\] act as full-fledged environments, delimiting the scope of declarations contained within them. A numbered displayed formula is produced by the equation environment. Section 4.2 describes commands for assigning names to equation numbers and referring to the numbers by name, so you don't have to keep track of the actual numbers.

The math, displaymath, and equation environments put TeX in math mode. TeX ignores spaces in the input when it's in math mode (but space characters may still be needed to mark the end of a command name). Section 3.3.7 describes how to add and remove space in formulas. Remember that TeX is in LR mode, where spaces in the input generate space in the output, when it begins processing the argument of an \mbox command—even one that appears inside a formula.

All the commands introduced in this section can be used only in math mode, unless it is explicitly stated that they can be used elsewhere. Except as noted, they are all robust. However, \begin, \end, \(, \), \[, and \] are fragile commands.

### 3.3.1   Some Common Structures

**Subscripts and Superscripts**

Subscripts and superscripts are made with the _ and ^ commands. These commands can be combined to make complicated subscript and superscript expressions.

$$x^{2y} \quad \texttt{x\^{}\{2y\}} \qquad x^{y^2} \quad \texttt{x\^{}\{y\^{}\{2\}\}} \qquad x_1^y \quad \texttt{x\^{}\{y\}\_\{1\}}$$

$$x_{2y} \quad \texttt{x\_\{2y\}} \qquad x^{y_1} \quad \texttt{x\^{}\{y\_\{1\}\}} \qquad x_1^y \quad \texttt{x\_\{1\}\^{}\{y\}}$$

**Fractions**

Fractions denoted by the / symbol are made in the obvious way.

Multiplying by $n/2$ gives $(m+n)/n$.        `Multiplying by $n/2$ gives \( (m+n)/n \).`

Most fractions in the running text are written this way. The `\frac` command is used for large fractions in displayed formulas; it has two arguments: the numerator and denominator.

$$x = \frac{y + z/2}{y^2 + 1}$$        `\[ x = \frac{y+z/2}{y^{2}+1} \]`

$$\frac{x+y}{1 + \frac{y}{z+1}}$$        `\[\frac{x+y}{1 + \frac{y}{z+1}}\]`

The `\frac` command can be used in an in-text formula to produce a fraction like $\frac{1}{2}$ (by typing `$\frac{1}{2}$`), but this is seldom done.

**Roots**

The `\sqrt` command produces the square root of its argument; it has an optional first argument for other roots. It is a fragile command.

A square root $\sqrt{x+y}$ and an $n$th root $\sqrt[n]{2}$.      `... \( \sqrt{x+y} \) ... \( \sqrt[n]{2} \).`

**Ellipsis**

The commands `\ldots` and `\cdots` produce two different kinds of ellipsis ($\ldots$).

A low ellipsis: $x_1, \ldots, x_n$.        `A low ellipsis: $x_{1}, \ldots ,x_{n}$.`
A centered ellipsis: $a + \cdots + z$.        `A centered ellipsis: $a + \cdots + z$.`

Use `\ldots` between commas and between juxtaposed symbols like $a \ldots z$; use `\cdots` between symbols like $+$, $-$, and $=$. TeX can also produce vertical and diagonal ellipses, which are used mainly in arrays.

    ⋮   \vdots          ⋰   \ddots

The \ldots command works in any mode, but \cdots, \vdots, and \ddots can be used only in math mode.

## 3.3.2   Mathematical Symbols

There are TeX commands to make almost any mathematical symbol you're likely to need. Remember that they can be used only in math mode.

**Greek Letters**

The command to produce a lowercase Greek letter is obtained by adding a \ to the name of the letter. For an uppercase Greek letter, just capitalize the first letter of the command name.

Making Greek letters is as easy as $\pi$ (or $\Pi$).               `... is as easy as $\pi$ (or $\Pi$).`

(The $'s are needed because these commands can be used only in math mode.) If the uppercase Greek letter is the same as its Roman equivalent, as in uppercase alpha, then there is no command to generate it. A complete list of the commands for making Greek letters appears in Table 3.3. Note that some of the lowercase letters have variant forms, made by commands beginning with \var. Also, observe that there's no special command for an omicron; you just use an o.

Lowercase

| | | | | | | | |
|---|---|---|---|---|---|---|---|
| $\alpha$ | \alpha | $\theta$ | \theta | $o$ | o | $\tau$ | \tau |
| $\beta$ | \beta | $\vartheta$ | \vartheta | $\pi$ | \pi | $\upsilon$ | \upsilon |
| $\gamma$ | \gamma | $\iota$ | \iota | $\varpi$ | \varpi | $\phi$ | \phi |
| $\delta$ | \delta | $\kappa$ | \kappa | $\rho$ | \rho | $\varphi$ | \varphi |
| $\epsilon$ | \epsilon | $\lambda$ | \lambda | $\varrho$ | \varrho | $\chi$ | \chi |
| $\varepsilon$ | \varepsilon | $\mu$ | \mu | $\sigma$ | \sigma | $\psi$ | \psi |
| $\zeta$ | \zeta | $\nu$ | \nu | $\varsigma$ | \varsigma | $\omega$ | \omega |
| $\eta$ | \eta | $\xi$ | \xi | | | | |

Uppercase

| | | | | | | | |
|---|---|---|---|---|---|---|---|
| $\Gamma$ | \Gamma | $\Lambda$ | \Lambda | $\Sigma$ | \Sigma | $\Psi$ | \Psi |
| $\Delta$ | \Delta | $\Xi$ | \Xi | $\Upsilon$ | \Upsilon | $\Omega$ | \Omega |
| $\Theta$ | \Theta | $\Pi$ | \Pi | $\Phi$ | \Phi | | |

Table 3.3: Greek Letters.

### Calligraphic Letters

TeX provides twenty-six uppercase calligraphic letters $\mathcal{A}$, $\mathcal{B}$, ..., $\mathcal{Z}$, also called script letters. They are produced by a special type style invoked with the `\mathcal` command.

Choose $\mathcal{F}$ such that $\mathcal{F}(x) > 0$.                    `Choose $\mathcal{F}$ such that...`

Only the twenty-six uppercase letters are available in the calligraphic type style.

### A Menagerie of Mathematical Symbols

TeX can make dozens of special mathematical symbols. A few of them, such as $+$ and $>$, are produced by typing the corresponding keyboard character. Others are obtained with the commands in Tables 3.4 through 3.7. The shaded symbols require the `latexsym` package to be loaded with a `\usepackage` command. (See Section 2.2.2.) Additional symbols can be made by stacking one symbol on top of another with the `\stackrel` command of Section 3.3.6 or the `array` environment of Section 3.3.3. You can also put a slash through a symbol by typing `\not` before it.

If $x \not< y$ then $x \not\leq y - 1$.                    `If $x \not< y$ then \( x \not\leq y-1 \).`

If the slash doesn't come out in exactly the right spot, put one of the math-mode spacing commands described in Section 3.3.7 between the `\not` command and the symbol.

There are some mathematical symbols whose size depends upon what kind of math environment they appear in; they are bigger in the `displaymath` and `equation` environments than in the ordinary `math` environment. These symbols are listed in Table 3.8, where both the large and small versions are shown. Subscript-sized expressions that appear above and below them are typed as ordinary subscripts and superscripts.

| | | | | | | | |
|---|---|---|---|---|---|---|---|
| $\pm$ | `\pm` | $\cap$ | `\cap` | $\diamond$ | `\diamond` | $\oplus$ | `\oplus` |
| $\mp$ | `\mp` | $\cup$ | `\cup` | $\bigtriangleup$ | `\bigtriangleup` | $\ominus$ | `\ominus` |
| $\times$ | `\times` | $\uplus$ | `\uplus` | $\bigtriangledown$ | `\bigtriangledown` | $\otimes$ | `\otimes` |
| $\div$ | `\div` | $\sqcap$ | `\sqcap` | $\triangleleft$ | `\triangleleft` | $\oslash$ | `\oslash` |
| $*$ | `\ast` | $\sqcup$ | `\sqcup` | $\triangleright$ | `\triangleright` | $\odot$ | `\odot` |
| $\star$ | `\star` | $\vee$ | `\vee` | $\lhd$ | `\lhd` | $\bigcirc$ | `\bigcirc` |
| $\circ$ | `\circ` | $\wedge$ | `\wedge` | $\rhd$ | `\rhd` | $\dagger$ | `\dagger` |
| $\bullet$ | `\bullet` | $\setminus$ | `\setminus` | $\unlhd$ | `\unlhd` | $\ddagger$ | `\ddagger` |
| $\cdot$ | `\cdot` | $\wr$ | `\wr` | $\unrhd$ | `\unrhd` | $\amalg$ | `\amalg` |

Table 3.4: Binary Operation Symbols. (Shaded ones require `latexsym` package.)

| ≤ \leq | ≥ \geq | ≡ \equiv | ⊨ \models |
|---|---|---|---|
| ≺ \prec | ≻ \succ | ∼ \sim | ⊥ \perp |
| ⪯ \preceq | ⪰ \succeq | ≃ \simeq | \| \mid |
| ≪ \ll | ≫ \gg | ⌢ \asymp | ‖ \parallel |
| ⊂ \subset | ⊃ \supset | ≈ \approx | ⋈ \bowtie |
| ⊆ \subseteq | ⊇ \supseteq | ≅ \cong | ⋈ \Join |
| ⊏ \sqsubset | ⊐ \sqsupset | ≠ \neq | ⌣ \smile |
| ⊑ \sqsubseteq | ⊒ \sqsupseteq | ≐ \doteq | ⌢ \frown |
| ∈ \in | ∋ \ni | ∉ \notin | ∝ \propto |
| ⊢ \vdash | ⊣ \dashv | | |

Table 3.5: Relation Symbols. (Shaded ones require `latexsym` package.)

| ← \leftarrow | ⟵ \longleftarrow | ↑ \uparrow |
|---|---|---|
| ⇐ \Leftarrow | ⟸ \Longleftarrow | ⇑ \Uparrow |
| → \rightarrow | ⟶ \longrightarrow | ↓ \downarrow |
| ⇒ \Rightarrow | ⟹ \Longrightarrow | ⇓ \Downarrow |
| ↔ \leftrightarrow | ⟷ \longleftrightarrow | ↕ \updownarrow |
| ⇔ \Leftrightarrow | ⟺ \Longleftrightarrow | ⇕ \Updownarrow |
| ↦ \mapsto | ⟼ \longmapsto | ↗ \nearrow |
| ↩ \hookleftarrow | ↪ \hookrightarrow | ↘ \searrow |
| ↼ \leftharpoonup | ⇀ \rightharpoonup | ↙ \swarrow |
| ↽ \leftharpoondown | ⇁ \rightharpoondown | ↖ \nwarrow |
| ⇌ \rightleftharpoons | ↝ \leadsto | |

Table 3.6: Arrow Symbols. (Shaded ones require `latexsym` package.)

| ℵ \aleph | ′ \prime | ∀ \forall | ∞ \infty |
|---|---|---|---|
| ℏ \hbar | ∅ \emptyset | ∃ \exists | □ \Box |
| ı \imath | ∇ \nabla | ¬ \neg | ◇ \Diamond |
| ȷ \jmath | √ \surd | ♭ \flat | △ \triangle |
| ℓ \ell | ⊤ \top | ♮ \natural | ♣ \clubsuit |
| ℘ \wp | ⊥ \bot | ♯ \sharp | ◇ \diamondsuit |
| ℜ \Re | ‖ \\| | \ \backslash | ♡ \heartsuit |
| ℑ \Im | ∠ \angle | ∂ \partial | ♠ \spadesuit |
| ℧ \mho | | | |

Table 3.7: Miscellaneous Symbols. (Shaded ones require `latexsym` package.)

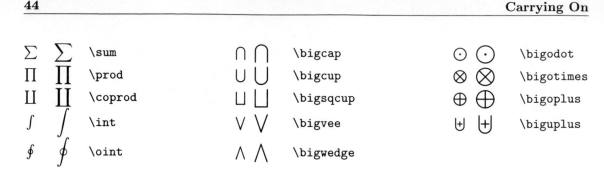

Table 3.8: Variable-sized Symbols.

Here's how they look when displayed:

$$\sum_{i=1}^{n} x_i = \int_{0}^{1} f$$

and in the text: $\sum_{i=1}^{n} x_i = \int_{0}^{1} f$.

```
Here's how they look when displayed:
\[\sum_{i=1}^{n} x_{i} = \int_{0}^{1} f \]
and in the text:
\(\sum_{i=1}^{n} x_{i} = \int_{0}^{1} f \).
```

Section 3.3.8 tells how to coerce TEX into producing $\sum_{i=1}^{n}$ in a displayed formula and $\sum_{i=1}^{n}$ in an in-text formula.

### Log-like Functions

In a formula like $\log(x + y)$, the "log", which represents the logarithm function, is a single word that is usually set in roman type. However, typing log in a formula denotes the product of the three quantities $l$, $o$, and $g$, which is printed as $log$. The logarithm function is denoted by the \log command.

Logarithms obey the law: $\log xy = \log x + \log y$.          . . . \( \log xy = \log x + \log y \).

Other commands like \log for generating function names are listed in Table 3.9. Two additional commands produce the "mod" (modulo) function: \bmod for a binary relation and \pmod for a parenthesized expression. (Remember b as in *binary* and p as in *parenthesized*.)

| \arccos | \cos | \csc | \exp | \ker | \limsup | \min | \sinh |
| \arcsin | \cosh | \deg | \gcd | \lg | \ln | \Pr | \sup |
| \arctan | \cot | \det | \hom | \lim | \log | \sec | \tan |
| \arg | \coth | \dim | \inf | \liminf | \max | \sin | \tanh |

Table 3.9: Log-like Functions.

$$\gcd(m,n) = a \bmod b$$
$$x \equiv y \pmod{a+b}$$

```
\( \gcd(m,n)  =  a \bmod b \)
\( x  \equiv  y \pmod{a+b} \)
```

Note that \pmod has an argument and produces parentheses, while \bmod produces only the "mod".

Some log-like functions act the same as the variable-sized symbols of Table 3.8 with respect to subscripts.

As a displayed formula:

$$\lim_{n \to \infty} x = 0$$

but in text: $\lim_{n\to\infty} x = 0$.

As a displayed formula:
```
\[ \lim_{n \rightarrow \infty} x = 0 \]
```
but in text:
```
\( \lim_{ ... } x = 0 \).
```

### 3.3.3   Arrays

**The array Environment**

Arrays are produced with the **array** environment. It has a single argument that specifies the number of columns and the alignment of items within the columns. For each column in the array, there is a single letter in the argument that specifies how items in the column should be positioned: c for centered, l for flush left, or r for flush right. Within the body of the environment, adjacent rows are separated by a \\ command and adjacent items within a row are separated by an & character.

$$
\begin{array}{clcr}
a+b+c & uv & x-y & 27 \\
a+b & u+v & z & 134 \\
a & 3u+vw & xyz & 2,978
\end{array}
$$

```
\( \begin{array}{clcr}
   a+b+c & uv    & x-y & 27    \\
   a+b   & u+v   & z   & 134   \\
   a     & 3u+vw & xyz & 2,978
\end{array} \)
```

There must be no & after the last item in a row and no \\ after the last row. TeX is in math mode when processing each array element, so it ignores spaces. Don't put any extra space in the argument.

In mathematical formulas, array columns are usually centered. However, a column of numbers often looks best flush right. Section 3.3.4 describes how to put large parentheses or vertical lines around an array to make a matrix or determinant.

Each item in an array is a separate formula, just as if it were in its own **math** environment. A declaration that appears in an item is local to the item; its scope is ended by the &, \\, or \end{array} that ends the item. The \\ command is fragile.

### Vertical Alignment

TEX draws an imaginary horizontal center line through every formula, at the height where a minus sign at the beginning of the formula would go. An individual array item is itself a formula with a center line. The items in a row of an array are positioned vertically so their center lines are all at the same height.

Normally, the center line of an array lies where you would expect it, halfway between the top and bottom. You can change the position of an array's center line by giving an optional one-letter argument to the `array` environment: the argument `t` makes it line up with the top row's center line, while `b` makes it line up with the bottom row's center line.

The box around each array in the following formula is for clarity; it is not produced by the input:

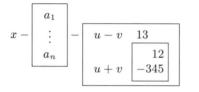

```
...\[ x - \begin{array}{c}
          a_{1} \\ \vdots \\ a_{n}
       \end{array}
     - \begin{array}{t}{cl}
          u-v & 13 \\
          u+v & \begin{array}[b]{r}
                   12 \\ -345
                \end{array}
       \end{array}                    \]
```

### More Complex Arrays

Visual formatting is sometimes necessary to get an array to look right. Section C.1.6 explains how to change the vertical space between two rows; Sections 3.3.7 and 6.4.2 describe commands for adding horizontal space within an item; and Section C.10.2 tells how to add horizontal space between columns. The `array` environment has a number of additional features for making more complex arrays; they are described in Section C.10.2. The LATEX *Companion* describes packages that provide additional features for the `array` environment.

The `array` environment can be used only in math mode and is meant for arrays of formulas; Section 3.6.2 describes an analogous `tabular` environment for making arrays of ordinary text items. The `array` environment is almost always used in a displayed formula, but it can appear in an in-text formula as well.

## 3.3.4  Delimiters

A *delimiter* is a symbol that acts logically like a parenthesis, with a pair of delimiters enclosing an expression. Table 3.10 lists every symbol that TEX regards as a delimiter, together with the command or input character that produces it. These commands and characters produce delimiters of the indicated size. However, delimiters in formulas should be big enough to "fit around" the expressions

| | | | | | |
|---|---|---|---|---|---|
| ( | ( | ) | ) | ↑ | \uparrow |
| [ | [ | ] | ] | ↓ | \downarrow |
| { | \{ | } | \} | ↕ | \updownarrow |
| ⌊ | \lfloor | ⌋ | \rfloor | ⇑ | \Uparrow |
| ⌈ | \lceil | ⌉ | \rceil | ⇓ | \Downarrow |
| ⟨ | \langle | ⟩ | \rangle | ⇕ | \Updownarrow |
| / | / | \ | \backslash | | |
| ∣ | ∣ | ∥ | \| | | |

Table 3.10: Delimiters.

that they delimit. To make a delimiter the right size, type a \left or \right command before it.

Big delimiters are most often used with arrays.

$$\left( \begin{array}{cc} x_{11} & x_{12} \\ x_{21} & x_{22} \\ & y \\ & z \end{array} \right.$$

```
...\[ \left( \begin{array}{c}
            \left| \begin{array}{cc}
                   ... \end{array}
            \right| \\
            y \\ z
      \end{array}    \right)  \]
```

The \left and \right commands must come in matching pairs, but the matching delimiters need not be the same.

$$\vec{x} + \vec{y} + \vec{z} = \left( \begin{array}{c} a \\ b \end{array} \right[$$

```
\[  ... = \left( \begin{array}{c}
          a \\ b
      \end{array}     \right[ \]
```

Some formulas require a big left delimiter with no matching right one, or vice versa. The \left and \right commands must match, but you can make an invisible delimiter by typing a "." after the \left or \right command.

$$x = \left\{ \begin{array}{ll} y & \text{if } y > 0 \\ z + y & \text{otherwise} \end{array} \right.$$

```
\[ x = \left\{ \begin{array}{ll}
       y    & \mbox{if $y>0$} \\
       z+y & \mbox{otherwise}
       \end{array}
\right. \]
```

### 3.3.5   Multiline Formulas

The `displaymath` and `equation` environments make one-line formulas. A formula is displayed across multiple lines if it is a sequence of separate formulas or is too long to fit on a single line. A sequence of equations or inequalities is displayed with the `eqnarray` environment. It is very much like a three-column `array` environment, with consecutive rows separated by \\ and consecutive items within a row separated by & (Section 3.3.3). However, an equation number is put on every line unless that line has a \nonumber command.

The middle column can be anything, not just a '='.

$$x \quad = \quad 17y \qquad\qquad\qquad\qquad\qquad\qquad (2)$$
$$y \quad > \quad a + b + c + d + e + f + g + h + i + j +$$
$$k + l + m + n + o + p \qquad\qquad (3)$$

```
...\begin{eqnarray}
    x & = & 17y \\
    y & > & a + ... + j +  \nonumber  \\
      &   & k + l + m + n + o + p
\end{eqnarray}
```

Section 4.2 describes how to let LaTeX handle references to equations so you don't have to remember equation numbers.

The `eqnarray*` environment is the same as `eqnarray` except it does not generate equation numbers.

$$x \quad \ll \quad y_1 + \cdots + y_n$$
$$\leq \quad z$$

```
\begin{eqnarray*}
   x  & \ll  & y_{1} + \cdots + y_{n} \\
      & \leq & z
\end{eqnarray*}
```

A + or − that begins a formula (or certain subformulas) is assumed to be a unary operator, so typing `$-x$` produces $-x$ and typing `$\sum -x_{i}$` produces $\sum -x_i$, with no space between the "−" and the "$x$". If the formula is part of a larger one that is being split across lines, TeX must be told that the + or − is a binary operator. This is done by starting the formula with an invisible first term, produced by an `\mbox` command with a null argument.

$$y \quad = \quad a + b + c + d + e + f + g + h + i + j$$
$$+ k + l + m + n + o + p$$

```
\begin{eqnarray*}
y & = & a + b + c + ...  + h + i + j \\
  &   & \mbox{} + k + ...
\end{eqnarray*}
```

A formula can often be split across lines using a `\lefteqn` command in an `eqnarray` or `eqnarray*` environment, as indicated by the following example:

$$w + x + y + z =$$
$$a + b + c + d + e + f + g + h + i + j +$$
$$k + l + m + n + o + p$$

```
\begin{eqnarray*}
\lefteqn{w+x+y+z = }  \\
& &   a + ... + j +  \\
& &   k + ... + o + p
\end{eqnarray*}
```

The `\lefteqn` command works by making TeX think that the formula it produces has zero width, so the left-most column of the `eqnarray` or `eqnarray*` environment is made suitably narrow. The indentation of the following lines can be increased by adding space (with the commands of Section 6.4.2) between the `\lefteqn` command and the \\.

Breaking a single formula across lines in this way is visual formatting, and I wish LaTeX could do it for you. However, doing it well requires more intelligence than LaTeX has, and doing it poorly can make the formula hard to understand, so you must do it yourself. This means that the formula may have to be reformatted if you change notation (changing the formula's length) or if you change the style of your document (changing the line length).

## 3.3.6  Putting One Thing Above Another

Symbols in a formula are sometimes placed one above another. The `array` environment is good for vertically stacking subformulas, but not smaller pieces— you wouldn't use it to put a bar over an $x$ to form $\bar{x}$. LaTeX provides special commands for doing this and some other common kinds of symbol stacking.

### Over- and Underlining

The `\overline` command puts a horizontal line above its argument.

You can have nested overlining: $\overline{\overline{x}^2 + 1}$.        `... \( \overline{\overline{x}^{2} + 1} \).`

There's an analogous `\underline` command for underlining that works in paragraph and LR mode as well as math mode, but it's seldom used in formulas.

The value is $\underline{3x}$.        `\underline{The} value is $\underline{3x}$.`

The `\underline` command is fragile.

Horizontal braces are put above or below an expression with the `\overbrace` and `\underbrace` commands.

$\overbrace{a + \underbrace{b + c} + d}$        `\overbrace{a+ \underbrace{b + c} + d}`

In a displayed formula, a subscript or superscript puts a label on the brace.

$$\underbrace{a + \overbrace{b + \cdots + y}^{24} + z}_{26}$$

`\[ \underbrace{a + \overbrace{b`
`          + \cdots + y}^{24} + z }_{26} \]`

### Accents

The accent commands described in Section 3.2.1 are for ordinary text and cannot be used in math mode. Accents in formulas are produced with the commands shown in Table 3.11. The letter $a$ is used as an illustration; the accents work with any letter.

Wide versions of the `\hat` and `\tilde` accent are produced by the `\widehat` and `\widetilde` commands. These commands try to choose the appropriate-sized accent to fit over their argument, but they can't produce very wide accents.

| $\hat{a}$ \hat{a} | $\acute{a}$ \acute{a} | $\bar{a}$ \bar{a} | $\dot{a}$ \dot{a} |
|---|---|---|---|
| $\check{a}$ \check{a} | $\grave{a}$ \grave{a} | $\vec{a}$ \vec{a} | $\ddot{a}$ \ddot{a} |
| $\breve{a}$ \breve{a} | $\tilde{a}$ \tilde{a} | | |

Table 3.11: Math Mode Accents.

Here are two sizes of wide hat: $\widehat{1-x} = \widehat{-y}$.              ... \( \widehat{1-x} = \widehat{-y} \).

The letters $i$ and $j$ should lose their dots when accented. The commands \imath and \jmath produce a dotless $i$ and $j$, respectively.

There are no dots in $\vec{\imath} + \tilde{\jmath}$.              ... \( \vec{\imath} + \tilde{\jmath} \).

### Stacking Symbols

The \stackrel command stacks one symbol above another.

$A \stackrel{a'}{\rightarrow} B \stackrel{b'}{\rightarrow} C$              \( A \stackrel{a'}{\rightarrow} B ...\)

$\vec{x} \stackrel{\mathrm{def}}{=} (x_1,\ldots,x_n)$              \( \vec{x} \stackrel{\mathrm{def}}{=} ...\)

See Section 3.3.8 for an explanation of the \mathrm command. The \stackrel command's first argument is printed in small type, like a superscript; use the \textstyle declaration of Section 3.3.8 to print it in regular-size type.

## 3.3.7   Spacing in Math Mode

In math mode, TEX ignores the spaces you type and formats the formula the way it thinks is best. Some authors feel that TEX cramps formulas, and they want to add more space. TEX knows more about typesetting formulas than many authors do. Adding extra space usually makes a formula prettier but harder to read, because it visually "fractures" the formula into separate units. Study how formulas look in ordinary mathematics texts before trying to improve TEX's formatting.

Although fiddling with the spacing is dangerous, you sometimes have to do it to make a formula look just right. One reason is that TEX may not understand the formula's logical structure. For example, it interprets y dx as the product of three quantities rather than as $y$ times the differential $dx$, so it doesn't add the little extra space after the $y$ that appears in $y\,dx$. Section 3.4 explains how to define your own commands for expressing this kind of logical structure, so you need worry about the proper spacing only when defining the commands, not when writing the formulas.

Like any computer program that makes aesthetic decisions, TEX sometimes needs human assistance. You'll have to examine the output to see if the spacing needs adjustment. Pay special attention to square root signs, integral signs, and quotient symbols (/).

The following five commands add the amount of horizontal space shown between the vertical lines:

| ‖ | \, | thin space | ‖ | \: | medium space | ‖ | \␣ | interword space |
| ‖ | \! | negative thin space | ‖ | \; | thick space | | | |

The \! acts like a backspace, removing the same amount of space that \, adds. The \, command can be used in any mode; the others can appear only in math mode. Here are some examples of their use, where the result of omitting the spacing commands is also shown.

$\sqrt{2}\,x$           `\sqrt{2} \, x`              instead of  $\sqrt{2}x$

$n/\log n$           `n / \! \log n`              instead of  $n/\log n$

$\iint z\,dx\,dy$           `\int\!\!\int z\,dx\,dy`      instead of  $\int\int zdxdy$

As with all such fine tuning, you should not correct the spacing in formulas until you've finished writing the document and are preparing the final output.

## 3.3.8   Changing Style in Math Mode

### Type Style

LaTeX provides the following commands for changing type style in math mode:

$\mathit{italic + 2^{ft} \Psi \log[\psi]}$                  `$\mathit{italic + 2^{ft} \Psi \log[\psi]}$`

$\mathrm{roman + 2^{ft} \Psi \log[\psi]}$                  `$\mathrm{roman  + 2^{ft} \Psi \log[\psi]}$`

$\mathbf{bold + 2^{ft} \Psi \log[\psi]}$                  `$\mathbf{bold    + 2^{ft} \Psi \log[\psi]}$`

$\mathsf{sans\ serif + 2^{ft}\Psi \log[\psi]}$                  `$\mathsf{sans\ serif + ... }$`

$\mathtt{typewriter + 2^{ft}\Psi\log[\psi]}$                  `$\mathtt{typewriter  + ... }$`

$\mathcal{CAL\ UPPERCASE\ LETTERS\ ONLY}$                  `$\mathcal{CAL\ UPPERCASE\ LETTERS\ ONLY}$`

They change the style only of letters, numbers, and uppercase Greek letters. Nothing else is affected. LaTeX normally uses an italic type style for letters in math mode. However, it interprets each letter as a separate mathematical symbol, and it produces very different spacing than an ordinary italic typestyle. You should use \mathit for multiletter symbols in formulas.

Is $different$ any $\mathit{different}$ from $dif^2e^2rnt$?          Is `$different$` any `$\mathit{different}$`...

As is evident from this example, you should not use $...$ as a shorthand for \emph{...} or \textit{...}.

The \boldmath declaration causes everything in a formula to be bold, including the symbols.

$\boldsymbol{diff + 2^{ft}\Psi\log[\psi]}$                  `\boldmath ${diff + 2^{ft}\Psi\log[\psi]}$`

This declaration cannot be used in math mode. To produce a bold subformula, put the subformula in an \mbox.

$x + \nabla f = 0$
$$\text{\\(x + \\mbox\{\\boldmath \$\\nabla f\$\} = 0\\)}$$

The \boldmath command generates a warning if any font (size and style of type) that you *might* use in a formula isn't available. For example, it might issue a warning that LaTeX does not have the font needed to produce a bold sans serif subsubscript, even though you never dreamed of producing such a subsubscript. You should examine your output to make sure that the fonts you do use are the right ones.

**Math Style**

TeX uses the following four *math styles* when typesetting formulas:

> **display** For normal symbols in a displayed formula.
>
> **text** For normal symbols in an in-text formula.
>
> **script** For subscripts and superscripts.
>
> **scriptscript** For further levels of sub- and superscripting, such as subscripts of superscripts.

Display and text math styles are the same except for the size of the variable-sized symbols in Table 3.8 on page 44 and the placement of subscripts and superscripts on these symbols, on some of the log-like functions in Table 3.9 on page 44, and on horizontal braces. TeX uses small type in script style and even smaller type in scriptscript style. The declarations \displaystyle, \textstyle, \scriptstyle, and \scriptscriptstyle force TeX to use the indicated style.

Compare the small superscript in $e^{x(i)}$ with the large one in $e^{y(i)}$.

```
... small superscript in \( e^{x(i)} \)
... large one in \( e^{\textstyle y(i)} \).
```

### 3.3.9   When All Else Fails

If you write a lot of complicated formulas, sooner or later you'll encounter one that can't be handled with the commands described so far. When this happens, the first thing to do is look at the advanced LaTeX features described in Sections C.7 and C.10.2. If you don't find what you need there, consider using the amstex package, described in the LaTeX *Companion*. This package was created for mathematicians by the American Mathematical Society.

If you are not a mathematician and don't write many complicated formulas, you may be satisfied with an *ad hoc* solution to your problem that uses visual formatting. Try the commands in Section 6.4.3 that move text around and change how big TeX thinks it is. LaTeX's picture environment, described in

Section 7.1, allows you to put a symbol anywhere you want, and to draw lines and arrows. The `graphics` package described in Section 7.2 contains commands to shrink, stretch, and rotate text. With a little effort, you can handcraft just about any kind of formula you want.

## 3.4   Defining Commands and Environments

The input file should display as clearly as possible the logical structures in your document. Any structure, such as a special mathematical notation, that appears several times in the document should be expressed with its own command or environment. The following two sections explain how to define commands and environments. Section 3.4.3 describes how to type theorems and similar structures.

### 3.4.1   Defining Commands

The simplest type of repeated structure occurs when the same text appears in different places. The `\newcommand` declaration defines a new command to generate such text; its first argument is the command name and its second argument is the text.

Let $\Gamma_i$ be the number of gnats per cubic meter, where $\Gamma_i$ is normalized with respect to $\nu(s)$.

```
\newcommand{\gn}{$\Gamma_{i}$}
...
Let \gn\ be the  ...  where \gn\ is  ...
```

The `\`$_\sqcup$ commands are needed because TEX ignores space characters following the command name `\gn`.

This example illustrates a common problem in defining commands to produce mathematical formulas. The `\Gamma` command can be used only in math mode, which is why the $'s are used in the `\newcommand` argument. However, the command `\gn` cannot be used in math mode because the first $ would cause TEX to leave math mode and encounter the `\Gamma` while in paragraph mode. To solve this problem, LATEX provides the `\ensuremath` command, which ensures that its argument is typeset in math mode, regardless of the current mode. Thus, `\ensuremath{x^{2}}` is equivalent to `$x^{2}$` if it appears in LR or paragraph mode, and it is equivalent to `x^{2}` if it appears in math mode. With `\ensuremath`, we define `\gn` so it can be used in any mode.

Let $\Gamma_i$ be the number of gnats per cubic meter, where $e^{\Gamma_i} = \nu(s)$.

```
\newcommand{\gn}{\ensuremath{\Gamma_{i}}}
...
Let \gn\ be the ... where $e^{\gn}=\nu(s)$.
```

You should use `\ensuremath` when defining a command to be used both in and out of math mode.

In addition to making the input more readable, defining your own commands can save typing. LaTeX's command and environment names have generally been chosen to be descriptive rather than brief. You can use \newcommand to define abbreviations for frequently used commands. For example, the declarations

```
\newcommand{\be}{\begin{enumerate}}
\newcommand{\ee}{\end{enumerate}}
```

define \be ... \ee to be equivalent to

```
\begin{enumerate} ... \end{enumerate}
```

For repetitive structures having components that vary, you can define commands with arguments by giving \newcommand an optional argument.

Since $gnu(5x; y)$ and $gnu(5x-1; y+1)$ represent adjacent populations, they are approximately equal.

```
\newcommand{\gnaw}[2]{\ensuremath{\mathit
                     {gnu}(#1;#2)}}
Since \gnaw{5x}{y} and \gnaw{5x-1}{y+1} ...
```

The optional argument 2 (in square brackets) specifies that \gnaw has two arguments. The #1 and #2 in the last argument of \newcommand are called *parameters*; they are replaced by the first and second arguments, respectively, of \gnaw when that command is used. A command may have up to nine arguments. Section C.8.1 explains how to define a command that has an optional argument.

When you define a command like \gnaw, the definition is saved exactly as it appears in the \newcommand declaration. When TeX encounters a use of \gnaw, it replaces \gnaw and its arguments by the definition, with the arguments substituted for the corresponding *parameters*—the #1 replaced by the first argument and the #2 replaced by the second. TeX then processes this text pretty much as if you had typed it instead of typing the \gnaw command. However, defining a command to have space at the end is usually a bad idea, since it can lead to extra space in the output when the command is used.

One command can be defined in terms of another.

The definition above of $gnu(0; 1)$ gives $gnu(5x; y)$ the expected value.

```
\newcommand{\usegnaw}{\gnaw{5x}{y}}
... of \gnaw{0}{1} gives \usegnaw\ the ...
```

It doesn't matter whether the \newcommand declaration defining \usegnaw comes before or after the one defining \gnaw, so long as they both come before any use of \usegnaw. However, a command cannot be defined in terms of itself, since TeX would chase its tail forever trying to figure out what such a definition meant.[2]

When TeX encounters a command, it looks for that command's arguments before interpreting it or any subsequent commands. Thus, you can't type

---

[2]This kind of recursive definition is possible using more advanced TeX commands, but it cannot be done with the LaTeX commands described in this book.

> `\newcommand{\gnawargs}{{5x}{y}} \gnaw\gnawargs is wrong`

because TeX expects the `\gnaw` command to be followed by two arguments enclosed in braces, not by another command.

The braces surrounding the last argument of the `\newcommand` declaration do not become part of the command's definition, and the braces surrounding an argument are thrown away before substituting the argument for the corresponding parameter. This means that the braces delimiting an argument do not delimit the scope of declarations in the argument. To limit the scope of declarations contained within an argument, you must add explicit braces in the command definition.

| | |
|---|---|
| *gnus(x; 54) is fine, but in gnus(x; 54), the scope of the emphasis declaration extends into the following text.* | `\newcommand{\good}[3]{{#1}$({#2};{#3})$}`<br>`\newcommand{\bad}[3]{#1$(#2;#3)$}`<br>`...`<br>`\good{\em gnus}{x}{54} is fine, but in`<br>`\bad{\em gnus}{x}{54}, the scope ...` |

Using `\newcommand` to define a command that already exists produces an error. The `\renewcommand` declaration redefines an already defined command; it has the same arguments as `\newcommand`. Don't redefine an existing command unless you know what you're doing. Even if you don't explicitly use a command, redefining it can produce strange and unpleasant results. Also, never define or redefine any command whose name begins with `\end`.

The `\newcommand` and `\renewcommand` commands are declarations; their scopes are determined by the rules given in Section 2.2.1. It's best to put all command definitions together in the preamble, with comments describing what the commands do. You're likely to re-use many of them in subsequent documents.

## 3.4.2   Defining Environments

The `\newenvironment` command is used to define a new environment. A command of the form

> `\newenvironment{cozy}{`*begin text*`}{`*end text*`}`

defines a `cozy` environment for which TeX replaces a `\begin{cozy}` command by the *begin text* and an `\end{cozy}` command by the *end text*. A new environment is usually defined in terms of an existing environment such as `itemize`, with the *begin text* beginning the `itemize` environment and the *end text* ending it.

Here is an example of a user-defined environment:

- *This environment produces items that are emphasized.*

- *It is defined in terms of LaTeX's* `itemize` *environment and* `\em` *command.*

```
\newenvironment{emphit}{\begin{itemize}
    \em}{\end{itemize}}
... example of a user-defined environment:
\begin{emphit}
 \item This environment produces ...
\end{emphit}
```

An optional argument of the `\newenvironment` command allows you to define an environment that has arguments; it works the same as described above for `\newcommand`.

Observe how a new logical structure—in this example, a labeled description of a single item—can be defined in terms of existing environments.

> *Armadillos*: This witty description of the armadillo was produced by the `descit` environment.

```
\newenvironment{descit}[1]{\begin{quote}
    \textit{#1}:}{\end{quote}}
...
defined in terms of existing environments.
\begin{descit}{Armadillos}
This witty description of the armadillo ...
\end{descit}
```

The parameters (the `#1`, `#2`, etc.) can appear only in the *begin text*. The comments made above about the scope of declarations that appear inside arguments of a command defined with `\newcommand` apply to the arguments of environments defined with `\newenvironment`. Section C.8.2 explains how to define an environment with an optional argument.

The `\newenvironment` command produces an error if the environment is already defined. Use `\renewenvironment` to redefine an existing environment. If `\newenvironment` complains that an environment you've never heard of already exists, choose a different environment name. Use `\renewenvironment` only when you know what you're doing; don't try redefining an environment that you don't know about.

### 3.4.3   Theorems and Such

Mathematical text usually includes theorems and/or theorem-like structures such as lemmas, propositions, axioms, conjectures, and so on. Nonmathematical text may contain similar structures: rules, laws, assumptions, principles, etc. Having a built-in environment for each possibility is out of the question, so LaTeX provides the `\newtheorem` declaration to define environments for the particular theorem-like structures in your document.

The `\newtheorem` command has two arguments: the first is the name of the environment, the second is the text used to label it.

Conjectures are numbered consecutively from the beginning of the document; this is the fourth one:

**Conjecture 4** *All conjectures are interesting, but some conjectures are more interesting than others.*

```
\newtheorem{guess}{Conjecture}
...
document; this is the fourth one:
\begin{guess}
  All conjectures ... than others.
\end{guess}
```

The \newtheorem declaration is best put in the preamble, but it can go anywhere in the document.

A final optional argument to \newtheorem causes the theorem-like environment to be numbered within the specified sectional unit.

This is the first Axiom of Chapter 3:

**Axiom 3.1** *All axioms are very dull.*

```
\newtheorem{axiom}{Axiom}[chapter]
...
\begin{axiom}
  All axioms are very dull.
\end{axiom}
```

Theorem-like environments can be numbered within any sectional unit; using section instead of chapter in the example above causes axioms to be numbered within sections.

Sometimes one wants different theorem-like structures to share the same numbering sequence—so, for example, the hunch immediately following Conjecture 5 should be Hunch 6.

**Conjecture 5** *Some good conjectures are numbered.*

**Hunch 6** *There are no sure-fire hunches.*

```
\newtheorem{guess}{Conjecture}
\newtheorem{hunch}[guess]{Hunch}
...
\begin{guess} Some good ... \end{guess}
\begin{hunch} There are ... \end{hunch}
```

The optional argument guess in the second \newtheorem command specifies that the hunch environment should be numbered in the same sequence as the guess environment.

A theorem-like environment defined with \newtheorem has an optional argument that is often used for the inventor or common name of a theorem, definition, or axiom.

**Conjecture 7 (Wiles, 1985)** *There do exist integers $n > 2$, $x$, $y$, and $z$ such that $x^n + y^n = z^n$.*

```
\begin{guess}[Wiles, 1985]
  There do exist integers $n>2$, $x$, ...
\end{guess}
```

See Section C.1.1 if the body of a theorem-like environment begins with a [.

## 3.5    Figures and Other Floating Bodies

### 3.5.1    Figures and Tables

TEX will break a sentence across pages to avoid a partially filled page. But some things, such as pictures, cannot be split; they must be "floated" to convenient places, like the top of the following page, to prevent half-empty pages. LaTeX provides two environments that cause their contents to float in this way: `figure` and `table`. There are packages that define or allow you to define other environments for floating objects, such as a `program` environment for computer programs. LaTeX doesn't care what you use any of these environments for; so far as it's concerned, the only difference between them is how they are captioned.

The caption on a figure or table is made with a `\caption` command having the caption's text as its argument. This is a moving argument, so fragile commands must be `\protect`'ed (see Section 2.2.3). The `figure` or `table` environment is placed in with the text, usually just past the point where the figure or table is first mentioned.

The body of the figure goes here. This figure happened to float to the top of the current page.

Figure 7: The caption goes here.

⋮

This is the place in the running text that mentions Figure 7 for the first time. The figure will not be put on an earlier page than the text preceding the `figure` environment.

```
This is the place in the running text that
mentions Figure~7 for the first time.
  \begin{figure}
    The body of the figure goes here.
    This figure ... the current page.
    \caption{The caption goes here.}
  \end{figure}
The figure will not be put on an ...
```

Tables are numbered separately from figures, using the same numbering scheme. Section 4.2 explains how to number cross-references automatically, so you never have to type the actual figure numbers.

You can put anything you want in the body of a figure or table; LaTeX processes it in paragraph mode just like any other text. The `figure` environment is generally used for pictures and the `table` environment for tabular information. Simple pictures can be drawn with the `picture` environment of Section 7.1. You can insert pictures prepared with other programs using the `graphics` package, described in Section 7.2. You can also use the `\vspace` command of Section 6.4.2 to leave room for a picture to be pasted in later. Tabular material can be formatted with the `tabular` environment of Section 3.6.2. Section 6.5 explains how to center the figure or table.

The body of a figure or table is typeset as a paragraph the same width as in the ordinary running text. Section 6.4.3 explains how to make paragraphs of different widths, position two half-width figures side by side, and do other formatting within a `figure` or `table` environment. More than one `\caption` command can appear in the same `figure` or `table` environment, producing a single floating object with multiple numbered captions. The `\caption` command can be used only in a `figure` or `table` environment.

LaTeX ordinarily tries to place a figure or table either above the text at the top of a page, below the text at the bottom of a page, or on a separate page containing nothing but figures and tables. Section C.9.1 describes the rules by which LaTeX decides where a floating object should float and how you can influence its decision; read that section if you don't understand why LaTeX put a figure or table where it did.

### 3.5.2   Marginal Notes

A marginal note is made with the `\marginpar` command, having the text as its argument. The note is placed in the margin, its first line even with the line of text containing the command. TeX is in paragraph mode when processing the marginal note. The following example shows how I typed this paragraph:

*This is a mar-ginal note.*

```
and, having the text as its           ... placed in the margin,
 line even with the line of           \marginpar{\em This is a marginal note.}
mode when processing the              its first line even with the line of
yped this paragraph.                  ... how I typed this paragraph.
```

*This is a mar-ginal note.*

The standard styles put notes in the right margin for one-sided printing (the default), in the outside margin for two-sided printing (specified by the `twoside` document-class option), and in the nearest margin for two-column formatting (the `twocolumn` option). Section C.9.2 describes commands for getting LaTeX to put them in the opposite margin.

You may want a marginal note to vary depending upon which margin it's in. For example, to make an arrow pointing to the text, you need a left-pointing arrow in the right margin and a right-pointing one in the left margin. If the `\marginpar` command is given an optional first argument, it uses that argument if the note goes in the left margin and uses the second (mandatory) argument if the note goes in the right margin. The command

```
\marginpar [$\Rightarrow$]{$\Leftarrow$}
```

makes an arrow that points towards the text, whichever margin the note appears in.[3]

A marginal note is never broken across pages; a note that's too long will extend below the page's bottom margin. LaTeX moves a marginal note down on the page to keep it from bumping into a previous one, warning you when it does

---

[3]The arrows won't be symmetrically placed, since both will be at the left of the space reserved for marginal notes. The `\hfill` command of Section 6.4.2 can be used to adjust their horizontal position.

so. When using notes more than two or three lines long, you may have to adjust
their placement according to where they happen to fall on the page. The vertical
position of a note is changed by beginning it with a vertical spacing command
(Section 6.4.2). You may also have to use the commands of Section 6.2.2 to
control where LaTeX starts a new page. This is visual design, which means
reformatting if you make changes to the document. Save this job until the very
end, after you've finished all the writing.

Marginal notes are not handled efficiently by LaTeX; it may run out of space if
you use too many of them. How many you can use before this happens depends
upon what computer you're running LaTeX on and how many figures and tables
you have.

## 3.6    Lining It Up in Columns

The `tabbing` and `tabular` environments both can align text in columns. The
`tabbing` environment allows you to set tab stops similar to the ones on a typewriter, while the `tabular` environment is similar to the `array` environment described in Section 3.3.3, except that it is for ordinary text rather than formulas.
The `tabbing` and `tabular` environments differ in the following ways:

- The `tabbing` environment can be used only in paragraph mode and makes
  a separate paragraph. The `tabular` environment can be used in any mode;
  it can put a table in the middle of a formula or line of text.

- TeX can start a new page in the middle of a `tabbing` environment, but
  not in the middle of a `tabular` environment. Thus, a long `tabbing` environment can appear in the running text, but a long `tabular` environment
  should go in a figure or table (Section 3.5.1).

- TeX automatically determines the widths of columns in the `tabular` environment; you have to do that yourself in the `tabbing` environment by
  setting tab stops.

- A change of format in the middle of the environment is easier in the
  `tabbing` than in the `tabular` environment. This makes the `tabbing` environment better at formatting computer programs.

If neither the `tabbing` nor the `tabular` environment does what you want, consult
the LaTeX *Companion*. It describes several packages that provide very powerful
commands to format tabular material.

### 3.6.1    The `tabbing` Environment

In the `tabbing` environment, you align text in columns by setting tab stops and
tabbing to them, somewhat as you would with an ordinary typewriter. Tab

stops are set with the \- command, and \> moves to the next tab stop. Lines
are separated by the \\ command.

| | |
|---|---|
| The `tabbing` environment starts a new line. | `... environment starts a new line.`<br>`\begin{tabbing}` |
| If it's raining<br>   then put on boots,<br>      take hat;<br>   else  smile.<br>Leave house. | `If \= it's raining          \\`<br>`   \> then \= put on boots,\\`<br>`   \>       \> take hat;   \\`<br>`   \> else \> smile.        \\`<br>`Leave house.`<br>`\end{tabbing}` |
| The text that follows starts on a new line, begin-ning a new paragraph if you leave a blank line after the \end{tabbing} command. | `The text that follows starts on a new ...` |

Unlike a typewriter's tabbing key, the \> command tabs to the logically next
tab stop, even if that means tabbing to the left.

| | |
|---|---|
| A short column<br>This is t~~oo~~ l~~ong~~ / / / | `\begin{tabbing}`<br>`     A short          \= column.      \\`<br>`     This is too long. \> / / / / / / /`<br>`\end{tabbing}`<br>`\mbox{}` |

Remember that the input file's format doesn't matter; one space is the same as
a hundred.

The \= command resets the logically next tab stop.

| | |
|---|---|
| Old Column 1 Old Col 2 Old Col 3<br>Col 1        Col 2<br>New Col 1 New 2        Same Col 3<br>Col 1       Col 2        Col 3 | `\begin{tabbing}`<br>`Old Column 1 \= Old Col 2  \= Old Col 3  \\`<br>`Col 1    \>        Col 2         \\`<br>`New Col 1  \= New 2        \> Same Col 3 \\`<br>`Col 1        \> Col 2      \> Col 3`<br>`\end{tabbing}` |

Spaces in the input are ignored after a \= or \> command, but not before it.

A line that ends with a \kill command instead of a \\ produces no output,
but can be used for setting tabs.

| | |
|---|---|
| Gnat     Gnu     Gnome<br>Armadillo Armament Armorer | `\begin{tabbing}`<br>`Armadillo \= Armament \=       \kill`<br>`Gnat       \> Gnu      \> Gnome  \\`<br>`Armadillo \> Armament \> Armorer`<br>`\end{tabbing}` |

A declaration made in a `tabbing` environment is local to the current item; its
scope is ended by the next \=, \>, \\, \kill, or \end{tabbing} command.

A lively *gnat*        A dull gnu                          `A lively \em gnat  \> A dull gnu \\`

The `tabbing` environment has a number of additional features that are described in Section C.10.1.

### 3.6.2   The `tabular` Environment

The `tabular` environment is similar to the `array` environment, so you should read Section 3.3.3 before reading any further here. It differs from the `array` environment in two ways: it may be used in any mode, not just in math mode, and its items are processed in LR mode instead of in math mode. This makes `tabular` better for tabular lists and `array` better for mathematical formulas. This section describes some features used mainly with the `tabular` environment, although they apply to `array` as well. Many additional features of these environments are described in Section C.10.2.

A | in the `tabular` environment's argument puts a vertical line extending the full height of the environment in the specified place. An `\hline` command after a `\\` or at the beginning of the environment draws a horizontal line across the full width of the environment. The `\cline{`*i-j*`}` command draws a horizontal line across columns *i* through *j*, inclusive.

| gnats | gram | $13.65 |
|---|---|---|
| | each | .01 |
| gnu | stuffed | 92.50 |
| emu | | 33.33 |
| armadillo | frozen | 8.99 |

```
\begin{tabular}{||l|lr||}          \hline
gnats       & gram      &\$13.65 \\ \cline{2-3}
            & each      &    .01 \\ \hline
gnu         & stuffed & 92.50
                    \\  \cline{1-1} \cline{3-3}
emu         &          & 33.33 \\ \hline
armadillo & frozen    &   8.99 \\ \hline
\end{tabular}
```

This is the only situation in which a `\\` goes after the last row of the environment.

Single (not doubled) | specifiers in the argument of a `tabular` (or `array`) environment do not change the width of the table. Tables not enclosed by vertical lines therefore have extra space around them. Section C.10.2 explains how to remove this space.

A single item that spans multiple columns is made with a `\multicolumn` command, having the form

   `\multicolumn{`*n*`}{`*pos*`}{`*item*`}`

where *n* is the number of columns to be spanned, *pos* specifies the horizontal positioning of the item—just as in the environment's argument—and *item* is the item's text. The *pos* argument replaces the portion of the environment's argument corresponding to the *n* spanned columns; it must contain a single `l`, `r`, or `c` character and may contain | characters.

Note the placement of "ITEM" and "PRICE":

```
...\begin{tabular}{llr}
   \multicolumn{2}{c}{ITEM} &
      \multicolumn{1}{c}{PRICE} \\
   gnat & (dozen) &    3.24        \\
   gnu  & (each)  & 24,985.47
\end{tabular}
```

| | ITEM | PRICE |
|---|---|---|
| gnat | (dozen) | 3.24 |
| gnu | (each) | 24,985.47 |

A \multicolumn command spanning a single column serves to override the item positioning specified by the environment argument.

When the environment argument has | characters, it's not obvious which of them get replaced by a \multicolumn's positioning argument. The rule is: *the part of the environment argument corresponding to any column other than the first begins with an l, r, or c character.* By this rule, the argument |l|l|r| is split into parts as |l| |l| |r|.

| *type* | *style* | |
|---|---|---|
| smart | red | short |
| rather silly | puce | tall |

```
\begin{tabular}{|l|l|r|}        \hline\hline
\emph{type} &
\multicolumn{2}{c|}{\emph{style}} \\ \hline
smart         & red  & short \\
rather silly & puce & tall   \\ \hline\hline
\end{tabular}
```

The tabular environment produces an object that TeX treats exactly like a single, big letter. You could put it in the middle of a paragraph, or in the middle of a word—but that would look rather strange. A tabular environment is usually put in a figure or table (Section 3.5.1), or else displayed on a line by itself, using the center environment of Section 6.5.

The tabular environment makes it easy to draw tables with horizontal and vertical lines. Don't abuse this feature. Lines usually just add clutter to a table; they are seldom helpful. The numbered tables in this book do not contain a single line.

## 3.7   Simulating Typed Text

A printed document may contain simulated typed text—for example, the instruction manual for a computer program usually shows what the user types. The \ttfamily declaration causes TeX to produce text in a typewriter type style (Section 3.1), but it doesn't stop TeX from breaking the text into lines as it sees fit. The verbatim environment allows you to type the text exactly the way you want it to appear in the document.

The `verbatim` environment is the one place where LaTeX pays attention to how the input file is formatted.

```
What the    #%|&$_\^~ is  ``going'' {on}
   here \today \\\\????
```

```
... to how the input file is formatted.
\begin{verbatim}
What the    #%|&$_\^~ is  ``going'' {on}
   here \today \\\\????
\end{verbatim}
```

Each space you type produces a space in the output, and new lines are begun just where you type them. Special characters such as \ and { are treated like ordinary characters in a `verbatim` environment. In fact, you can type anything in the body of a `verbatim` environment except for the fourteen-character sequence `\end{verbatim}`.

The `verbatim` environment begins on a new line of output, as does the text following it. A blank line after the `\end{verbatim}` starts a new paragraph as usual.

The `\verb` command simulates a short piece of typed text inside an ordinary paragraph. Its argument is not enclosed in braces, but by a pair of identical characters.

The %\} {@& gnat and --#$ gnus are silly.

```
The \verb+%\} {@&+ gnat and \verb2--#$2 ...
```

The argument of the first `\verb` command is contained between the two + characters, the argument of the second between two 2 characters. Instead of + or 2, you can use any character that does not appear in the argument except a space, a letter, or a *.

There are also a `verbatim*` environment and a `\verb*` command. They are exactly like `verbatim` and `\verb` except that a space produces a ␣ symbol instead of a blank space.

You can type $x␣=␣y$ or ␣$x=y$␣.

```
... \verb*|$x = y$| or \verb*/ $x=y$ /.
```

The `verbatim` environment and `\verb` command are inherently anomalous, since characters like $ and } don't have their usual meanings. This results in the following restrictions on their use:

- A `verbatim` environment or `\verb` command may not appear within an argument of any other command. (However, they may appear inside another environment.)

- There may be no space between a `\verb` or `\verb*` command and its argument. The command and its argument must all appear on a single line of the input file.

- There may be no space between `\end` and { in `\end{verbatim}`.

The `verbatim` environment is for simulating typed text; it is not intended to turn LaTeX into a typewriter. If you're tempted to use it for visual formatting, don't; use the `tabbing` environment of Section 3.6.1 instead.

# CHAPTER 4

# Moving Information Around

LaTeX often has to move information from one place to another. For example, the information contained in a table of contents comes from the sectioning commands that are scattered throughout the input file. Similarly, the LaTeX command that generates a cross-reference to an equation must get the equation number from the `equation` environment, which may occur several sections later. This chapter describes the features that cause LaTeX to move information around. You also move information around when you send your document to friends and colleagues. Section 4.7 describes commands that make this easier.

LaTeX requires two passes over the input to move information around: one pass to find the information and a second pass to put it into the text. (It occasionally even requires a third pass.) To compile a table of contents, one pass determines the titles and starting pages of all the sections and a second pass puts this information into the table of contents. Instead of making two passes every time it is run, LaTeX reads your input file only once and saves the cross-referencing information in special files for use the next time. For example, if `sample2e.tex` had a command to produce a table of contents, then LaTeX would write the necessary information into the file `sample2e.toc`. It would use the information in the current version of `sample2e.toc` to produce the table of contents, and would write a new version of that file to produce the table of contents the next time LaTeX is run with `sample2e.tex` as input.

LaTeX's cross-referencing information is therefore always "old", since it was gathered on a previous execution. This will be noticeable mainly when you are first writing the document—for example, a newly added section won't be listed in the table of contents. However, the last changes you make to your document will normally be minor ones that polish the prose rather than add new sections or equations. The cross-referencing information is unlikely to change the last few times you run LaTeX on your file, so all the cross-references will almost always be correct in the final version. In any case, if the cross-referencing is incorrect, LaTeX will type a warning message when it has finished. (But, LaTeX won't warn you about changes to table-of-contents entries.) Running it again on the same input will correct any errors.[1]

An error in your input file could produce an error in one of the special cross-referencing files. The error in the cross-referencing file will not manifest itself until that file is read, the next time you run LaTeX. Section 8.1 explains how to recognize such an error.

## 4.1   The Table of Contents

A `\tableofcontents` command produces a table of contents. More precisely, it does two things:

---

[1] If you're a computer wizard or are very good at mathematical puzzles, you may be able to create a file in which a reference to a page number always remains incorrect. The chance of that happening by accident is small.

- It causes LaTeX to write a new `toc` file—that is, a file with the same first name as the input file and the extension `toc`—with the information needed to generate a table of contents.

- It reads the information from the previous version of the `toc` file to produce a table of contents, complete with heading.

The commands `\listoffigures` and `\listoftables` produce a list of figures and a list of tables, respectively. They work just like the `\tableofcontents` command, except that LaTeX writes a file with extension `lof` when making a list of figures and a file with extension `lot` when making a list of tables.

Occasionally, you may find that you don't like the way LaTeX prints a table of contents or a list of figures or tables. You can fine-tune an individual entry by using the optional argument to the sectioning command or `\caption` command that generates it; see Sections C.4.1 and C.9.1. Formatting commands can also be introduced with the `\addtocontents` command described in Section C.4.3. If all else fails, you can edit the `toc`, `lof`, and `lot` files yourself. Edit these files only when preparing the final version of your document, and use a `\nofiles` command (described in Section C.11.1) to suppress the writing of new versions of the files.

## 4.2  Cross-References

One reason for numbering things like figures and equations is to refer the reader to them, as in: "See Figure 3 for more details." You don't want the "3" to appear in the input file because adding another figure might make this one become Figure 4. Instead, you can assign a *key* of your choice to the figure and refer to it by that key, letting LaTeX translate the reference into the figure number. The key is assigned a number by the `\label` command, and the number is printed by the `\ref` command. A `\label` command appearing in ordinary text assigns to the key the number of the current sectional unit; one appearing inside a numbered environment assigns that number to the key.

Equation 4.12 in Section 2.3 below is Euler's famous result.

⋮

### 2.3 Early Results

Euler's equation

$$e^{i\pi} + 1 = 0 \qquad (4.12)$$

combines the five most important numbers in mathematics in a single equation.

```
Equation~\ref{eq:euler} in
Section~\ref{sec-early} below
...
\subsection{Early Results}
\label{sec-early}
Euler's equation
\begin{equation}
  e^{i\pi} + 1 = 0      \label{eq:euler}
\end{equation}
combines the five most important ...
```

In this example, the `\label{eq:euler}` command assigns the key `eq:euler` to the equation number, and the command `\ref{eq:euler}` generates that equation number.

A key can consist of any sequence of letters, digits, or punctuation characters (Section 2.1). Upper- and lowercase letters are different, so `gnu` and `Gnu` are distinct keys. In addition to sectioning commands, the following environments also generate numbers that can be assigned to keys with a `\label` command: `equation`, `eqnarray`, `enumerate` (assigns the current item's number), `figure`, `table`, and any theorem-like environment defined with the `\newtheorem` command of Section 3.4.3.

The `\label` command can usually go in any natural place. To assign the number of a sectional unit to a key, you can put the `\label` command anywhere within the unit except within a command argument or environment in which it would assign some other number, or you can put it in the argument of the sectioning command. To refer to a particular equation in an `eqnarray` environment, put the `\label` command anywhere between the `\\` or `\begin{eqnarray}` that begins the equation and the `\\` or `\end{eqnarray}` that ends it. The position of the `\label` command in a figure or table is less obvious: it must go after the `\caption` command or in its argument.

Figure 17 shows the evolution of the salamander (order Urodela) from its origin in the Jurassic ...

Body of Figure

Figure 17: Newts on parade.

```
Figure~\ref{fig:newt} shows the evolution
\begin{figure}
    \centering Body of Figure
\caption{Newts on parade.} \label{fig:newt}
\end{figure}
of the salamander...
```

(See Section 2.2.1 for an explanation of the ~ command.) A `\caption` command within its `figure` or `table` environment acts like a sectioning command within the document. Just as a document has multiple sections, a figure or table can have multiple captions.

The `\pageref` command is similar to the `\ref` command except it produces the page number of the place in the text where the corresponding `\label` command appears.

See page 42 for more details.
⋮

*Text on page 42*:
The meaning of life, the universe, and ...

```
See page~\pageref{`meaning'} for more
...
The \label{`meaning'} meaning of life, ...
```

A `\ref` or `\pageref` command generates only the number, so you have to type the **page** to produce "page 42".

The numbers generated by `\ref` and `\pageref` were assigned to the keys the previous time you ran LaTeX on your document. Thus, the printed output

will be incorrect if any of these numbers have changed. LATEX will warn you
if this may have happened, in which case you should run it again on the input
file to make sure the cross-references are correct. (This warning will occur if
any number assigned to a key by a \label command has changed, even if that
number is not referenced.) Each \ref or \pageref referring to an unknown key
produces a warning message; such messages appear the first time you process
any file containing these commands.

A \label can appear in the argument of a sectioning or \caption command,
but in no other moving argument.

Using keys for cross-referencing saves you from keeping track of the actual
numbers, but it requires you to remember the keys. You can produce a list of
the keys by running LATEX on the input file lablst.tex. (You probably do this
by typing "latex lablst"; check your *Local Guide* to be sure.) LATEX will then
ask you to type in the name of the input file whose keys you want listed, as
well as the name of the document class specified by that file's \documentclass
command.

## 4.3   Bibliography and Citation

A citation is a cross-reference to another publication, such as a journal article,
called the *source*. The modern method of citing a source is with a cross-reference
to an entry in a list of sources at the end of the document. With LATEX, the
citation is produced by a \cite command having the citation key as its argument.

Knudson [67] showed that, in the Arctic ...        Knudson~\cite{kn:gnus} showed ...

You can cite multiple sources with a single \cite, separating the keys by commas. The \cite command has an optional argument that adds a note to the
citation.

Although they had disappeared from Fiji [4,15,36],        ... Fiji~\cite{tom-ix,dick:ens,harry+d},
Knudson [67, pages 222–333] showed that ...        Knudson~\cite[pages 222--333]{kn:gnus} ...

A citation key can be any sequence of letters, digits, and punctuation characters,
except that it may not contain a comma. As usual in LATEX, upper- and lowercase
letters are considered to be different.

In the preceding examples, LATEX has to determine that citation key kn:gnus
corresponds to source label 67. How LATEX does this depends on how you produce
the list of sources. The best way to produce the source list is with a separate
program called BIBTEX, described in Section 4.3.1. You can also produce it
yourself, as explained in Section 4.3.2.

### 4.3.1   Using B<small>IB</small>T<sub>E</sub>X

B<small>IB</small>T<sub>E</sub>X is a separate program that produces the source list for a document, obtaining the information from a bibliographic database. To use B<small>IB</small>T<sub>E</sub>X, you must include in your L<sup>A</sup>T<sub>E</sub>X input file a \bibliography command whose argument specifies one or more files that contain the database. The names of the database files must have the extension bib. For example, the command

> \bibliography{insect,animal}

specifies that the source list is to be obtained from entries in the files insect.bib and animal.bib. There must be no space following the comma. Appendix B explains how to make bibliographic database files.

B<small>IB</small>T<sub>E</sub>X creates a source list containing entries for all the citation keys specified by \cite commands. The data for the source list is obtained from the bibliographic database, which must have an entry for every citation key. A \nocite command in the L<sup>A</sup>T<sub>E</sub>X input file causes the specified entries to appear in the source list, but produces no output. For example, \nocite{g:nu,g:nat} causes B<small>IB</small>T<sub>E</sub>X to put bibliography database entries having keys g:nu and g:nat in the source list. The command \nocite{*} causes all entries in the bibliographic database to be put in the source list. A \nocite command can go anywhere after the \begin{document} command, but it is fragile.

To use B<small>IB</small>T<sub>E</sub>X, your L<sup>A</sup>T<sub>E</sub>X input file must contain a \bibliographystyle command. This command specifies the *bibliography style*, which determines the format of the source list. For example, the command

> \bibliographystyle{plain}

specifies that entries should be formatted as specified by the plain bibliography style. The \bibliographystyle command can go anywhere after the \begin{document} command. L<sup>A</sup>T<sub>E</sub>X's standard bibliography styles are:

plain Formatted more or less as suggested by van Leunen in *A Handbook for Scholars* [7]. Entries are sorted alphabetically and are labeled with numbers.

unsrt The same as plain except that entries appear in the order of their first citation.

alpha The same as plain except that source labels like "Knu66", formed from the author's name and the year of publication, are used.

abbrv The same as plain except that entries are more compact because first names, month names, and journal names are abbreviated.

Dozens of other bibliography styles exist, including ones that produce source lists in the formats used by a number of scientific journals. Consult the L<sup>A</sup>T<sub>E</sub>X

*Companion* and the *Local Guide* to find out what styles are available. Documentation for the BIBTEX program explains how to create your own bibliography style.

The source list is normally formatted in what van Leunen calls a *compressed* style. The `openbib` document-class option causes it to be formatted in an *open* style. (Document-class options are specified by the `\documentclass` command; see Section 2.2.2.)

Once you've created an input file containing the appropriate LATEX commands, you perform the following sequence of steps to produce the final output:

- Run LATEX on the input file, which I assume is called `myfile.tex`. LATEX will complain that all your citations are undefined, since there is no source list yet.

- Run BIBTEX by typing something like `bibtex myfile`. (Consult your *Local Guide* to find out what you actually type.) BIBTEX will generate the file `myfile.bbl` containing LATEX commands to produce the source list.

- Run LATEX again on `myfile.tex`. LATEX's output will now contain the source list. However, LATEX will still complain that your citations are undefined, since the output produced by a `\cite` command is based on information obtained from the source list the last time LATEX was run on the file.

- Run LATEX one more time on `myfile.tex`.

If you add or remove a citation, you will have to go through this whole procedure again to get the citation labels and source list right. But they don't have to be right while you're writing, so you needn't do this very often.

BIBTEX almost always produces a perfectly fine source list. However, it is only a computer program, so you may occasionally encounter a source that it does not handle properly. When this happens, you can usually correct the problem by modifying the bibliographic database—perhaps creating a special database entry just for this document. As a last resort, you can edit the `bbl` file that BIBTEX generated. (Of course, you should do this only when you are producing the final output.)

## 4.3.2   Doing It Yourself

A source list is created with the `thebibliography` environment, which is like the `enumerate` environment described in Section 2.2.4 except that:

- Each list item is begun with a `\bibitem` command whose argument is the citation key. (The `\bibitem` and `\cite` commands work much like the `\label` and `\ref` commands of Section 4.2.)

- The `thebibliography` environment has an argument that should be a piece of text the same width as or slightly wider than the widest item label in the source list.

Knudson [67] showed that, in the Arctic ...

⋮

**References**

⋮

[67] D. E. Knudson. *1966 World Gnus Almanac.* Permafrost Press, Novosibirsk.

```
Knudson~\cite{kn:gnus} showed ...
...
\begin{thebibliography}{99}
...
\bibitem{kn:gnus} D. E. Knudson.
\emph{1966 World Gnus Almanac.}
...
\end{thebibliography}
```

In most type styles, "99" is at least as wide as all other two-digit numbers.

Instead of using numbers, you can choose your own labels for the sources by giving an optional argument to the `\bibitem` command.

Knudson [Knud 66] showed that, in the Arctic ...

⋮

**References**

⋮

[Knud 66] D. E. Knudson. *1966 World Gnus Almanac.* Permafrost Press, Novosibirsk.

```
Knudson~\cite{kn:gnus} showed ...
...
\begin{thebibliography}{Dillo 83}
...
\bibitem[Knud 66]{kn:gnus} D. E. Knudson.
\emph{1966 World Gnus Almanac.}
...
\end{thebibliography}
```

In this example, "[Dillo 83]" should be the longest label. The optional argument of `\bibitem` is a moving argument.

As in any kind of cross-reference, citations are based upon the information gathered the previous time LaTeX was run on the file. So, when you change the source list, you have to run LaTeX two more times to change the citations.

## 4.4  Splitting Your Input

A large document requires a lot of input. Rather than putting the whole input in a single large file, you may find it more convenient to split the input into several smaller files. Regardless of how many separate files you use, there is one that is the *root* file; it is the one whose name you type when you run LaTeX.

The `\input` command provides the simplest way to split your input into several files. The command `\input{gnu}` in the root file causes LaTeX to insert the contents of the file `gnu.tex` right at the current spot in your manuscript—just as if the `\input{gnu}` command were removed from the root file and replaced by the contents of the file `gnu.tex`. (However, the input files are not changed.) The file `gnu.tex` may also contain an `\input` command, calling another file that may have its own `\input` commands, and so on.

Besides splitting your input into conveniently sized chunks, the \input command also makes it easy to use the same input in different documents. While text is seldom recycled in this way, you might want to reuse declarations. You can keep a file containing declarations that are used in all your documents, such as the definitions of commands and environments for your own logical structures (Section 3.4). You can even begin your root file with an \input command and put the \documentclass command in your declarations file.

Another reason for splitting the input into separate files is to run LATEX on only part of the document so, when you make changes, only the parts that have changed need to be processed. For this, you must use the \include command instead of \input. The two commands are similar in that \include{gnu} also specifies that the contents of the file gnu.tex should be inserted in its place. However, with the \include command, you can tell LATEX either to insert the file or to omit it and process all succeeding text as if the file had been inserted, numbering pages, sections, equations, etc., as if the omitted file's text had been included.

To run LATEX on only part of the document, the preamble must contain an \includeonly command whose argument is a list of files (first names only). The file specified by an \include command is processed only if it appears in the argument of the \includeonly command. Thus, if the preamble contains the command

\includeonly{gnu,gnat,gnash}

then an \include{gnat} command causes the file gnat.tex to be included, while the command \include{rmadlo} causes LATEX *not* to include the file rmadlo.tex, but to process the text following it as if the file had been included. More precisely, it causes LATEX to process the succeeding text under the assumption that the omitted file is exactly the same as it was the last time it was included. LATEX does not read an omitted file and is unaware of any changes made to the file since it was last included.

The entire root file is always processed. If the preamble does not contain an \includeonly command, then every \include command inserts its file. The command \includeonly{} (with a null argument) instructs LATEX to omit all \include'd files. An \include can appear only after the \begin{document} command.

The \include command has one feature that limits its usefulness: the included text always starts a new page, as does the text immediately following the \include command. It therefore works right only if the \include'd text and the text following it should begin on a new page—for example, if it consists of one or more complete chapters. While writing a chapter, you might want to split it into smaller files with \include commands. When you've finished writing that chapter, you can combine those files into a single one.

Another difficulty with the \include mechanism is that changing the document may require reprocessing some unchanged \include'd files in order to get the correct numbering of pages, sections, etc. When skipping an \include'd file, the numbering in the succeeding text is based upon the numbering in the file's text the last time it was processed. Suppose that the root file contains the commands

```
\include{gnu}
\chapter{Armadillo}
```

and an \includeonly in the preamble causes the \include command to omit file gnu.tex. If the text in gnu.tex ended in Chapter 5 on page 56 the last time it was processed, even if you've added seven more chapters and sixty pages of text before the \include command since then, the \chapter command will produce Chapter 6 starting on page 57. In general, to make sure everything is numbered correctly, you must reprocess an \include'd file if a change to the preceding text changes the numbering in the text produced by that file.

When writing a large document, you should probably make each chapter a separate \include'd file. (You may find it convenient to enter the \includeonly command from the terminal, using the \typein command described in Section 4.6.) Process each file separately as you write or revise it, and don't worry about numbers not matching properly. If the inconsistent numbering gets too confusing, generate a coherent version by processing all the files at once. (You can do this by removing the \includeonly command before running LaTeX.) When you've finished making changes, run LaTeX on the entire document. You can then produce the final output either all at once by running LaTeX again on the entire document, or a few chapters at a time by using the \includeonly command.

## 4.5   Making an Index or Glossary

There are two steps in making an index or glossary: gathering the information that goes in it, and generating the LaTeX input to produce it. Section 4.5.1 describes the first step. The easiest way to perform the second step is with the *MakeIndex* program, described in Appendix A. Section 4.5.2 describes how to produce an index or glossary if you don't use *MakeIndex*.

### 4.5.1   Compiling the Entries

Compiling an index or a glossary is not easy, but LaTeX can help by writing the necessary information onto a special file. If the root file is named myfile.tex, index information is written on the "idx file" myfile.idx. LaTeX makes an idx file if the preamble contains a \makeindex command. The information on the file is written by \index commands; the command \index{gnu} appearing with the text for page 42 causes LaTeX to write

```
    \indexentry{gnu}{42}
```

on the `idx` file. If there is no `\makeindex` command, the `\index` command does nothing. The `showidx` package causes LaTeX to print the arguments of all index commands in the margin.

The `\index` command produces no text, so you type

```
A gnat\index{gnat} with gnarled wings gnashed ...
```

to index this instance of "gnat". It's best to put the `\index` command next to the word it references, with no space between them; this keeps the page number from being off by one if the word ends or begins a page. I find it best to put index entries on a separate line, as in

```
When in the Course of
    \index{human events}%
    \index{events, human}%
human events, it becomes necessary for one people
```

This use of the `%` character is explained on page 19.

The procedure for making a glossary is completely analogous. In place of `\index` there is a `\glossary` command. The `\makeglossary` command produces a file with the extension `glo` that is similar to the `idx` file except with `\glossaryentry` entries instead of `\indexentry` entries.

The argument of `\index` or `\glossary` can contain any characters, including special characters like `\` and `$`. However, curly braces must be properly balanced, each `{` having a matching `}`. The `\index` and `\glossary` commands are fragile. Moreover, an `\index` or `\glossary` command should not appear in the argument of any other command if its own argument contains any of LaTeX's ten special characters (Section 2.1).

## 4.5.2   Producing an Index or Glossary by Yourself

If you don't use the *MakeIndex* program, you can use the `theindex` environment to produce an index in two-column format. Each main index entry is begun by an `\item` command. A subentry is begun with `\subitem`, and a subsubentry is begun with `\subsubitem`. Blank lines between entries are ignored. An extra vertical space is produced by the `\indexspace` command, which is usually put before the first entry that starts with a new letter.

```
gnats 13, 97
gnus 24, 37, 233
    bad, 39, 236
        very, 235
    good, 38, 234

harmadillo 99, 144
```

```
\item gnats 13, 97
\item gnus 24, 37, 233
    \subitem bad, 39, 236
        \subsubitem very, 235
    \subitem good, 38, 234
\indexspace
\item harmadillo 99, 144
```

There is no environment expressly for glossaries. However, the `description` environment of Section 2.2.4 may be useful.

## 4.6   Keyboard Input and Screen Output

When creating a large document, it's often helpful to leave a reminder to yourself in the input file—for example, to note a paragraph that needs rewriting. The use of the `%` character for putting comments into the text is described in Section 2.2.1. However, a passive comment is easy to overlook, so LaTeX provides the `\typeout` command for printing messages on the terminal. In the examples in this section, the left column shows what is produced on the terminal by the input in the right column; the oval represents the terminal.

```
Don't forget to revise this!
```
                                `\typeout{Don't forget to   revise this!}`

Remember that everything LaTeX writes on the terminal is also put in the `log` file.

It is sometimes useful to type input to LaTeX directly from your keyboard—for example, to enter an `\includeonly` command. This is done with a `\typein` command, such as the following:

```
Enter 'includeonly', boss!

\@typein=
```
                                `\typein {Enter 'includeonly', boss!}`

When this appears on your terminal, LaTeX is waiting for you to enter a line of input, ended by pressing the *return* key. LaTeX then processes what you typed just as if it had appeared in the input file in place of the `\typein` command.

The `\typein` command has an optional first argument, which must be a command name. When this optional argument is given, instead of processing your typed input at that point, LaTeX defines the specified command to be equivalent to the text that you have typed.

```
Enter lover's name.

\lover=
```
                                `\typein [\lover]{Enter lover's name.}`
                                `I love \lover\ very much.`

Typing `Chris` and pressing the return key causes the `\typein` command to define the command `\lover` to be equivalent to `Chris`—just like the `\newcommand` or `\renewcommand` commands of Section 3.4. Thus, the input following this `\typein` command would produce

I love Chris very much.

The argument of the `\typeout` or `\typein` command is a moving argument. Both of these commands are fragile.

## 4.7   Sending Your Document

Today, you are likely to send a document electronically—by e-mail or on a diskette—rather than on paper.  Putting a file in an e-mail message or on a diskette is no problem.  However, to process your document, LaTeX must read a number of files in addition to the main input file.  Some files, such as the `toc` file (Section 4.1), are generated by LaTeX itself.  The rest must be sent if the recipient does not already have them.  These files include the `bbl` file (Section 4.3.1), files required by any nonstandard packages the document uses, and files that are read by `\input` or `\include` commands.  You can combine all these files into a single LaTeX input file by using the `filecontents` environment.  Instead of sending the file `name.tex` separately, put the environment

> `\begin{filecontents}{name.tex}`
> *contents of file*
> `\end{filecontents}`

at the beginning of your input file.  When LaTeX is run on this input file, it writes the file `name.tex` if no file by that name already exists.  If such a file does exist, LaTeX prints a warning message.  You can put any number of `filecontents` environments in an input file, but they must all precede the `\documentclass` command.

To find out what files you need to send, put a `\listfiles` command in the preamble.  LaTeX will then print out a list of the files it reads when processing the document.  The list will not include files generated by LaTeX, and it will identify standard files that are always present on a computer that runs LaTeX. However, the list may not tell you in what directories the files are.  The terminal output might include complete file names. (As explained in Section 8.1, when LaTeX starts to read a file, it writes the file's name on the terminal and in the `log` file.)  You can also consult the *Local Guide* to find out what directories contain the files read by packages.

When sending files by e-mail, don't forget about the problem of lines beginning with `From␣` that is discussed in Section 2.4.

# CHAPTER 5

# Other Document Classes

## 5.1   Books

Books differ from reports mainly in their front and back matter. The front matter of a book usually includes a half-title page, a main title page, a copyright page, a preface or foreword, and a table of contents. It may also contain acknowledgements, a dedication, a list of figures, a list of other books in the same series, and so on. The back matter usually includes an index and may contain an afterword, acknowledgements, a bibliography, a colophon, etc.

The `book` document class does not attempt to provide commands for all the logical structures that could appear in a book's front and back matter. It is just the same as the `report` class except for the differences described below. Individual publishers might have packages with additional commands for the particular structures they want in their books.

The front matter, main matter (the main body of the book, including appendices), and back matter are begun with the three commands `\frontmatter`, `\mainmatter`, and `\backmatter`, respectively. In the standard `book` class, front matter pages are numbered with roman numerals; main and back matter pages are numbered with arabic numerals. In the front and back matter, the `\chapter` command does not produce a chapter number, but it does make a table of contents entry. Thus, you can begin a preface with

> `\chapter{Preface}`

Only the ∗ forms of other sectioning commands should be used in the front and back matter (see Section C.4.1).

Two-sided printing is the norm for books, so the `twoside` option is the default in the `book` class. Another default option is `openright`, which causes new chapters to begin on a right-hand page. The contrary option, `openany`, is the default for the `report` class.

A book can have more than one title page, and each title page can contain a variety of information besides the title and author—for example, the publisher, series, and illustrator. The `\maketitle` command is therefore of little use in a book.

You will probably have to do a considerable amount of customizing of the style parameters for a book—especially of the page-style parameters, described in Section C.5.3. The time this takes should be infinitesimal compared with the time you spend writing the book.

## 5.2   Slides

The `slides` document class is used for making slides. Slides are usually printed or photocopied onto transparencies for projection on a screen.

Producing good slides requires visual formatting, which means that LaTeX is not well suited for the task. Here are a few reasons why you may want to use LaTeX anyway:

- Your slides are based on material from a LaTeX document.

- Your slides have a lot of mathematical formulas.

- You don't make slides often enough to bother learning how to use another system.

The `slides` document class's default fonts were specially designed to be easy to read from a distance. To my knowledge, no other system makes slides that are so readable. The `slides` class's fonts are much larger than the usual ones; `\normalsize` produces roughly the same size characters as `\LARGE` in other document classes (Section 6.7.1). Moreover, the roman family is similar to the ordinary sans serif family. The only type families generally available are roman and typewriter, and the only type shapes are upright and italic. (See Section 3.1.) The `\emph` command works as usual.

## 5.2.1   Slides and Overlays

An individual slide is produced with a `slide` environment:

<table>
<tr>
<td>

GNATS and GNUS

Gnats are very small and have a bad temper.

Gnus are big.



3

</td>
<td>

```
\begin{slide}
 \begin{center}
   GNATS and GNUS
 \end{center}

 Gnats are very small and have a bad
 temper.

 Gnus are big.
\end{slide}
```

</td>
</tr>
</table>

The text appearing on a slide is produced with ordinary LaTeX commands. Any commands that make sense for slides can be used. Commands that *don't* make sense include sectioning commands, `figure` and `table` environments, and page-breaking commands. The latter make no sense in a slide because each slide must fit on a single page. To make colored slides, use the `color` package described in Section 7.3.

The `overlay` environment is used for an overlay—a slide that is meant to be put on top of another slide. It is the same as the `slide` environment except for the numbering; the first overlay following slide number 3 is numbered "3-a", the second one is numbered "3-b", and so on. The best way to get the text on the slide and the overlay to line up properly is to have all the text on both of them and make text that isn't supposed to appear invisible by coloring it white (Section 7.3).

Superimposing this slide and overlay yields the preceding slide (plus an extra "-a" next to the slide number). If the `color` package is not available on your computer, you can use the commands of Section 6.4.2 to produce the blank spaces.

### 5.2.2 Notes

When giving a lecture, it helps if you put notes to yourself in with the slides to remind you of what to say. The `note` environment produces a one-page note. Notes that follow slide number 3 are numbered "3-1", "3-2", etc. I always make a note to accompany each slide. (You can print the slides and notes separately by using the `\onlyslides` and `\onlynotes` commands described below.)

A good lecturer plans a talk carefully and does not run out of time. The `slides` document class's `clock` option helps you keep track of time during your lecture. Right before or after each slide, put an `\addtime` command giving the number of seconds you should spend on that slide. The total amount of time (in minutes) that you should have taken so far will be printed at the bottom of each note.

```
\documentclass[clock]{slides}
...
\addtime{180}  % Slide 1: 3 minutes
...
\addtime{150}  % Slide 2: 2-1/2 minutes
...
\addtime{120}  % Slide 3: 2 minutes

\begin{note}
Don't forget to swat those gnats.
\end{note}
```

Don't forget to swat those gnats.

7 min          3-1

LaTeX will also type out on your terminal the total elapsed time at the end of the document.

You can reset the elapsed time with the `\settime` command. The command `\settime{120}` sets the total elapsed time to 120 seconds (2 minutes). Do not put an `\addtime` or `\settime` command inside a `slide`, `overlay`, or `note` environment.

### 5.2.3 Printing Only Some Slides and Notes

For making corrections, it's convenient to generate only some of the slides and notes from your input file. The command

```
\onlyslides{4,7-13,23}
```

in the preamble will cause LaTeX to generate only slides numbered 4, 7–13 (inclusive), and 23, plus all of their overlays. The slide numbers in the argument must be in ascending order, and can include nonexistent slides—for example, you can type

```
\onlyslides{10-9999}
```

to produce all but the first nine slides. The argument of the \onlyslides command must be nonempty.

There is also an analogous \onlynotes command to generate a subset of the notes. Notes numbered 11-1, 11-2, etc. will all be generated by specifying page 11 in the argument of the \onlynotes command. If the input file has an \onlyslides command but no \onlynotes command, then no notes are produced, and vice versa. Including both an \onlyslides and an \onlynotes command has the expected effect of producing only the specified slides and notes. The \onlyslides and \onlynotes commands may not work right if a slide, overlay, or note environment appears in the argument of any command.

### 5.2.4   Other Text

Your input file can include text that appears outside a slide, overlay, or note environment. Such other text is formatted like a slide, but without a slide number. It can be used to make a title page. This other text is always printed, even when an \onlyslides or \onlynotes command is given.

Text outside a slide or note differs from text inside one only in that page-breaking commands are allowed. Use a \pagebreak command if you want to tell LaTeX where to start a new page in the middle of the text.

## 5.3   Letters

For making letters—the kind that are put in an envelope and mailed—LaTeX provides the letter document class. To use this class, begin your input file with a \documentclass command having letter as its main (nonoptional) argument (Section 2.2.2).

You can make any number of letters with a single input file. Your name and address, which are likely to be the same for all letters, are specified by declarations. The return address is declared by an \address command, with multiple output lines separated by \\ commands.

```
\address{1234 Ave.\ of the Armadillos\\
         Gnu York, G.Y. 56789}
```

The \signature command declares your name, as it appears at the end of the letter, with the usual \\ commands separating multiple lines.

```
\signature{R. (Ma) Dillo  \\  Director of Cuisine}
```

These declarations are usually put in the preamble, but they are ordinary declarations with the customary scoping rules and can appear anywhere in the document.

Each letter is produced by a separate `letter` environment, having the name and address of the recipient as its argument. The argument of the `letter` environment is a moving argument. The letter itself begins with an `\opening` command that generates the salutation.

1234 Ave. of the Armadillos
Gnu York, G.Y. 56789

July 4, 1996

Dr. G. Nathaniel Picking
Acme Exterminators
33 Swat Street
Hometown, Illinois 62301

Dear Nat,

I'm afraid that the armadillo problem is still with us. I did everything …

```
\begin{letter}{Dr.\ G. Nathaniel Picking \\
   Acme Exterminators\\ 33 Swat Street \\
   Hometown, Illinois 62301}

\opening{Dear Nat,}

I'm afraid that the armadillo problem
is still with us.  I did everything
...
```

The return address is determined by the `\address` declaration; LaTeX supplies the date. An `\address` and/or `\signature` command that applies just to this letter can be put between the `\begin{letter}` and the `\opening` command.

The main body of the letter is ordinary LaTeX input, but commands like `\section` that make no sense in a letter should not be used. The letter closes with a `\closing` command.

… and I hope you can get rid of the nasty beasts this time.

Best regards,

R. (Ma) Dillo
Director of Cuisine

```
... and I hope you can get rid of the nasty
beasts this time.

\closing{Best regards,}
```

The name comes from the `\signature` declaration.

The `\cc` command can be used after the closing to list the names of people to whom you are sending copies.

cc: Bill Clinton
    George Bush

```
\cc {Bill Clinton \\ George Bush}
```

There's a similar `\encl` command for a list of enclosures.

Additional text after the closing must be preceded by a \ps command. This command generates no text—you'll have to type the "P.S." yourself—but is needed to format the additional text correctly.

You can change the date on your letters by using \renewcommand (Section 3.4.1) to redefine \today. Put the \renewcommand in the preamble to change the date on all letters; put it right before the \opening command to change the date on a single letter.

1234 Ave. of the Armadillos
Gnu York, G.Y. 56789

    Thursday, 15842 B.C.

Mr. A. Oop
Kingdom of Moo

Dear Mr. Oop:

In your last shipment of stegosaur steaks, ...

```
\begin{letter}{Mr.\ A. Oop \\
   Kingdom of Moo}

\renewcommand{\today}{Thursday, 15842 B.C.}

\opening{Dear Mr.\ Oop:}
In your last shipment of stegosaur steaks,
...
```

Redefining \today will not alter the postmark printed on the envelope by the post office.

A \makelabels command in the preamble will cause LaTeX to print a list of mailing labels, one for each letter environment, in a format suitable for xerographic copying onto "peel-off" labels. A mailing label without a corresponding letter is produced by an empty letter environment—one with nothing between the argument and the \end{letter} command.

There may be other features for making letters—especially if you are using LaTeX at a company or university. For example, you may be able to format letters for copying onto the company letterhead. Consult the *Local Guide* for more information.

# CHAPTER 6
# Designing It Yourself

The preceding chapters describe LaTeX commands and environments for specifying a document's logical structure. This chapter explains how to specify its visual appearance. Before reading it, you should review the discussion in Section 1.4 of the dangers of visual design. Commands specifying the visual appearance of the document are usually confined to the preamble, either as style declarations or in the definitions of commands and environments for specifying logical structures. The notable exceptions are the line- and page-breaking commands of Section 6.2 and the picture-drawing commands of Section 7.1.

## 6.1   Document and Page Styles

### 6.1.1   Document-Class Options

The style of the document can be changed by using the optional argument of the `\documentclass` command to specify style options. The `11pt`, `12pt`, `twoside`, and `twocolumn` options are described in Section 2.2.2. Three other standard options are:

`titlepage` Causes the `\maketitle` command to generate a separate title page and the `abstract` environment to make a separate page for the abstract. This option is the default for the `report` document class.

`leqno` Causes the formula numbers produced by the `equation` and `eqnarray` environments to appear on the left instead of the right.

`fleqn` Causes formulas to be aligned on the left, a fixed distance from the left margin, instead of being centered.

A complete list of the standard options appears in Section C.5.1. The *Local Guide* will tell you if there are any other options available on your computer.

The `twocolumn` option is used for a document that consists mostly of double-column pages. It sets various style parameters, such as the amount of paragraph indentation, to values appropriate for such pages. You may want double-column pages for just part of the document, such as a glossary. The `\twocolumn` declaration starts a new page and begins producing two-column output. It does not change any style parameters except the ones required to produce two-column output. The inverse `\onecolumn` declaration starts a new page and begins producing single-column output.

In books, it is conventional for the height of the text to be the same on all full pages. The `\flushbottom` declaration makes all text pages the same height, adding extra vertical space when necessary to fill out the page. The `\raggedbottom` declaration has the opposite effect, letting the height of the text vary a bit from page to page. The default is `\raggedbottom` except when the `twoside` option is in effect. You can change the default by putting the appropriate declaration in the preamble.

## 6.1.2   Page Styles

A page of output consists of three units: the *head*, the *body*, and the *foot*. In most pages of this book, the head contains a page number, a chapter or section title, and a horizontal line, while the foot is empty; but in the table of contents and the preface, the page head is empty and the foot contains the page number. The body consists of everything between the head and foot: the main text, footnotes, figures, and tables.

The information in the head and foot, which usually includes a page number, helps the reader find his way around the document. You can specify arabic page numbers with a `\pagenumbering{arabic}` command and roman numerals with a `\pagenumbering{roman}` command, the default being arabic numbers. The `\pagenumbering` declaration resets the page number to one, starting with the current page. To begin a document with pages i, ii, etc. and have the first chapter start with page 1, put `\pagenumbering{roman}` anywhere before the beginning of the text and `\pagenumbering{arabic}` right after the first `\chapter` command.

Page headings may contain additional information to help the reader. They are most useful in two-sided printing, since headings on the two facing pages convey more information than the single heading visible with one-sided printing. Page headings are generally not useful in a short document, where they tend to be distracting rather than helpful.

The *page style* determines what goes into the head and foot; it is specified with a `\pagestyle` declaration having the page style's name as its argument. There are four standard page styles:

`plain`   The page number is in the foot and the head is empty. It is the default page style for the `article` and `report` document classes.

`empty`   The head and foot are both empty. LaTeX still assigns each page a number, but the number is not printed.

`headings`   The page number and other information, determined by the document style, is put in the head; the foot is empty.

`myheadings`   Similar to the `headings` page style, except you specify the "other information" that goes in the head, using the `\markboth` and `\markright` commands described below.

The `\pagestyle` declaration obeys the normal scoping rules. What goes into a page's head and foot is determined by the page style in effect at the end of the page, so the `\pagestyle` command usually comes after a command like `\chapter` that begins a new page.

The `\thispagestyle` command is like `\pagestyle` except it affects only the current page. Some commands, such as `\chapter`, change the style of the current page. These changes can be overridden with a subsequent `\thispagestyle` command.

The contents of the page headings in the `headings` and `myheadings` styles are set by the following commands:

>     `\markboth{`*left_head*`}{`*right_head*`}`
>     `\markright{`*right_head*`}`

The *left_head* and *right_head* arguments specify the information to go in the page heads of left-hand and right-hand pages, respectively. In two-sided printing, specified with the `twoside` document-class option, the even-numbered pages are the left-hand ones and the odd-numbered pages are the right-hand ones. In one-sided printing, all pages are considered to be right-hand ones.

In the `headings` page style, the sectioning commands choose the headings for you; Section C.5.3 explains how to use `\markboth` and `\markright` to override their choices. In the `myheadings` option, you must use these commands to set the headings yourself. The arguments of `\markboth` and `\markright` are processed in LR mode; they are moving arguments.

### 6.1.3 The Title Page and Abstract

The `\maketitle` command produces a title page when the `titlepage` document-class option is in effect; it is described in Sections 2.2.2 and C.5.4. You can also create your own title page with the `titlepage` environment. This environment creates a page with the `empty` page style, so it has no printed page number or heading. It causes the following page to be numbered 1.

You are completely responsible for what appears on a title page made with the `titlepage` environment. The following commands and environments are useful in formatting a title page: the type-size-changing commands of Section 6.7.1, the type-style-changing commands of Section 3.1, and the `center` environment of Section 6.5. Recall also that the `\today` command, described in Section 2.2.1, generates the date. You will probably produce several versions of your document, so it's important to include a date on the title page.

An abstract is made with the `abstract` environment.

| | |
|---|---|
| **Abstract**<br>    The mating habits of insects are quite different from those of large mammals. | `\begin{abstract}`<br>`The mating habits of insects are quite`<br>`different from those of large mammals.`<br>`\end{abstract}` |

The abstract is placed on a separate page if the `titlepage` document-class option is in effect; otherwise, it acts like an ordinary displayed-paragraph environment.

### 6.1.4    Customizing the Style

If you don't like the style of the output produced by LaTeX with the standard
style options, you should check the LaTeX *Companion* and the *Local Guide* to
see if there are other options available. If there aren't, you must change the
style of your document yourself. Changing the style means changing the way
the standard structures such as paragraphs and itemized lists are formatted,
not creating new structures. Section 3.4 describes how to define new logical
structures.

Before changing your document's style, remember that many authors make
elementary errors when they try to design their own documents. The only way
to avoid these errors is by consulting a trained typographic designer or reading
about typographic design. All I can do here is warn you against the very common
mistake of making lines that are too wide to read easily—a mistake you won't
make if you follow this suggestion: *Use lines that contain no more than 75
characters, including punctuation and spaces.*

The style of a particular document can be customized by adding declarations
to its preamble. If the same style modifications are used in several documents,
it is more convenient to put them in a separate package. A package is created
by writing the appropriate declarations in a `sty` file—a file whose first name is
the package name and whose extension is `sty`. For example, to define a package named `vacation`, you would create the file `vacation.sty`. The command
`\usepackage{vacation}` would then cause LaTeX to read the file `vacation.sty`.

When reading a package's `sty` file, TeX regards an `@` character as a letter,
so it can be part of a command name like `\@listi`. Such a command name
cannot be used in your document, since TeX would interpret it as the command
`\@` followed by the text characters `listi`. Many of LaTeX's internal commands
have an `@` in their name to prevent their accidental use within the document;
these include some parameters described in Appendix C that you may want to
change.

The simplest way to modify a document's style is by changing parameters
such as the ones that control the height and width of the text on the page.
LaTeX's style parameters are described in this chapter and in Appendix C. Other
modifications require redefining LaTeX commands. For example, if you want to
change the style of chapter headings, you will have to redefine the `\chapter`
command. If the change is complicated—for example, if you want the chapter
heading to list the titles of all preceding chapters—then you will need to learn
advanced TeX commands. However, it isn't hard to figure out how to make
most of the changes you are likely to want. To illustrate the process, I will now
describe how you would make a typical style change: printing chapter titles in
a bold sans serif type style, rather than in the standard bold roman style.

You have to change the definition of `\chapter`, so the first problem is finding that definition. Commands that exist in all document classes are usually
*preloaded*. The file `source2e.tex` lists the names of the files in which the defi-

nitions of preloaded commands can be found. (Consult the *Local Guide* to find
out in what directory these files are.) Commands like `\chapter` that exist only
in some document classes or are defined by a package are not preloaded. The
definitions of these commands are in files read by LaTeX when it processes your
document. Section 4.7 explains how to find out what files LaTeX reads.

For this example, I assume that your document uses the `report` document
class. You will find that LaTeX reads the file `report.cls`. Searching this file for
"`\chapter`", you will come across

```
\newcommand\chapter{\if@openright\cleardoublepage\else...
              \thispagestyle{plain}%
              \global\@topnum\z@
              \@afterindentfalse
              \secdef\@chapter\@schapter}
```

This is where the `\chapter` command is defined. (Macho TeX programmers
sometimes remove the braces around the first argument of `\newcommand`; don't
do it yourself.) Looking at this definition, it's not hard to guess that the chapter heading is produced by `\@chapter` or `\@schapter`. Immediately below the
definition of `\chapter` is

```
\def\@chapter[#1]#2{...
```

This is where `\@chapter` is defined. (Macho TeX programmers also use the TeX
command `\def` to define commands; don't you do it.) Examining this definition
will lead you to suspect that the heading is produced by the `\@makechapterhead`
command. The definition of `\@makechapterhead` contains two `\bfseries` commands. An obvious guess is that adding `\sffamily` commands right before or
after these `\bfseries` commands will produce bold sans serif chapter headings.
So, you will create a file named `sfchap.sty` containing the modified definition
of `\@makechapterhead`, add a `\usepackage{sfchap}` command to the preamble
of your document, and run LaTeX. You will then discover that you have guessed
right; LaTeX has produced the bold sans serif headings you wanted.

This detective work was good practice, but there's a way to avoid much of it.
Comments at the beginning of `report.cls` indicate that this file was generated
from a source file named `classes.dtx`. (The file `source2e.tex` also directs
you to `classes.dtx`.) A `dtx` file contains comments and additional formatting
commands. You can run a `dtx` file through LaTeX to produce a printed version,
or you can just read the `dtx` file itself. The file `classes.dtx` reveals that the
`\@schapter` command prints unnumbered chapter headings. (Such headings
are produced by the `\chapter*` command described in Section C.4.1.) Aided
by the comments, you should now be able to figure out how to change the way
unnumbered chapter headings are printed.

This example shows how to modify a command; modifying an environment
is similar. To find its definition, you need to know that some environments are

defined with TeX's \def command instead of \newenvironment. For example, the equation environment is defined by defining \equation, which is executed by the \begin{equation} command, and \endequation, which is executed by \end{equation}.

Remember that before creating your own package of style changes, you should check the LaTeX *Companion* and the *Local Guide* to see if someone has already created a document class or package that does what you want.

## 6.2   Line and Page Breaking

TeX usually does a good job of breaking text into lines and pages, but it sometimes needs help. Don't worry about line and page breaks until you prepare the final version. Most of the bad breaks that appear in early drafts will disappear as you change the text. Many LaTeX users waste time formatting when they should be writing. **Don't worry about line and page breaks until you prepare the absolutely final version.**

### 6.2.1   Line Breaking

Let's return to the line-breaking problem that we inserted into the sample2e input file in Section 2.3. Recall that it produced the following warning message:

```
Overfull \hbox (10.51814pt too wide) in paragraph at lines 195--200
[]\OT1/cmr/m/n/10 Mathematical for-mu-las may also be dis-played. A dis-played
for-mula is gnomonly
```

TeX could not find a good place to break the line and left the word "gnomonly" extending past the right margin. The first line of this warning message states that the output line extends 10.51814 points past the right margin—a point is about $1/72^{nd}$ of an inch—and is in the paragraph generated by lines 195 through 200 of the input file. The next part of the message shows the input that produced the offending line, except TeX has inserted a "-" character every place that it's willing to hyphenate a word. The draft document class option causes TeX to put a black box next to the extra-long line, making it easy to find.

TeX is quite good at hyphenating words; an English-language version never[1] incorrectly hyphenates an English word and usually finds all correct possibilities. However, it does miss some. For example, it does not know how to hyphenate the word *gnomonly* (which isn't a very gnomonly used word), nor can it hyphenate *gnomon*.

A \- command tells TeX that it is allowed to hyphenate at that point. We could correct our sample hyphenation problem by changing gnomonly to gno\-monly, allowing TeX to break the line after *gno*. However, it's better to change it to gno\-mon\-ly, which also allows TeX to break right before the *ly*.

---

[1] Well, hardly ever.

While TeX will still break this particular sample line after *gno*, further changes to the text might make *gnomon-ly* better.

TeX will not hyphenate a word with a nonletter in the middle, where it treats any sequence of nonspace characters as a single word. While it hyphenates *ra-di-a-tion* properly, it does not hyphenate *x-radiation*—though it will break a line after the *x-*. You must type `x-ra\-di\-a\-tion` for TeX to consider all possible hyphenation points. However, it is generally considered a bad idea to hyphenate a hyphenated compound; you should do so only when there is no better alternative.

When writing a paper about sundials, in which the word *gnomon* appears frequently, it would be a nuisance to type it as `gno\-mon` everywhere it is used. You can teach TeX how to hyphenate words by putting one or more `\hyphenation` commands in the preamble. The command

```
\hyphenation{gno-mon gno-mons gno-mon-ly}
```

tells TeX how to hyphenate *gnomon*, *gnomons*, and *gnomonly*—but it still won't know how to hyphenate *gnomonic*.

While it's very good at hyphenating English, an English-language version of LaTeX does not respect the hyphenation rules of other languages. For example, it uses the English hyphenation *re-spect* rather than the Romanian *res-pect*. If your document contains only a few phrases in Romanian, you can correct hyphenation errors as they occur by using `\hyphenation` or `\-` commands to tell TeX where it can hyphenate a word. If your document contains a lot of text in Romanian or some other language(s), use the `babel` package described in the LaTeX *Companion*.

Not all line-breaking problems can be solved by hyphenation. Sometimes there is just no good way to break a paragraph into lines. TeX is normally very fussy about line breaking; it lets you solve the problem rather than producing a paragraph that doesn't meet its high standards. There are three things you can do when this happens. The first is to rewrite the paragraph. However, having carefully polished your prose, you may not want to change it just to produce perfect line breaks.

The second way to handle a line-breaking problem is to use a `sloppypar` environment or `\sloppy` declaration, which direct TeX not to be so fussy about where it breaks lines. Most of the time, you just enclose the entire paragraph that contains the bad line break between `\begin{sloppypar}` and `\end{sloppypar}` commands. However, sometimes it's easier to use a `\sloppy` declaration. To explain how to use this declaration, it helps to introduce the concept of a *paragraph unit*. A paragraph unit is a portion of text that is treated as a single string of words to be broken into lines at any convenient point. For example, a paragraph containing a displayed equation would consist of two paragraph units—the parts of the paragraph that come before and after the equation. (Since the equation itself can't be broken across lines, it is not a paragraph unit.) Similarly, each item in a list-making environment begins a new paragraph unit.

TeX does its line breaking for a paragraph unit when it encounters the command or blank line that ends the unit, based upon the declarations in effect at that time. So, the scope of the `\sloppy` declaration should include the command or blank line that ends the paragraph unit with the bad line break. You can either delimit the scope of the `\sloppy` declaration with braces, or else use a countermanding `\fussy` declaration that restores TeX to its ordinary compulsive self. The `\begin{sloppypar}` command is equivalent to a blank line followed by {`\sloppy`, and `\end{sloppypar}` is equivalent to a blank line followed by a }.

The third way to fix a bad line break is with a `\linebreak` command, which forces TeX to break the line at that spot. The `\linebreak` is usually inserted right before the word that doesn't fit. An optional argument converts the `\linebreak` command from a demand to a request. The argument must be a digit from 0 through 4, a higher number denoting a stronger request. The command `\linebreak[0]` allows TeX to break the line there, but neither encourages nor discourages its doing so, while `\linebreak[4]` forces the line break just like an ordinary `\linebreak` command. The arguments 1, 2, and 3 provide intermediate degrees of insistence, and may succeed in coaxing TeX to overcome a bad line break. They can also be used to help TeX find the most aesthetically pleasing line breaks. The `\linebreak[0]` command allows a line break where it would normally be forbidden, such as within a word.

Both of these methods handle line-breaking problems by sweeping them under the rug. The "lump in the carpet" that they may leave is one or more lines with too much blank space between words. Such a line will produce an "Underfull \hbox" warning message.

Although unwanted line breaks are usually prevented with the ~ and `\mbox` commands described in Section 2.2.1, LaTeX also provides a `\nolinebreak` command that forbids TeX from breaking the line at that point. Like the `\linebreak` command, `\nolinebreak` takes a digit from 0 through 4 as an optional argument to convert the prohibition into a suggestion that this isn't a good place for a line break—the higher the number, the stronger the suggestion. A `\nolinebreak[0]` command is equivalent to `\linebreak[0]`, and `\nolinebreak[4]` is equivalent to `\nolinebreak`.

A `\linebreak` command causes TeX to justify the line, stretching the space between words so the line extends to the right margin. The `\newline` command ends a line without justifying it.

I can think of no good reason why you would want
to make a short line like this
in the middle of a paragraph, but perhaps you can
think of one.

```
I can think of no good reason why you would
want to make a short line like this
  \newline
in the middle of a paragraph,
but perhaps you can think of one.
```

You can type \\, which is the usual LaTeX command for ending a line, in place of \newline. In fact, LaTeX provides the \newline command only to maintain a complete correspondence between the line-breaking commands and the page-breaking commands described below.

The \linebreak, \nolinebreak, and \newline commands can be used only in paragraph mode. They are fragile commands. See Section C.1.1 if a [ follows a \linebreak or \nolinebreak command that has no optional argument.

Remember, **don't worry about line breaks until you prepare the ultimate, absolutely final version.**

### 6.2.2  Page Breaking

TeX is as fussy about page breaks as it is about line breaks. As with line breaking, sometimes TeX can find no good place to start a new page. A bad page break usually causes TeX to put too little rather than too much text onto the page. When the \flushbottom declaration (Section 6.1.1) is in effect, this produces a page with too much extra vertical space; with the \raggedbottom declaration, it produces a page that is too short. In the first case, TeX warns you about the extra space by generating an "Underfull \vbox" message. With \raggedbottom in effect, TeX does not warn you about bad page breaks, so you should check your final output for pages that are too short.

The LaTeX page-breaking commands are analogous to the line-breaking commands described in Section 6.2.1 above. As with line breaking, LaTeX provides commands to demand or prohibit a page break, with an optional argument transforming the commands to suggestions. The \pagebreak and \nopagebreak commands are the analogs of \linebreak and \nolinebreak. When used between paragraphs, they apply to that point; when used in the middle of a paragraph, they apply immediately after the current line. Thus, a \pagebreak command within a paragraph insists that TeX start a new page after the line in which the command appears, and \nopagebreak[3] suggests rather strongly that TeX *not* start a new page there.

You will sometimes want to squeeze a little more text on a page than TeX thinks you should. The best way of doing this is to make room on the page by removing some vertical space, using the commands of Section 6.4.2. If that doesn't work, you can try using a \nopagebreak command to prevent TeX from breaking the page before you want it to. However, TeX often becomes adamant about breaking a page at a certain point, and it will not be deterred by \nopagebreak. When this happens, you can put extra text on the page as follows:

- Add the command \enlargethispage*{1000pt} to the text on the current page, before the point where TeX wants to start a new page.

- Add a \pagebreak command to break the page where you want.

Squeezing in extra text in this way will make the page longer than normal, which may look bad in two-sided printing. Section C.12.2 describes a less heavy-handed approach. But **don't worry about page breaks until you prepare the ultimate, absolutely final, no-more-changes (really!) version.**

The \newpage command is the analog of \newline, creating a page that ends prematurely right at that point. Even when a \flushbottom declaration is in effect, a shortened page is produced. The \clearpage command is similar to \newpage, except that any leftover figures or tables are put on one or more separate pages with no text. The \chapter and \include commands (Section 4.4) use \clearpage to begin a new page. Adding an extra \newpage or \clearpage command will not produce a blank page; two such commands in a row are equivalent to a single one. To generate a blank page, you must put some invisible text on it, such as an empty \mbox.

When using the twoside style option for two-sided printing, you may want to start a sectional unit on a right-hand page. The \cleardoublepage command is the same as \clearpage except that it produces a blank page if necessary so that the next page will be a right-hand (odd-numbered) one.

When used in two-column format, the \newpage and \pagebreak commands start a new column rather than a new page. However, the \clearpage and \cleardoublepage commands start a new page.

The page-breaking commands can be used only where it is possible to start a new page—that is, in paragraph mode and not inside a box (Section 6.4.3). They are all fragile.

## 6.3 Numbering

Every number that LaTeX generates has a *counter* associated with it. The name of the counter is usually the same as the name of the environment or command that produces the number, except with no \. Below is a list of the counters used by LaTeX's standard document styles to control numbering.

| | | | |
|---|---|---|---|
| part | paragraph | figure | enumi |
| chapter | subparagraph | table | enumii |
| section | page | footnote | enumiii |
| subsection | equation | mpfootnote | enumiv |
| subsubsection | | | |

The counters enumi ... enumiv control different levels of enumerate environments, enumi for the outermost level, enumii for the next level, and so on. The mpfootnote counter numbers footnotes inside a minipage environment (Section 6.4.3). In addition to these, an environment created with the \newtheorem command (Section 3.4.3) has a counter of the same name unless an optional argument specifies that it is to be numbered the same as another environment.

There are also some other counters used for document-style parameters; they are described in Appendix C.

The value of a counter is a single integer—usually nonnegative. Multiple numbers are generated with separate counters, the "2" and "4" of "Subsection 2.4" coming from the `section` and `subsection` counters, respectively. The value of a counter is initialized to zero and is incremented by the appropriate command or environment. For example, the `subsection` counter is incremented by the `\subsection` command before the subsection number is generated, and it is reset to zero when the `section` counter is incremented, so subsection numbers start from one in a new section.

The `\setcounter` command sets the value of a counter, and `\addtocounter` increments it by a specified amount.

Because[18] counters[17] are stepped before being used, you set them to one less than the number you want.

```
\setcounter{footnote}{17}
Because\footnote{...}
\addtocounter{footnote}{-2}%
counters\footnote{...} are stepped ...
```

When used in the middle of a paragraph, these commands should be attached to a word to avoid adding extra space.

The `\setcounter` and `\addtocounter` commands affect only the specified counter; for example, changing the `section` counter with these commands does not affect the `subsection` counter. The commands to change counter values are global declarations (Section C.1.4); their effects are not limited by the normal scope rules for declarations.

The `page` counter is used to generate the page number. It differs from other counters in that it is incremented *after* the page number is generated, so its value is the number of the current page rather than the next one. A `\setcounter{page}{27}` command in the middle of the document therefore causes the current page to be numbered 27. For this reason, the `page` counter is initialized to one instead of zero.

LaTeX provides the following commands for printing counter values; the list shows what they produce when the `page` counter has the value four.

| | | | | | |
|---|---|---|---|---|---|
| 4 | `\arabic{page}` | iv | `\roman{page}` | d | `\alph{page}` |
| | | IV | `\Roman{page}` | D | `\Alph{page}` |

To generate a printed number, LaTeX executes a command whose name is formed by adding `\the` to the beginning of the appropriate counter's name; redefining this command changes the way the number is printed. For example, a subsection number is made by the `\thesubsection` command. To change the numbering of sections and subsections so the fourth subsection of the second section is numbered "II-D", you type the following (see Section 3.4 for an explanation of `\renewcommand`):

```
\renewcommand{\thesection}{\Roman{section}}
\renewcommand{\thesubsection}{\thesection-\Alph{subsection}}
```

Since sections are usually numbered the same throughout the document (at least until the appendix), the obvious place for this command is in the preamble.

A new counter is created with a \newcounter command having the name of the counter as its argument. The new counter's initial value is zero, and its initial \the... command prints the value as an arabic numeral. See Section 6.6 for an example of how a new counter is used in defining an environment. The \newcounter declaration should be used only in the preamble.

## 6.4   Length, Spaces, and Boxes

In visual design, one specifies how much vertical space to leave above a chapter heading, how wide a line of text should be, and so on. This section describes the basic tools for making these specifications.

### 6.4.1   Length

A length is a measure of distance. An amount of space or a line width is specified by giving a length as an argument to the appropriate formatting command. A length of one inch is specified by typing 1in; it can also be given in metric units as 2.54cm or 25.4mm, or as 72.27pt, where pt denotes *point*—a unit of length used by printers. A length can also be negative—for example, -2.54cm.

The number 0 by itself is not a length. A length of zero is written 0in or 0cm or 0pt, not 0. Writing 0 as a length is a common mistake.

While inches, centimeters, and points are convenient units, they should be avoided because they specify fixed lengths. A .25-inch horizontal space that looks good in one-column output may be too wide in a two-column format. It's better to use units of length that depend upon the appropriate style parameters. The simplest such units are the em and the ex, which depend upon the font (the size and style of type). A 1em length is about equal to the width of an "M", and 1ex is about the height of an "x". The em is best used for horizontal lengths and the ex for vertical lengths. An em ruler for the current font is given below, and an ex ruler is in the margin.

In addition to writing explicit lengths such as 1in or 3.5em, you can also express lengths with *length commands*. A length command has a *value* that is a length. For example, \parindent is a length command whose value specifies the width of the indentation at the beginning of a normal paragraph. Typing

`\parindent` as the argument of a command is equivalent to typing the current value of `\parindent`. You can also type `2.5\parindent` for a length that is 2.5 times as large as `\parindent`, or `-2.5\parindent` for the negative of that length; `-\parindent` is the same as `-1.0\parindent`.

A length such as `1.5em` or `\parindent` is a *rigid* length. Specifying a space of width `1cm` always produces a one-centimeter-wide space. (It may not be exactly one centimeter wide because your output device might uniformly change all dimensions—for example, enlarging them by 5%.) However, there are also *rubber* lengths that can vary.[2] Space specified with a rubber length can stretch or shrink as required. For example, TeX justifies lines (produces an even right margin) by stretching or shrinking the space between words to make each line the same length.

A rubber length has a natural length and a degree of elasticity. Of particular interest is the special length command `\fill` that has a natural length of zero but is infinitely stretchable, so a space of width `\fill` tends to expand as far as it can. The use of such stretchable space is described in Section 6.4.2 below. Multiplying a length command by a number destroys its elasticity, producing a rigid length. Thus, `1\fill` and `.7\fill` are rigid lengths of value zero inches.

Most lengths used in LaTeX are rigid. Unless a length is explicitly said to be rubber, you can assume it is rigid. All length commands are robust; a `\protect` command should never precede a length command.

Below are some of LaTeX's *length parameters*—length commands that define a document's style parameters; others are given in Appendix C. By expressing lengths in terms of these parameters, you can define formatting commands that work properly with different styles.

`\parindent`  The amount of indentation at the beginning of a normal paragraph.

`\textwidth`  The width of the text on the page.

`\textheight`  The height of the body of the page—that is, the normal height of everything on a page excluding the head and foot (Section 6.1.2).

`\parskip`  The extra vertical space inserted between paragraphs. It is customary not to leave any extra space between paragraphs, so `\parskip` has a natural length of zero (except in the `letter` document class). However, it is a rubber length, so it can stretch to add vertical space between paragraphs when the `\flushbottom` declaration (Section 6.1.1) is in effect.

`\baselineskip`  The normal vertical distance from the bottom of one line to the bottom of the next line in the same paragraph. Thus, `\textheight` $\div$ `\baselineskip` equals the number of lines of text that would appear on a page if it were all one paragraph.[3]

---

[2] A rigid length is called a ⟨dimen⟩ and a rubber length is called a ⟨skip⟩ in the *TeXbook*.

[3] This is only approximately correct—see the `\topskip` command in Section C.5.3 to find out why.

LATEX provides the following declarations for changing the values of length commands and for creating new ones. These declarations obey the usual scoping rules.

`\newlength` Defines a new length command.  You type `\newlength{\gnat}` to make `\gnat` a length command with value 0cm.  An error occurs if a `\gnat` command is already defined.

`\setlength` Sets the value of a length command. The value of `\parskip` is set to 1.01 millimeters by the command `\setlength{\parskip}{1.01mm}`.

`\addtolength` Increments the value of a length command by a specified amount. If the current value of `\parskip` is .01 inches, then executing the command `\addtolength{\parskip}{-.1\parskip}` changes its value to .009 inches—the original value plus $-.1$ times its original value.

`\settowidth` Sets the value of a length command equal to the width of a specified piece of text. The command `\settowidth{\parindent}{\em small}` sets the value of `\parindent` to the width of *small*—the text produced by typesetting {`\em small`} in LR mode.

`\settoheight`, `\settodepth` These commands act like `\settowidth`, except they set the value of the length command to the height and depth, respectively, of the text. For example, `\settoheight{\parskip}{Gnu}` sets the value of `\parskip` to the height of the letter "G" in the current font, while `\settodepth{\parskip}{gnu}` sets the value of `\parskip` to the distance the letter "g" extends below the line.  Height and depth are explained below, in Section 6.4.3.

The value of a length command created with `\newlength` can be changed at any time. This is also true for some of LATEX's length parameters, while others should be changed only in the preamble and still others should never be changed. Consult Appendix C to find out when you can safely change the value of a LATEX parameter.

## 6.4.2  Spaces

A horizontal space is produced with the `\hspace` command. Think of `\hspace` as making a blank "word", with spaces before or after it producing an interword space.

```
Here         is a .5 inch space.          Here\hspace{.5in}is a .5 inch space.
Here         is a .5 inch space.          Here \hspace{.5in}is a .5 inch space.
Here         is a .5 inch space.          Here \hspace{.5in} is a .5 inch space.
Negative space is a backspace—like this.  ...---like this.\hspace{-.5in}/////
```

TEX removes space from the beginning or end of each line of output text, except at the beginning and end of a paragraph—including space added with \hspace. The \hspace* command is the same as \hspace except that the space it produces is never removed, even when it comes at the beginning or end of a line. The \hspace and \hspace* commands are robust.

The \vspace command produces vertical space. It is most commonly used between paragraphs; when used within a paragraph, the vertical space is added after the line in which the \vspace appears.

You seldom add space like this between lines in
  .25 in
a paragraph, but you sometimes remove space between them by adding some negative space.
  7 mm
You more often add space between paragraphs—especially before or after displayed material.

```
You\vspace{.25in} seldom add space like
this between lines in a paragraph, but you
... by adding some negative space.

\vspace{7 mm}

You more often add space between ...
```

Just as it removes horizontal space from the beginning and end of a line, TEX removes vertical space that comes at the beginning or end of a page. The \vspace* command creates vertical space that is never removed.

If the argument of an \hspace or \vspace command (or its *-form) is a rubber length, the space produced will be able to stretch and shrink. This is normally relevant only for the fine tuning of the formatting commands of a package or document class. However, a space made with an infinitely stretchable length such as \fill is useful for positioning text because it stretches as much as it can, pushing everything else aside. The command \hfill is an abbreviation for \hspace{\fill}.

Here is a                          stretched space.
Here are             two           equal ones.

```
Here is a \hfill stretched space.
Here are \hfill two \hfill equal ones.
```

Note that when two equally stretchable spaces push against each other, they stretch the same amount. You can use stretchable spaces to center objects or to move them flush against the right-hand margin. However, LATEX provides more convenient methods of doing that, described in Section 6.5.

Infinitely stretchable space can be used in the analogous way for moving text vertically. The \vfill command is equivalent to a blank line followed by \vspace{\fill}. Remember that spaces produced by \hfill or \vfill at the beginning and end of a line or page disappear. You must use \hspace*{\fill} or \vspace*{\fill} for space that you don't want to disappear.

The \dotfill command acts just like \hfill except it produces dots instead of spaces. The command \hrulefill works the same way, but it produces a horizontal line.

Gnats and gnus ..................... see pests.            Gnats and gnus \dotfill\  see pests.
This is _____ really _____ it.            This is \hrulefill\ really \hrulefill\ it.

## 6.4.3  Boxes

A *box* is a chunk of text that TEX treats as a unit, just as if it were a single letter.
No matter how big it is, TEX will never split a box across lines or across pages.
The \mbox command introduced in Section 2.2.1 prevents its argument from
being split across lines by putting it in a box. Many other LATEX commands and
environments produce boxes. For example, the array and tabular environments
(Section 3.6.2) both produce a single box that can be quite big, as does the
picture environment described in Section 7.1.

A box has a *reference point*, which is at its left-hand edge. TEX produces
lines by putting boxes next to one another with their reference points aligned,
as shown in Figure 6.1. The figure also shows how the width, height, and depth
of a box are computed.

LATEX provides additional commands and environments for making three
kinds of boxes: LR boxes, in which the contents of the box are processed in LR
mode; parboxes, in which the contents of the box are processed in paragraph
mode; and rule boxes, consisting of a rectangular blob of ink.

A box-making command or environment can be used in any mode. LATEX
uses the declarations in effect at that point when typesetting the box's contents,
so the contents of a box appearing in the scope of an \em declaration will be
emphasized—usually by being set in an italic type style. However, box-making
commands that appear in a mathematical formula are not affected by the commands described in Section 3.3.8 that change the type style in the formula.

The \mbox in the formula $x = y * ab+xyz+cd/z$ uses         ... in the formula
the same type style as the surrounding text.              $x = y * \mathbf{\scriptstyle ab +
                                                          \mbox{xyz} + cd} \textstyle / z$ uses ...

Since the input that produces a box's contents is either the argument of a box-
making command or the text of a box-making environment, any declarations
made inside it are local to the box.

Figure 6.1: Boxes and how TEX puts them together.

A box is often displayed on a line by itself. This can be done by treating the box as a formula and using the `displaymath` environment (\[ ... \]). The `center` environment described in Section 6.5 can also be used.

### LR Boxes

The `\mbox` command makes an LR box—a box whose contents are obtained by processing the command's argument in LR mode. It is an abbreviated version of the `\makebox` command; `\makebox` has optional arguments that `\mbox` doesn't. The box created by an `\mbox` command is just wide enough to hold its contents. You can specify the width of the box with a `\makebox` command that has an optional first argument. The default is to center the contents in the box, but this can be overridden by a second optional argument that consists of a single letter: `l` to move the contents to the left side of the box, and `r` to move it to the right.

|   |   |
|---|---|
| Good    *gnus*    are here at last. | `Good \makebox[1in]{\em gnus}  are here ...` |
| Good *gnus*    are here at last. | `Good \makebox[1in][l]{\em gnus} are ...` |
| Good       *gnus* are here at last. | `Good \makebox[1in][r]{\em gnus} are ...` |

A box is treated just like a word; space characters on either side produce an interword space.

The `\framebox` command is exactly the same as `\makebox` except it puts a frame around the outside of the box. There is also an `\fbox` command, the abbreviation for a `\framebox` command with no optional arguments.

|   |   |
|---|---|
| There was not a ⎵gnu⎵ or ⎵armadillo⎵ in sight. | `There was not a \framebox[1in][l]{gnu}` <br> `or \fbox{armadillo} in sight.` |

When you specify a box of a fixed width, TeX acts as if the box has exactly that width. If the contents are too wide for the box, they will overflow into the surrounding text.

|   |   |
|---|---|
| X X⎵wide armadillos⎵X X | `X X X\framebox[.5in]{wide armadillos}X X X` |

### Parboxes

A *parbox* is a box whose contents are typeset in paragraph mode, with TeX producing a series of lines just as in ordinary text. The `figure` and `table` environments (Section 3.5.1) create parboxes. There are two ways to make a parbox at a given point in the text: with the `\parbox` command and the `minipage` environment. They can be used to put one or more paragraphs of text inside a picture or in a table item.

For TeX to break text into lines, it must know how wide the lines should be. Therefore, `\parbox` and the `minipage` environment have the width of the parbox as an argument. The second mandatory argument of the \parbox command is the text to be put in the parbox.

|←——— 1 in ———→|

Breaking lines in a narrow parbox is hard.  YOU CAN  expect to get a lot of bad line breaks if you try this sort of thing.

```
\parbox{1in}{Breaking lines in a narrow
    parbox is hard.} \ YOU CAN \
\parbox{1in}{expect to get a lot of bad
    line breaks if you try ...}
```

There is no indentation at the beginning of a paragraph in these parboxes; LaTeX sets the \parindent parameter, which specifies the amount of indentation, to zero in a parbox. You can set it to any other value with \setlength (Section 6.4.1).

In the example above, the parboxes are positioned vertically so the center of the box is aligned with the center of the text line. An optional first argument of t (for *top*) or b (*bottom*) aligns the top or bottom line of the parbox with the text line. More precisely, the optional argument causes the reference point of the box to be the reference point of the top or bottom line of its contents.

This is a parbox aligned on its bottom line.   AND THIS  one is aligned on its top line.

```
\parbox[b]{1in}{This is a parbox aligned
    on its bottom line.}
\ AND THIS \
\parbox[t]{1in}{one is aligned on its top
    line.}
```

Finer control of the vertical positioning is obtained with the \raisebox command described below.

The \parbox command is generally used for a parbox containing a small amount of text. For a larger parbox or one containing a tabbing environment, a list-making environment, or any of the paragraph-making environments described in Section 6.5, you should use a minipage environment. The minipage environment has the same optional positioning argument and mandatory width argument as the \parbox command.

When used in a minipage environment, the \footnote command puts a footnote at the bottom of the parbox produced by the environment. This is particularly useful for footnotes inside figures or tables. Moreover, unlike in ordinary text, the \footnote command can be used anywhere within the environment— even inside another box or in an item of a tabular environment. To footnote something in a minipage environment with an ordinary footnote at the bottom of the page, use the \footnotemark and \footnotetext commands described in Section C.3.3.

| | | |
|---|---|---|
| *gnat*: a tiny bug that is very hard to find. | AND | *gnu*: a beast[a] that is hard to miss. |
| | | ───── |
| | | [a]See armadillo. |

```
\begin{minipage}[t]{1in}
  {\em gnat}: a tiny bug ...
\end{minipage} \ AND \
\begin{minipage}[t]{1in}
  {\em gnu}: a beast\footnote{See
    armadillo.} that is hard to miss.
\end{minipage}
```

If you have one `minipage` environment nested inside another, footnotes may appear at the bottom of the wrong one.

You may find yourself wishing that TeX would determine the width of a parbox by itself, making it just wide enough to hold the text inside. This is normally impossible because TeX must know the line width to do its line breaking. However, it doesn't have to know a line width when typesetting a `tabbing` environment because the input specifies where every line ends. Therefore, if a `minipage` environment consists of nothing but a `tabbing` environment, then TeX will set the width of the parbox to be either the width specified by the `minipage` environment's argument or the actual width of the longest line, choosing whichever is smaller.

### Rule Boxes

A rule box is a rectangular blob of ink. It is made with the `\rule` command, whose arguments specify the width and height of the blob. The reference point of the rule box is its lower-left corner. There is also an optional first argument that specifies how high to raise the rule (a negative value lowers it).

Rule 1: (figure)     Rule 2: (figure)

```
Rule 1: \rule{1mm}{5mm}
Rule 2: \rule[.1in]{.25in}{.02in}
```

A thin enough rule is just a line, so the `\rule` command can draw horizontal or vertical lines of arbitrary length and thickness.

A rule box of width zero is called a *strut*. Having no width, a strut is invisible; but it does have height, and TeX will adjust the vertical spacing to leave room for it.

Compare this box with this box .

```
Compare \fbox{this box} with
\fbox{\rule[-.5cm]{0cm}{1cm}this box}.
```

Struts provide a convenient method of adding vertical space in places where `\vspace` can't be used, such as within a mathematical formula.

### Raising and Lowering Boxes

The \raisebox command raises text by a specified length (a negative length lowers the text). It makes an LR box, just like the \mbox command.

| | |
|---|---|
| You can *raise* or ~lower~ text. | `You can \raisebox{.6ex}{\em raise} or`<br>`\raisebox{-.6ex}{\em lower} text.` |

It is sometimes useful to change how big TeX thinks a piece of text is without changing the text. The \makebox command tells TeX how wide the text is, while a strut can increase the text's apparent height but cannot decrease it. Optional arguments of \raisebox tell TeX how tall it should pretend that the text is. The command

```
\raisebox{.4ex}[1.5ex][.75ex]{\em text}
```

not only raises *text* by .4ex, but also makes TeX think that it extends 1.5ex above the bottom of the line and .75ex below the bottom of the line. (The bottom of the line is where most characters sit; a letter like $y$ extends below it.) If you omit the second optional argument, TeX will think the text extends as far below the line as it actually does. By changing the apparent height of text, you change how much space TeX leaves for it. This is sometimes used to eliminate space above or below a formula or part of a formula.

### Saving Boxes

If a single piece of text appears in several places, you can define a command with \newcommand (Section 3.4) to generate it. While this saves typing, TeX doesn't save any time because it must do the work of typesetting the text whenever it encounters the command. If the text is complicated—especially if it contains a picture environment (Section 7.1)—TeX could waste a lot of time typesetting it over and over again.

TeX can typeset something once as a box and then save it in a named *storage bin*, from which it can be used repeatedly. The name of a storage bin is an ordinary command name; a new bin is created and named by the \newsavebox declaration. The \savebox command makes a box and saves it in a specified bin; it has the bin name as its first argument and the rest of its arguments are the same as for the \makebox command. The \usebox command prints the contents of a bin.

| | |
|---|---|
| | `\newsavebox{\toy}`<br>`\savebox{\toy}[.65in]{gnats}` |
| ⊢— .65 in —⊣ | `...` |
| It's   gnats   and   gnats   and   gnats   , | `It's \usebox{\toy} and \usebox{\toy} and` |
| wherever we go. | `\usebox{\toy}, wherever we go.` |

The \sbox command is the short form of \savebox, with no optional arguments. The \savebox and \sbox commands are declarations that have the usual scope. However, the \newsavebox declaration is global (Section C.1.4) and does not obey the customary scoping rules.

The lrbox environment is like an \sbox command, except that it ignores spaces at the beginning and end of the text. Thus,

```
\begin{lrbox}{\jewel}
   Text
\end{lrbox}
```

is equivalent to \sbox{\jewel}{Text}. This environment is used to define an environment in terms of a command. For example, suppose we want to define a boxit environment that produces a boxed, 1-inch-wide paragraph.

Here is a
```
silly boxed para-
graph that no one
will ever use
```
for anything.

```
... a   \begin{boxit}
           silly boxed paragraph ...
       \end{boxit}   for anything.
```

We define this environment by using its body (the text between \begin{boxit} and \end{boxit}) as the argument of an \fbox command. Making the paragraph box with a minipage environment, we can define the boxit environment by:

```
\newsavebox{\savepar}
\newenvironment{boxit}{\begin{lrbox}{\savepar}
  \begin{minipage}[b]{1in}}
 {\end{minipage}\end{lrbox}\fbox{\usebox{\savepar}}}
```

### 6.4.4   Formatting with Boxes

Many LaTeX users fail to realize how much they can do with the box-making commands described above. I will illustrate the power of these commands with a silly example: defining a \face command to put a funny face around a word, like the faces around "funny" and "face" in this sentence. The face is composed of two diamonds (◇) produced with the \diamond command, and a smile (⌣) produced with \smile. The trick, of course, is positioning these symbols correctly relative to the word being "faced".

The left eye of the face (the one near the "f") is positioned above the word and 15% of the way from the word's left edge to its right edge. First, we see how to put a piece of text a fixed distance to the right of the left-hand edge of a word. Recall that if the specified width of a \makebox is less than the width of its contents, the contents extend outside the box. With the l position specified, the contents extend to the right of the box. In the extreme case of a zero-width box, the entire contents lie to the right.

⊢ 1 cm ⊢

The gnuuuuu began to moooooꞓooooo.        ...to \makebox[0pt][l]{\hspace{1cm}X}moo...

Because the box produced by this \makebox command has zero width, it doesn't change the position of the "moo...".

We want the face's left eye to be shifted to the right by .15 times the width of the word and raised by the height of the word. So, the \face command must measure the width and height of its argument using the \settoheight and \settowidth commands. These lengths are saved in two new length commands, \faceht and \facewd, that are defined with \newlength. The eye is raised with the \raisebox command. Before figuring out how to draw the rest of the face, we define a \lefteye command so \lefteye{\emph{moooo}} produces m̊oooo.

```
\newlength{\facewd}  \newlength{\faceht}       %% Define length commands
\newcommand{\lefteye}[1]{%                    Definition of \lefteye:
  \settowidth{\facewd}{#1}\settoheight{\faceht}{#1}%   – Save width & height
  \raisebox{\faceht}{%                         – Raise by height
    \makebox[0pt][l]{\hspace{.15\facewd}%      – Move right .15 * width
      $\diamond$}}%                            – Print eye
  #1}%                                         – Print argument
```

Each line in the definition of \lefteye ends with a %. This both allows comments and splits the definition across lines without introducing unwanted interword spaces. (See Section 2.2.1.) Unintentional spaces are a common source of error in command definitions; be careful not to introduce any.

To make the right eye of the \face command, we put immediately after the word a zero-width box whose contents extend to the left. Such a box is produced by a \makebox command with the r positioning specifier:

```
\makebox[0pt][r]{$\diamond$\hspace{.15\facewd}}
```

The right eye, like the left, is raised with a \raisebox command.

The face's smile is centered beneath the word. To achieve the correct horizontal positioning, \makebox is used to center the smile in a box the same width as the word. This box is in turn put inside and extending to the right of a zero-width box that is placed before the word.

```
\makebox[0pt][l]{\makebox[\facewd]{$\smile$}}
```

A bit of experimentation reveals that the smile should be lowered (raised by a negative distance of) 1.4 ex.

The complete definition of \face appears in Figure 6.2. (Like all such definitions, it should go in the preamble.) The definition has been refined to solve two problems. First, the eyes and smile would normally increase the height and depth of the line, causing TeX to add extra space above and below it. To prevent this, the optional arguments to \raisebox have been used to make TeX pretend that the eyes have zero height and the smile has zero (height and) depth.

```
\newlength{\facewd}  \newlength{\faceht}   %% Define length commands
\newcommand{\face}[1]{%
  \settowidth{\facewd}{#1}\settoheight{\faceht}{#1}%    * Save width & height.
  \raisebox{\faceht}[0pt]{\makebox[0pt][l]{%            * Print left eye.
    \hspace{.15\facewd}$\diamond$}}%
  \raisebox{-1.4ex}[0pt][0pt]{\makebox[0pt][l]{%        * Print smile.
    \makebox[\facewd]{$\smile$}}}%
  {#1}%                                                 * Print argument
  \raisebox{\faceht}[0pt]{\makebox[0pt][r]{%            * Print right eye.
    $\diamond$\hspace{.15\facewd}}}}}
```

Figure 6.2: The complete definition of the \face command.

The second problem occurs in the definition of \lefteye given above. As explained in Section 3.4.1, that definition fails to limit the scope of declarations that appear in its argument.

The \em declaration in *g̊nu escapes its argument.*         ... in \lefteye{\em gnu} escapes ...

This problem is solved by putting an extra pair of braces around the part of the definition that prints the argument.

A \face command uses the argument three times—to measure its height, to measure its width, and to print it. Each time, the argument is processed anew by LaTeX. This could be a problem. For example, if the argument contains a \typein command, each occurrence of \face causes LaTeX to request three separate inputs. We can modify the definition to make \face process its argument only once by using a \savebox command to save the argument and replacing the three uses (the #1's) with \usebox commands.

Solving a formatting problem is often a matter of figuring out how to position some text. The definition of the \face command shows how we can use space- and box-making commands to put one object (for example, an eye or a smile) in any desired position relative to another object. The two objects can be arbitrarily far apart. Consider the box around this complete line of text. It is easy to produce the box itself by putting a strut (a zero-width rule) and some horizontal space in an \fbox command.

$$\text{\fbox{\rule{0pt}{.5\baselineskip}\hspace{\textwidth}}}$$

But, how did I position the box? I could have positioned it relative to the first or last word on the line. However, that would have required knowing where the line breaks occur, and they change every time I revise the paragraph. Instead, I positioned the box relative to an invisible marginal note, produced with an \mbox{} inside a \marginpar command (described in Section 3.5.2).

Suppose you want to put a box around an entire page of text. Again, producing a box of the right size is easy; the problem is positioning it. Since the box appears at a fixed point on the page, it must be positioned relative to some object that appears at a fixed location on the page. One such object is the page heading; another is the page number. You just have to add a suitable zero-width box to either of these objects. Section C.5.3 describes how to set page headings; the page number is produced by the `\thepage` command (Section 6.3).

# 6.5   Centering and "Flushing"

The `center` environment is used to produce one or more lines of centered text; a `\\` command starts a new line.

This is the last line of text in the preceding paragraph.

Here are three<br>
centered<br>
lines of text.

This is the text immediately following the environment. It begins a new paragraph only if you leave a blank line after the `\end{center}`.

```
... of text in the preceding paragraph.
\begin{center}
  Here are three\\  centered \\
  lines of text.
\end{center}
This is the text immediately ...
```

LaTeX is in paragraph mode inside the `center` environment, so it breaks lines where necessary to keep them from extending past the margins.

The `flushleft` and `flushright` environments are similar, except instead of each line of text being centered, it is moved to the left or right margin, respectively.

These are the last lines of text from the preceding paragraph.

These are two<br>
flushed right lines.

```
... of text from the preceding paragraph.
\begin{flushright}
  These are two \\ flushed right lines.
\end{flushright}
```

The `center` and `flushright` environments are most commonly used with each new line started by an explicit `\\` command. There is little purpose to using the `flushleft` environment in this way, since the `\\` command in ordinary text produces a flushed-left line. By letting TeX do the line breaking, `flushleft` produces ragged-right text.

Notice how TeX leaves these lines uneven, without stretching them out to reach the right margin. This is known as "ragged-right" text.

```
\begin{flushleft}
  Notice how \TeX\ leaves these lines
  uneven, without stretching them out ...
\end{flushleft}
```

The centering and flushing environments work by using certain declarations that change how TeX makes paragraphs. These declarations are available as

LaTeX commands; the declaration that corresponds to each environment is shown below:

| *environment*: | center | flushleft | flushright |
| *declaration*: | \centering | \raggedright | \raggedleft |

These declarations can be used inside an environment such as `quote` or in a parbox (Section 6.4.3).

This is text that comes at the end of the preceding paragraph.

Here is a quote environment<br>whose lines are<br>flushed right.

```
... at the end of the preceding paragraph.
\begin{quote}
  \raggedleft Here is a quote environment\\
  whose lines are \\  flushed right.
\end{quote}
```

The text of a figure or table can be centered on the page by putting a `\centering` declaration at the beginning of the `figure` or `table` environment.

Unlike the environments, the centering and flushing declarations do not start a new paragraph; they simply change how TeX formats paragraph units (Section 6.2.1). To affect a paragraph unit's format, the scope of the declaration must contain the blank line or `\end` command (of an environment like `quote`) that ends the paragraph unit.

## 6.6   List-Making Environments

A *list* is a sequence of items typeset in paragraph mode with indented left and right margins, each item begun with a label. A label can be empty and an indentation can be of length zero, so an environment not normally thought of as a list can be regarded as one. In fact, almost every one of LaTeX's environments that begins on a new line is defined as a list. The list-making environments are: `quote`, `quotation`, `verse`, `itemize`, `enumerate`, `description`, `thebibliography`, `center`, `flushleft`, and `flushright`, as well as the theorem-like environments declared by `\newtheorem`.

LaTeX provides two primitive list-making environments: `list` and `trivlist`, the latter being a restricted version of `list`. They are flexible enough to produce most lists and are used to define the environments listed above.

### 6.6.1   The `list` Environment

The `list` environment has two arguments. The first specifies how items should be labeled when no argument is given to the `\item` command; the second contains declarations to set the formatting parameters. The general form of a list and the meaning of most of its formatting parameters are shown in Figure 6.3. The vertical-space parameters are rubber lengths; the horizontal-space parame-

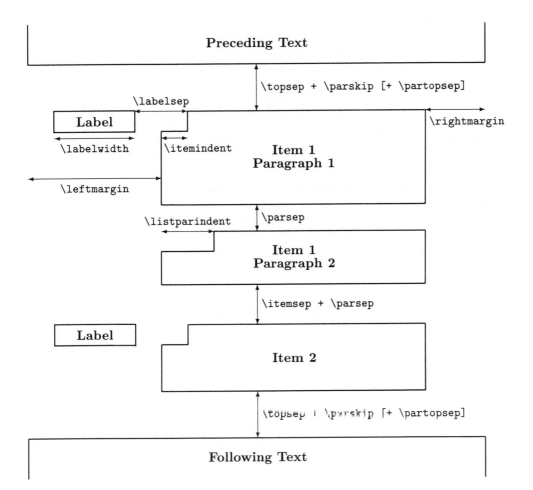

Figure 6.3: The format of a list.

ters are rigid ones. The extra \partopsep space is added at the top of the list only if the input file has a blank line before the environment. The vertical space following the environment is the same as the one preceding it.

Inside the list, the values of \parskip and \parindent are set to the values of \parsep and \listparindent, respectively. When one list is nested inside another, the \leftmargin and \rightmargin distances of the inner list are measured from the margins of the outer list.

The default values of these parameters are determined by the document class (and its options), as described in Section C.6.3; they depend upon the level of nesting of the list. These default values can be changed by declarations in the list environment's second argument. It is best to maintain the same spacing in all lists, so the default values of the vertical spacing and margin parameters should be used. However, the width and placement of the label may differ in different kinds of lists.

The label is typeset in LR mode. If it fits within a box of width \labelwidth, it is placed flush with the right-hand edge of a box of that width, which is positioned as shown in Figure 6.3. (It can be moved to a different position with the \hfill command of Section 6.4.2.) If the label is wider than \labelwidth, it extends to the right of the position shown in Figure 6.3 and the indentation of the first line of the item is increased by the extra width of the label.

The first argument of the environment is the text to be used as the label for any \item command with no optional argument. To number the items automatically, the second argument of the list environment should contain a \usecounter{ctr} command whose argument is the name of a counter—usually one defined with \newcounter (Section 6.3). This counter is reset to zero at the beginning of the environment and is incremented by one before the execution of any \item command that has no optional argument, so it can be used to generate a label number.

This sentence represents the end of the text that precedes the list.

B–I This is the first item of the list. Observe how the left and right margins are indented by the same amount.

B–II This is the second item.

As usual, the following text starts a new paragraph only if the list environment is followed by a blank line.

```
\newcounter{bean}
... the text that precedes the list.
\begin{list}
  {B--\Roman{bean}}{\usecounter{bean}
    \setlength{\rightmargin}{\leftmargin}}
  \item This is the first item of the list.
    Observe how the left and ...
  \item This is the second item.
\end{list}
As usual, the following text starts a ...
```

A list environment like this would be used to produce a one-of-a-kind list. The list environment is more commonly used with the \newenvironment command (Section 3.4) to define a new environment. Having many different list formats tends to confuse the reader. Instead of formatting each list individually, you should define a small number of list-making environments.

### 6.6.2  The `trivlist` Environment

The `trivlist` environment is a restricted form of the `list` environment in which margins are not indented and an `\item` command with no optional argument produces no text. The environment has no arguments and is very much like a `list` environment whose second argument sets `\leftmargin`, `\rightmargin`, `\labelwidth`, and `\itemindent` to a length of zero.

The `trivlist` environment is used to define other environments that create a one-item list, usually with an empty label. For example, the `center` environment (Section 6.5) is equivalent to

```
\begin{trivlist} \centering \item  ...  \end{trivlist}
```

## 6.7  Fonts

A *font* is a particular size and style of type. Section 3.1 explains how to change the type style; Section 6.7.1 explains how to change the size. As its default, LaTeX uses the Computer Modern fonts designed by Donald Knuth. There are a variety of packages that cause LaTeX to use fonts other than Computer Modern. Many of these packages are described in the LaTeX *Companion*; your *Local Guide* will tell you which of them are available on your computer. You should use one of these packages to change the fonts that are used throughout the document.

### 6.7.1  Changing Type Size

LaTeX's normal default type size is ten-point, but the `11pt` document-class option makes the default size eleven-point and the `12pt` option makes it twelve-point. LaTeX provides the following declarations for changing the type size within a document.

| | | | | | |
|---|---|---|---|---|---|
| Gnu | `\tiny` | Gnu | `\normalsize` | Gnu | `\LARGE` |
| Gnu | `\scriptsize` | Gnu | `\large` | Gnu | `\huge` |
| Gnu | `\footnotesize` | Gnu | `\Large` | Gnu | `\Huge` |
| Gnu | `\small` | | | | |

These declarations can be combined in the natural way with the commands for changing the type style described in Section 3.1.

get big and bigger **and bolder**    `\sffamily get \large big and \Large bigger`
`\bfseries and \LARGE bolder`

The precise size of type produced by these declarations depends upon the default type size; the examples appearing here are for a ten-point default size. The `\normalsize` declaration produces the default size, `\footnotesize` produces the size used for footnotes, and \scriptsize produces the size used for subscripts and superscripts in \normalsize formulas.

When you typeset an entire paragraph unit (Section 6.2.1) in a certain size, the scope of the size-changing declaration should include the blank line or \end command that ends the paragraph unit. A size-changing command may not be used in math mode. To set part of a formula in a different size of type, you can put it in an \mbox containing the size-changing command. All size-changing commands are fragile.

Not every type style is available in every size. If you try to use a font that is not available, LaTeX will issue a warning and substitute a font of the same size that is as close as possible in style to the one you wanted.

### 6.7.2   Special Symbols

You may need a special symbol not normally provided by LaTeX. Such symbols can exist in special fonts. The *Local Guide* should tell you what special fonts are available; the LaTeX *Companion* describes how to get LaTeX to use a special font.

A symbol in a special font is often identified by its *character-code*, which is a number from 0 to 255. When describing a special font, the *Local Guide* should tell you how to find the character codes for its special symbols. The command \symbol{26} produces the symbol with character code 26 in the currently chosen font. Character codes are often given in octal (base 8) or hexadecimal (base 16). An octal character code is prefaced by ' and a hexadecimal one by ", so \symbol{'32} and \symbol{"1A} produce the same symbol as \symbol{26}, since 32 is the octal and $1A$ the hexadecimal representation of 26.

# CHAPTER 7
# Pictures and Colors

This chapter explains how to draw pictures, include graphics prepared with other programs in your document, and produce colors. Of these features, only simple picture-drawing commands are implemented in standard TEX. The others are implemented by the `graphics` and `color` packages, which need special help from the device driver—the program that turns the `dvi` file into the output you see. Different device drivers may require different `dvi` files, which are created by giving different options to the `\usepackage` commands that load the `graphics` and `color` packages.

Eventually, these special features should be available with all device drivers. However, when LATEX 2$_\varepsilon$ is first released, some drivers will not implement these features, and some drivers may implement only some of them. Check the *Local Guide* to find out about the device drivers on your computer.

## 7.1   Pictures

The `picture` environment is used to draw pictures composed of text, straight lines, arrows, circles, and simple curves. This environment and its associated commands are implemented with standard TEX; they do not require special support from the device driver. However, the `pict2e` package uses device-driver support to provide enhanced versions of these commands that remove some of their restrictions. The enhanced commands can draw straight lines and arrows of any slope, circles of any size, and lines (straight and curved) of any thickness.

In the `picture` environment, you position objects in a picture by specifying their $x$ and $y$ coordinates. So, before getting to the picture-making commands, let us first review a little bit of coordinate geometry.

A *coordinate* is a number such as 5, $-7$, 2.3, or $-3.1416$. Given an *origin* and a *unit length*, a pair of coordinates specifies a position. As shown in Figure 7.1, the coordinate pair $(-1.8, 1)$ specifies the position reached by starting at the origin and moving left 1.8 units and up 1 unit.

The unit length used in determining positions in a `picture` environment is the value of the length command `\unitlength`. Not just positions but all lengths in a `picture` environment are specified in terms of `\unitlength`. Its default value is 1 point (about $1/72^{nd}$ of an inch or .35mm), but it can be changed with the `\setlength` command described in Section 6.4.1. Changing the value of `\unitlength` magnifies or reduces a picture—halving the value halves the lengths of all lines and the diameters of all circles. This makes it easy to adjust the size of a picture. However, changing `\unitlength` does not change the widths of lines or the size of text characters, so it does not provide true magnification and reduction. (The `graphics` package, described in Section 7.2, provides true magnifying and reducing commands.)

LATEX provides two standard thicknesses for the lines in a picture—thin as in ☐ and thick as in ☐. They are specified by the declarations `\thinlines`

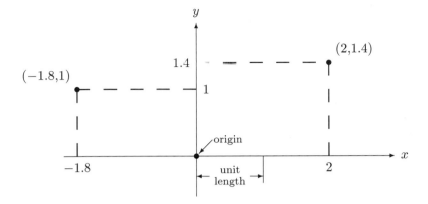

Figure 7.1: Points and their coordinates.

and \thicklines, with \thinlines as the default. These commands are ordinary declarations and can be used at any time.

Many picture-drawing commands have a coordinate pair as an argument. Such an argument is not enclosed in braces, but is just typed with parentheses and a comma, as in (-2,3.7) or (0,-17.2).

## 7.1.1   The picture Environment

The picture environment has a coordinate-pair argument that specifies the picture's size (in terms of \unitlength). The environment produces a box (Section 6.4.3) whose width and height are given by the two coordinates. The origin's default position is the lower-left corner of this box. However, the picture environment has an optional second coordinate-pair argument that specifies the coordinates of the box's lower-left corner, thereby determining the position of the origin. For example, the command

        \begin{picture}(100,200)(10,20)

produces a picture of width 100 units and height 200 units, whose lower-left corner has coordinates $(10, 20)$, so the upper-right corner has coordinates $(110, 220)$. Unlike ordinary optional arguments, the picture environment's optional argument is not enclosed in square brackets.

When first drawing a picture, you will usually omit the optional argument, leaving the origin at the lower-left corner. Later, if you want to modify the picture by shifting everything, you just add the appropriate optional argument.

The environment's first argument specifies the nominal size of the picture, which is used by TeX to determine how much room to leave for it. This need bear no relation to how large the picture really is; LATEX allows you to draw things outside the picture, or even off the page.

The `\begin{picture}` command puts LATEX in *picture mode*, a special mode that occurs nowhere else.[1] The only things that can appear in picture mode are `\put`, `\multiput`, `\qbezier`, and `\graphpaper` commands (described below) and declarations such as `\em`, `\thicklines`, and `\setlength`. You should not change `\unitlength` in picture mode.

The examples in this section all illustrate commands in picture mode, but the `\begin{picture}` and `\end{picture}` commands are not shown. To help you think in terms of arbitrary unit lengths, the examples assume different values of `\unitlength`. They are all drawn with the `\thicklines` declaration in effect. The pictures in the examples also contain lines and arrows, not produced by the commands being illustrated, that indicate positions and dimensions; these are drawn with `\thinlines` in effect, allowing you to compare the two line thicknesses.

Remember that the `picture` environment produces a box, which TEX treats just like a single (usually) large letter. See Section 6.5 for commands and environments to position the entire picture on the page. All the picture-drawing commands described in this section are fragile.

## 7.1.2   Picture Objects

Most things in a picture are drawn by the `\put` command. The command

    \put (11.3,-.3){*picture object*}

puts the *picture object* in the picture with its *reference point* having coordinates $(11.3, -.3)$. The various kinds of picture objects and their reference points are described below.

### Text

The simplest kind of picture object is ordinary text, which is typeset in LR mode to produce a box with the usual reference point (see Section 6.4.3).

gang of armadillos                         `\put(2.3,5){gang of armadillos}`

$(2.3, 5)$

### Boxes

A box picture object is made with the `\makebox` or `\framebox` command. These commands, and the related `\savebox` command, have a special form for use with pictures. The first argument is a coordinate pair that specifies the width and height of the box.

---

[1] LATEX's picture mode is really a restricted form of LR mode.

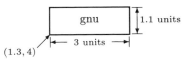

`\put(1.3,4){\framebox(3,1.1){gnu}}`

The reference point is the lower-left corner of the box. The default is to center the text both horizontally and vertically within the box, but an optional argument specifies other positioning. This argument consists of one or two of the following letters: `l` (left), `r` (right), `t` (top), and `b` (bottom). The letters in a two-letter argument can appear in either order.

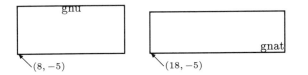

`\put(8,-5){\framebox(8,3.5)[t]{gnu}}`
`\put(18,-5){\framebox(10,3)[br]{gnat}}`

Unlike the ordinary `\framebox` command described in Section 6.4.3, the picture-making version adds no space between the frame and the text. There is a corresponding version of `\makebox` that works the same as `\framebox` except it does not draw the frame. These picture-making versions are used mainly as picture objects, although they can be used anywhere that an ordinary box-making command can.

The discussion of zero-width boxes in Section 6.4.4 should explain why a `\makebox(0,0)` command with no positioning argument puts the center of the text on the reference point, and with a positioning argument puts the indicated edge or corner of the text on the reference point.

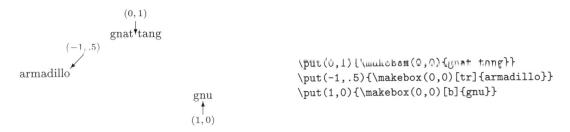

`\put(0,1){\makebox(0,0){gnat tang}}`
`\put(-1,.5){\makebox(0,0)[tr]{armadillo}}`
`\put(1,0){\makebox(0,0)[b]{gnu}}`

A `\makebox(0,0)` command is very useful for positioning text in a picture.

The `\dashbox` command is similar to `\framebox` but draws the frame with dashed lines. It has an additional first argument that specifies the width of each dash.

`\put(4,2.2){\dashbox{.5}(5,2)[t]{gnat}}`

A dashed box looks best when the width and the height are both multiples of the dash length—in this example, the width is ten times and the height four times the length of a dash.

**Straight Lines**

Straight lines can be drawn with only a fixed, though fairly large, choice of slopes. A line is not specified by giving its endpoints, since that might produce a slope not in LATEX's repertoire. Instead, the slope and length of the line are specified. LATEX's method of describing slope and length was chosen to make designing pictures easier, but it requires a bit of explanation.

The \line command produces a picture object that is a straight line, with one end of the line as its reference point. The command has the form

> \line(x,y){len}

where the coordinate pair $(x, y)$ specifies the slope and *len* specifies the length, in a manner I will now describe. (Figure 7.2 illustrates the following explanation with a particular example.) Let $p_0$ be the reference point, and suppose its coordinates are $(x_0, y_0)$. Starting at $p_0$, move $x$ units to the right and $y$ units up to find the point $p_1$, so $p_1$ has coordinates $(x_0 + x, y_0 + y)$. (Negative distances have the expected meaning: moving right a distance of $-2$ units means moving 2 units to the left, and moving up $-2$ units means moving down 2 units.) The line drawn by this command lies along the straight line through $p_0$ and $p_1$. It starts at $p_0$ and goes in the direction of $p_1$ a distance determined as follows by *len*. If the line is not vertical ($x \neq 0$), it extends *len* units horizontally to the right or left of $p_0$ (depending upon whether $x$ is positive or negative). If the line is vertical ($x = 0$), it extends *len* units above or below $p_0$ (depending upon whether $y$ is positive or negative).

The *len* argument therefore specifies the line's horizontal extent, except for a vertical line, which has no horizontal extent, where it specifies the vertical

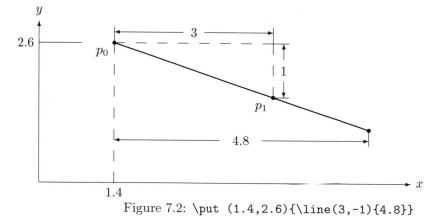

Figure 7.2: \put (1.4,2.6){\line(3,-1){4.8}}

distance. It equals the actual length of the line only for horizontal and vertical lines. The value of *len* must be nonnegative.

Since only a fixed number of slopes are available, there are only a limited number of values that $x$ and $y$ can assume. They must both be integers (numbers without decimal points) between $-6$ and $+6$, inclusive. Moreover, they can have no common divisor bigger than one. In other words, $x/y$ must be a fraction in its simplest form, so you can't let $x = 2$ and $y = -4$; you must use $x = 1$ and $y = -2$ instead. The following are all *illegal* arguments of a \line command: (1.4,3), (3,6), (0,2), and (1,7).

LaTeX draws slanted (neither horizontal nor vertical) lines using a special font whose characters consist of small line segments. This means that there is a smallest slanted line that LaTeX can draw—its length is about 10 points, or 1/7 inch. If you try to draw a smaller slanted line, LaTeX will print nothing. It also means that LaTeX must print lots of line segments to make up a long slanted line, so drawing a lot of slanted lines can take a long time and can use up a lot of TeX's memory. However, LaTeX draws a horizontal or vertical line of any length quickly, without using much memory.

## Arrows

An arrow—a straight line ending in an arrowhead—is made by the \vector command. It works exactly like the \line command.

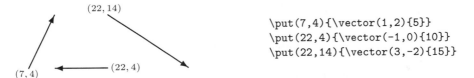

```
\put(7,4){\vector(1,2){5}}
\put(22,4){\vector(-1,0){10}}
\put(22,14){\vector(3,-2){15}}
```

The tip of the arrowhead lies on the endpoint of the line opposite the reference point. This makes any normal-length arrow point away from the reference point. However, for an arrow of length zero, both endpoints lie on the reference point, so the tip of the arrow is at the reference point.

LaTeX can't draw arrows with as many different slopes as it can draw lines. The pair of integers specifying the slope in a \vector command must lie between $-4$ and $+4$, inclusive; as with the \line command, they must have no common divisor.

## Stacks

The \shortstack command produces a box containing a single column of text with the reference point at its lower-left corner. Its argument contains the text, rows being separated by a \\ command. The \shortstack command is much like a one-column **tabular** environment (Section 3.6.2), but the space between rows is designed for a vertical column of text in a picture. The default alignment is to center each row in the column, but an optional positioning argument of l (left) or r (right) aligns the text on the indicated edge.

|                | May    | Sh |
|----------------|--------|----|
| Gnats          |        | o  |
| and            | break  | e  |
| gnus           | my     | s  |

```
\put(1,7){\shortstack{Gnats\\ and \\ gnus}}
\put(3,7){\shortstack[r]{May\\ break \\my}}
\put(5,7){\shortstack[l]{Sh\\o\\e\\s}}
```

Unlike an ordinary `tabular` environment, rows are not evenly spaced. You can change the inter-row spacing by using either the \\ command's optional argument (Section C.1.6) or a strut (Section 6.4.3). The \shortstack command is an ordinary box-making command that can be used anywhere, but it seldom appears outside a `picture` environment.

### Circles

The \circle command draws a circle of the indicated diameter, with the center of the circle as reference point, and the \circle* command draws a disk (a circle with the center filled in). LaTeX has only a fixed collection of circles and disks; the \circle and \circle* commands choose the one whose diameter is closest to the specified diameter.

```
\put(20,0){\circle{20}}
\put(20,0){\vector(0,1){10}}
\put(50,0){\circle*{5}}
```

On my computer, the largest circle that LaTeX can draw has a diameter of 40 points (a little more than 1/2 inch) and the largest disk has a diameter of 15 points (about .2 inch). Consult the *Local Guide* to find out what size circles and disks are available on your computer.

### Ovals and Rounded Corners

An oval is a rectangle with rounded corners—that is, a rectangle whose corners are replaced by quarter circles. It is generated with the \oval command, whose argument specifies the width and height, the reference point being the center of the oval. LaTeX draws the oval with corners as round as possible, using quarter circles with the largest possible radius.

```
\put(1.1,-4){\oval(8,3.1)}
```

Giving an optional argument to the \oval command causes LaTeX to draw only half or a quarter of the complete oval. The argument is one or two of the letters l (left), r (right), t (top), and b (bottom), a one-letter argument specifying a half oval and a two-letter argument specifying a quarter oval. The size and reference point are determined as if the complete oval were being drawn; the optional argument serves only to suppress the unwanted part.

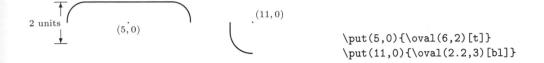

```
\put(5,0){\oval(6,2)[t]}
\put(11,0){\oval(2.2,3)[bl]}
```

Joining a quarter oval to straight lines produces a rounded corner. It takes a bit of calculating to figure out where to \put the quarter oval.

```
\put(5,4){\line(0,-1){2}}
\put(6,2){\oval(2,2)[bl]}
\put(6,1){\vector(1,0){6}}
```

**Framing**

The \framebox command puts a frame of a specified size around an object. It is often convenient to let the size of the object determine the size of the frame. The \fbox command described in Section 6.4.3 does this, but it puts extra space around the object that you may not want in a picture. The \frame command works very much like \fbox except it doesn't add any extra space.

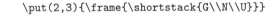

```
\put(2,3){\frame{\shortstack{G\\N\\U}}}
```

## 7.1.3   Curves

The \qbezier command takes three points as arguments and draws a quadratic Bezier curve with those as its control points. A quadratic Bezier curve with control points $P_1$, $P_2$, $P_3$ is a curve from $P_1$ to $P_3$ such that the line from $P_1$ to $P_2$ is tangent to the curve at $P_1$, and the line from $P_3$ to $P_2$ is tangent to the curve at $P_3$.

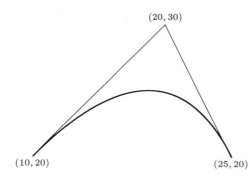

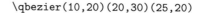

`\qbezier(10,20)(20,30)(25,20)`

For two curves (or a curve and a straight line) to join smoothly, they must have the same tangent at the point where they meet. Bezier control points therefore provide a convenient way of specifying a curve.

LaTeX draws curves by drawing lots of individual points. (This does not apply to the `pict2e` package's enhanced version.) Each point takes time to draw and takes memory space, so LaTeX does not draw a completely smooth curve. The `\qbeziermax` command specifies the maximum number of points LaTeX will normally plot for a single `\qbezier` command. (It can be changed with `\renewcommand`.) However, an optional argument to `\qbezier` allows you to tell LaTeX exactly how many points to plot.

`\qbezier[37](10,20)(20,30)(25,20)`

### 7.1.4   Grids

The `graphpap` package defines the `graphpaper` command, which draws a numbered coordinate grid. The command's first argument specifies the coordinates of the lower-left corner of the grid, and its second argument specifies the grid's width and height.

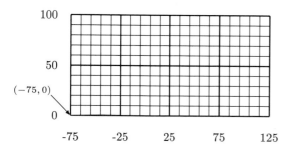

`\graphpaper(-75,0)(200,100)`

The grid normally consists of one line every 10 units, but an optional first argument allows you to specify a different spacing.

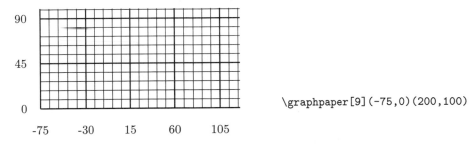

\graphpaper[9](-75,0)(200,100)

The arguments of \graphpaper can contain only integers.

## 7.1.5 Reusing Objects

The \savebox command described in Section 6.4.3 is similar to \makebox except that, instead of being drawn, the box is saved in the indicated storage bin. Like \makebox, the \savebox command has a form in which the size of the box is indicated by a coordinate pair, with positioning determined by an optional argument.

```
\savebox{\toy}(3,1.3)[tr]{gnu}
...
\put(-2,4){\frame{\usebox{\toy}}}
\put(2,4){\frame{\usebox{\toy}}}
```

The storage bin \toy in this example must be defined with \newsavebox. A \savebox command can be used inside a picture environment to save an object that appears several times in that picture, or outside to save an object that appears in more than one picture. Remember that \savebox is a declaration with the normal scoping rules.

It can take LaTeX a long time to draw a picture, especially if it contains slanted lines, so it's a good idea to use \savebox whenever an object appears in different pictures or in different places within the same picture. However, a saved box also uses memory, so a picture should be saved no longer than necessary. The space used by a saved box is reclaimed upon leaving the scope of the \savebox declaration. You can also use a command like \sbox{\toy}{}, which destroys the contents of storage bin \toy and reclaims its space.

## 7.1.6 Repeated Patterns

Pictures often contain repeated patterns formed by regularly spaced copies of the same object. Instead of using a sequence of \put commands, such a pattern can be drawn with a `\multiput` command. For any coordinate pairs $(x, y)$ and $(\Delta x, \Delta y)$, the command

> `\multiput(`$x$`,`$y$`)(`$\Delta x$`,`$\Delta y$`){17}{`*object*`}`

puts 17 copies of *object* in the picture, starting at position $(x, y)$ and stepping the position by $(\Delta x, \Delta y)$ units each time. It is equivalent to the 17 commands

> `\put(`$x$`,`$y$`){`*object*`}`
> `\put(`$x + \Delta x$`,`$y + \Delta y$`){`*object*`}`
> `\put(`$x + 2\Delta x$`,`$y + 2\Delta y$`){`*object*`}`
> ...
> `\put(`$x + 16\Delta x$`,`$y + 16\Delta y$`){`*object*`}`

as illustrated by the following example:

$(3, 2.4)$ ● |← 5.2 units →|     ↕ 1.3 units     `\multiput(3,2.4)(5.2,-1.3){4}{\circle*{.3}}`

You can make a two-dimensional pattern by using a `picture` environment containing another `\multiput` in the argument of a `\multiput` command. However, `\multiput` typesets the object anew for each copy it makes, so it is much more efficient to make a two-dimensional pattern by saving a one-dimensional pattern made with `\multiput` in a storage bin, then repeating it with another `\multiput`. Saving the object in a bin can also save processing time for a one-dimensional pattern. However, patterns with too many repetitions in all may cause TeX to run out of memory.

### 7.1.7   Some Hints on Drawing Pictures

As you gain experience with the `picture` environment, you'll develop your own techniques for designing pictures. Here are a few hints to get you started.

If you use a small unit length, such as the default value of 1 point, you will seldom need decimals.

It can take quite a bit of trial and error to get a picture right. Use a screen previewer, and run LaTeX on a file containing just the picture.

Make a coordinate grid with the `\graphpaper` command, and use it for placing objects.

If you are not afraid of math, you will find that a few simple calculations can save a lot of trial and error—especially when drawing slanted lines and arrows.

It's a good idea to break a complicated picture into "subpictures". The subpicture is drawn in a separate `picture` environment inside a `\put` argument, as in

        `\put(13,14.2){\begin{picture}(10,7) ... \end{picture}}`

This permits easy repositioning of the subpicture and allows you to work in terms
of local coordinates relative to the subpicture's origin instead of calculating the
position of every picture component with respect to a single origin. You can also
magnify or reduce just the subpicture by changing the value of `\unitlength` with
a `\setlength` command in the `\put` command's argument—but don't leave any
space after the `\setlength` command.

A small mistake in a picture-drawing command can produce strange results.
It's usually simple to track down such an error, so don't panic when a picture
turns out all wrong. If you find that some part of the picture is incorrectly
positioned by a small amount, check for stray spaces in the argument of the
`\put` command. Remember that this argument is typeset in LR mode, so a
space before or after an object produces space in the output.

## 7.2   The graphics **Package**

The `graphics` package defines commands for performing geometric transformations and including graphics prepared with other computer programs. The
geometric transformations are scaling, rotation, and reflection. These transformations may be applied to any text including ordinary letters and words, but
they are usually applied to pictures made with the `picture` environment and
included graphics. This package requires support from the device driver; see the
remarks at the beginning of this chapter.

The package provides two scaling commands, `\scalebox` and `\resizebox`.
The `\scalebox` command allows you to enlarge or reduce any text by a constant
scale factor.

# great big gnat
regular gnat

<small>tiny gnat</small>

```
\scalebox{2}{great big gnat}
regular gnat
\scalebox{.5}{tiny gnat}
```

An optional second argument specifies a separate vertical scale factor.

<small>tall skinny gnat</small>

```
\scalebox{.75}[2]{tall skinny gnat}
```

The `\resizebox` allows you to scale text to a desired size. Its two arguments
specify the width and height of the box that it produces. Using ! for either
argument maintains the aspect ratio of the text.

```
\resizebox{5cm}{.4cm}{fat gnat}

\resizebox{2cm}{!}{fat gnat}
```

Both \scalebox and \resizebox typeset their text argument in LR mode. They produce a box whose reference point is the same as the reference point of the original unscaled box.

The \rotatebox command rotates text by a specified angle. In the following examples, the sizes and reference points of boxes are shown.

          gnu    \rotatebox{30}{gnu}

The \rotatebox command typesets its text argument in LR mode. It produces a box whose reference point is at the same height as the rotated reference point of the original text.

          gnu
                                                    \rotatebox{180}{gnu}
                                                        \rotatebox{270}{gnu}

The \reflectbox command typesets its argument in LR mode and then produces its mirror image.

                               gnu    \reflectbox{gnu}

Graphics produced by another program can be included in your document with the \includegraphics command. The following example assumes that the file LA83.fun contains a picture in a form that the device driver can handle.

                                    \includegraphics{LA83.fun}

In this example, the size of the box is specified by the file LA83.fun. Some graphics files do not include a size specification. In that case, LaTeX will produce an error message, and you will have to specify the size yourself using optional arguments to the \includegraphics command. In the next example, the first

picture shows what is actually in the file `jason.eps` and the second shows the
output of the `\includegraphics` command.[2]

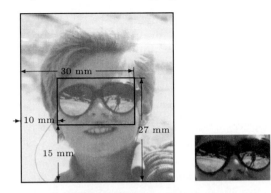

```
\includegraphics*
    [10mm,15mm][30mm,27mm]{jason.eps}
```

The optional arguments to `\includegraphics` override any size specification
in the file itself. However, the box specified by the file (and produced by
`\includegraphics` with no optional argument) might not contain the entire
picture. A command such as

```
\resizebox{\textwidth}{!}
    {\includegraphics[0in,0in][8in,10in]{jason.eps}}
```

will show you what is actually in the file `jason.eps`.

The `draft` option causes the `\includegraphics` command to print a box
containing the name of the file rather than the contents of the file. This option
is specified either by typing

```
\usepackage[draft]{graphics}
```

or by specifying the `draft` document-class option (Section 2.2.2). A `final` option in the `\usepackage` command counteracts the effects of a `draft` document-
class option.

## 7.3   Color

You can produce colored text with the `\textcolor` command or the corresponding `\color` declaration. (To keep the cost of this book down, colors are indicated
by shades of gray.)

CECI N'EST PAS UNE PIPE ROUGE.                `... UNE \textcolor{red}{PIPE} ROUGE.`

```
\color{red}
CECI N'EST PAS UNE PIPE NOIRE.                    ... UNE {\color{black} PIPE} NOIRE.
```

---

[2]Without the * after `\includegraphics`, the entire picture would be printed, although TeX
would leave only enough space for the small rectangle.

The \colorbox command typesets its argument in LR mode on a rectangular background of a specified color.

`UNE PIPE ROUGE`

\colorbox{red}{UNE PIPE ROUGE}

The command \fcolorbox{blue}{red}{UNE...} puts a blue border around the red rectangle.

A \pagecolor{green} declaration causes the background of the entire page to be green. It is a global declaration that applies to the current page and all subsequent pages, until countermanded by another \pagecolor command.

The following colors are predefined: black, white, red, green, blue, yellow, cyan, and magenta. The \definecolor command allows you to define your own colors in terms of a *color model*. In the rgb color model, a color is specified by three numbers, ranging from 0 to 1, that represent the amounts of red, green, and blue light required to produce it. For example, magenta is produced by mixing equal amounts of red and blue light, so it is defined by

\definecolor{magenta}{rgb}{1,0,1}

A darker shade of magenta is defined by

\definecolor{darkmagenta}{rgb}{.5,0,.5}

In the gray color model, a shade of gray is specified by a single number ranging from 0 (black) to 1 (white).

`A dark gray box.`

\definecolor{dark}{gray}{.5}
  \colorbox{dark}{A dark gray box.}

`A light gray box.`

\definecolor{light}{gray}{.75}
  \colorbox{light}{A light gray box.}

LaTeX also supports the cmyk model, popular with (human) printers, in which a color is specified by values of cyan, magenta, yellow, and black ranging from 0 to 1. Other color models may be available on your computer, including ones in which a color is specified by a name. Check your *Local Guide*.

After LaTeX 2ε is released, there may be a period when some drivers will not handle color commands properly. Check your output carefully, especially when the scope of a color declaration spans pages—for example if the declaration appears in a footnote that is split across pages.

# CHAPTER 8
# Errors

Section 2.3 describes first aid for handling errors; it explains how to deal with simple errors. This chapter is for use when you encounter an error or warning message that you don't understand. The following section tells how to locate the error; the remaining sections explain the meaning of specific error and warning messages.

As you saw in Section 2.3, an error can confuse LaTeX and cause it to produce spurious error messages when processing subsequent text that is perfectly all right. Such spurious errors are not discussed here. When TeX writes a page of output, it has usually recovered from the effects of any previous errors, so the next error message probably indicates a real error. The following section explains how to tell when TeX has written an output page.

## 8.1   Finding the Error

As described in Section 2.3, an error message includes an error indicator stating what TeX thinks the problem is, and an error locator that shows how much of your input file TeX had read when it found the error. Most of the time, the line printed in the error locator displays an obvious error in the input. Typing H can also provide useful information. If you don't see what's wrong, look up the error message in the following sections to find its probable cause. If you still don't see what's wrong, the first thing to do is locate exactly where the error occurred.

The error locator starts with a line number such as 1.14, meaning that the error was found while LaTeX was processing the fourteenth line from the beginning of the file. If your input is all on a single file, then the error locator unambiguously identifies where TeX thinks the problem is. However, if you're using the commands of Section 4.4 to split your input into several files, then you also must know what file the error is in. Whenever TeX starts processing a file, it prints on your terminal (and on the log file) a "(" followed by the file name, and it prints a ")" when it finishes processing the file. For example, the terminal output

```
... (myfile.tex [1] [2] [3] (part1.tex [4]   [5]) (part2.tex [6] [7]
! Undefined control sequence.
l.249 \todzy
?
```

tells you that the error (a misspelled \today command) is on line 249 of the file part2.tex, which was included by an \input or \include command contained in the file myfile.tex. TeX had completely processed the file part1.tex, which was also read by a command in myfile.tex.

The error locator tells you how much of the input file TeX had processed before it discovered the error; the last command that TeX processed is usually the source of the problem. There is one important exception; but before discussing it, a digression is in order.

Logically, typesetting can be viewed as a two-step process: first the document is typeset on one continuous scroll that unrolls vertically, then the scroll is cut into individual pages to which headings and page numbers are added. (Since a 50-yard scroll of metal type is somewhat unwieldy, printers partition the logical scroll into convenient lengths called galleys.) Instead of first producing the entire scroll and then cutting it into pages, TEX does both steps together, alternately putting output on the scroll with one hand and cutting off a page with the other. It usually puts text on the scroll one paragraph unit (Section 6.2.1) at a time. After each paragraph unit, it checks whether there's enough for a page. If so, it cuts off the page, adds the heading and page number, and writes the page on the `dvi` file. This way, TEX doesn't have to keep much more than one page of text in the computer's memory at a time.

Whenever TEX writes a page on its output file, it prints the page number on the terminal, enclosed in square brackets. Thus, any message that appears on the terminal after TEX prints [27] and before it prints [28] was generated between the time TEX wrote output pages 27 and 28. Whatever generated the message probably appeared in the text printed on page 28. However, it might also be in the text that was left on the scroll when TEX cut off page 28, putting it in the first paragraph of page 29. Most of LATEX's warning messages are generated by TEX's scroll-making hand. It reports that a problem is on page 28 if it is detected between the time TEX writes pages 27 and 28, so the problem could actually appear at the top of page 29.

Now, let's get back to locating an error. Most errors are discovered while TEX is producing the scroll, but some errors, which I will call *outputting* errors, are detected while it is cutting off a page. TEX identifies an outputting error by printing `<output>` on the terminal at the beginning of a line somewhere above the error locator. For an outputting error, the error locator shows how far TEX got when it was producing the scroll; the actual error occurred at or before that point. An outputting error is usually caused by a fragile command in a moving argument.

An error can occur while LATEX is processing the `\begin{document}` or `\end{document}` command, when it reads the auxiliary files it has written. You can tell that this has happened because the output on your terminal shows that TEX is reading a file with the extension `aux`. Such an error means that there is bad information on the auxiliary file. An error while processing the `\begin{document}` was caused by an error the last time you ran LATEX. An error while processing the `\end{document}` is usually caused by a fragile command in a moving argument.

An error that occurs while LATEX is processing a `toc`, `lof`, or `lot` file means that there is an error in a table of contents, list of figures, or list of tables entry. This error was caused by an error in a `\caption` or sectioning command— perhaps a fragile command in the argument—the previous time LATEX was run on the file.

When the terminal output doesn't quickly lead you to the source of the error, look at the printed output (on your screen previewer). If LaTeX reaches the end of your input or is stopped with a \stop command, the printed output will contain everything it has put on the scroll, and the location of the error will probably be obvious. If you stopped LaTeX by typing an X, then it will not print what was left on the scroll after the last full page was written out. Since the error probably occurred in this leftover text, the output will just narrow the possible location of the error.

If you still can't find the error, your next step is to find the smallest piece of your input file that produces the error. Start by eliminating everything between the \begin{document} and the last page or so of output. Then keep cutting the input in half, throwing away the part that does not cause the error. This should quickly lead to the source of the problem.

When all else fails, consult your *Local Guide* to find a LaTeX expert near you.

## 8.2 LaTeX's Error Messages

Here is an alphabetical list of most of LaTeX's error indicators (with the initial "! LaTeX Error:" omitted), together with their causes. Not listed are indicators for errors caused by a bad document class, some errors for which typing H provides a clear explanation, and many errors produced only when a particular package is used.

Bad \line or \vector argument.
A \line or \vector command specified a negative length or an illegal slope. Look up the constraints on these commands in Section 7.1.

Bad math environment delimiter.
LaTeX has found either a math-mode-starting command such as \[ or \( when it is already in math mode, or else a math-mode-ending command such as \) or \] while in LR or paragraph mode. The problem is caused by either unmatched math mode delimiters or unbalanced braces.

\begin{...} on input line ... ended by \end{...}.
LaTeX has found an \end command that doesn't match the corresponding \begin command. You probably misspelled the environment name in the \end command, have an extra \begin, or else forgot an \end.

Can be used only in preamble.
LaTeX has encountered, after the \begin{document}, a command that should appear only in the preamble, such as \usepackage, \nofiles, \includeonly, or \makeindex. The error is also caused by an extra \begin{document} command.

`Cannot determine size of graphic in ... (no BoundingBox).`
An \includegraphics command with no optional arguments read a file that does not specify the size of the box to be produced (**graphics** package only).

`Command ... already defined`
You are using \newcommand, \newenvironment, \newlength, \newsavebox, or \newtheorem to define a command or environment name that is already defined, or \newcounter to define a counter that already exists. (Defining an environment named **gnu** automatically defines the command \gnu.)   You'll have to choose a new name or, in the case of \newcommand or \newenvironment, switch to the \renew... command.

`Command ... invalid in math mode.`
The indicated command is not permitted in math mode but was used there.

`Counter too large.`
Some object that is numbered with letters or with footnote symbols has received too large a number. You're probably either making a very long enumerated list or resetting counter values.

`Environment ... undefined.`
LATEX has encountered a \begin command for a nonexistent environment. You probably misspelled the environment name. This error can be corrected on the spot by typing an I followed by the correct command, ending with a *return*. (This does not change the input file.)

`File ... not found.`
LATEX is trying to read a file that apparently doesn't exist. If the missing file has the extension **tex**, then LATEX is trying to \input or \include a nonexistent file; if it has the extension **cls**, then you have specified a nonexistent document class; if it has the extension **sty**, then you have specified a nonexistent package. LATEX is waiting for you either to type another file name followed by *return*, or to type *return* to continue without reading any file.

`Illegal character in array arg.`
There is an illegal character in the argument of an **array** or **tabular** environment, or in the second argument of a \multicolumn command.

`\include cannot be nested.`
Your document \include's a file containing an \include command.

`Lonely \item--perhaps a missing list environment.`
An \item command appears outside any list environment.

`Missing \begin{document}.`
LaTeX produced printed output before encountering a `\begin{document}` command. Either you forgot the `\begin{document}` command or there is something wrong in the preamble. The problem may be a stray character or an error in a declaration—for example, omitting the braces around an argument or forgetting the `\` in a command name.

`Missing p-arg in array arg.`
There is a `p` that is not followed by an expression in braces in the argument of an `array` or `tabular` environment, or in the second argument of a `\multicolumn` command.

`Missing @-exp in array arg.`
There is an `@` character not followed by an `@`-expression in the argument of an `array` or `tabular` environment, or in the second argument of a `\multicolumn` command.

`No counter '...' defined.`
You have specified a nonexistent counter in a `\setcounter` or `\addtocounter` command, or in an optional argument to a `\newcounter` or `\newtheorem` command. You probably mistyped the counter name. However, if the error occurred while a file with the extension `aux` is being read, then you probably used a `\newcounter` command in an `\include`'d file.

`No \title given.`
A `\maketitle` command is not preceded by a `\title` command.

`Not in outer par mode.`
You had a `figure` or `table` environment or a `\marginpar` command in math mode or inside a parbox.

`Option clash for package ...`
The same package was loaded twice with different options. The package might have been loaded by another package.

`\pushtabs and \poptabs don't match.`
LaTeX found a `\poptabs` with no matching `\pushtabs`, or has come to the `\end{tabbing}` command with one or more unmatched `\pushtabs` commands.

`Something's wrong--perhaps a missing \item.`
There are many possible causes, including an omitted `\item` command in a list-making environment and a missing argument of a `thebibliography` environment.

`Tab overflow.`

A `\=` command has exceeded the maximum number of tab stops that LATEX permits.

`There's no line here to end.`

A `\newline` or `\\` command appears between paragraphs, where it makes no sense. If you are trying to "leave a blank line", use a `\vspace` command (Section 6.4.2).

`This file needs format ... but this is ...`

The document uses a document class or package that is not compatible with the version of LATEX you are running. If you are using only standard files, then there is something wrong with the installation of LATEX on your computer.

`This may be a LaTeX bug.`

LATEX has become thoroughly confused. This is probably due to a previously detected error, but it is possible that you have discovered an error in LATEX itself. If this is the first error message produced by the input file and you can't find anything wrong, save the file and contact the person listed in your *Local Guide*.

`Too deeply nested.`

There are too many list-making environments nested within one another. How many levels of nesting are permitted may depend upon what computer you are using, but at least four levels are provided, which should be enough.

`Too many columns in eqnarray environment.`

An `eqnarray` environment contains three `&` column separators without an intervening `\\` command.

`Too many unprocessed floats.`

While this error can result from having too many `\marginpar` commands on a page, a more likely cause is forcing LATEX to save more figures and tables than it has room for. When typesetting its continuous scroll, LATEX saves figures and tables separately and inserts them as it cuts off pages. This error occurs when LATEX is forced to save too many `figure` and/or `table` environments. A likely cause is a logjam—a figure or table that cannot be printed, causing others to pile up behind it, since LATEX will not print figures or tables out of order. The jam can be started by a figure or table that won't fit where its optional placement argument (Section C.9.1) says it must go. See the discussion of LATEX's figure-placement algorithm in Section C.9.1.

`Undefined color '...'.`
The indicated color name is used without having been defined by a `\definecolor` command (`color` package only).

`Undefined color model '...'.`
A `\definecolor` command specifies an unknown color model (`color` package only).

`Undefined tab position.`
A `\>`, `\+`, `\-`, or `\<` command is trying to go to a nonexistent tab position—one not defined by a `\=` command.

`Unknown graphics extension ...`
The `graphics` package's `\includegraphics` command uses the file's extension to determine what kind of program produced the file. This error occurs when the file name does not have an extension known to the package. Consult the *Local Guide* to see what file extensions you can use.

`Unknown option ... for ...`
The `\documentclass` command or a `\usepackage` command specifies an illegal option for the class or package.

`\verb ended by end of line.`
The argument of a `\verb` command extends beyond the current line. You may have forgotten the character that ends the argument.

`\verb illegal in command argument.`
A `\verb` command appears in the argument of another command.

`\< in mid line.`
A `\<` command appears in the middle of a line in a `tabbing` environment. This command should come only at the beginning of a line.

## 8.3   TeX's Error Messages

Here is an alphabetical list of some of TeX's error messages and what may have caused them.

`!  Double subscript.`
There are two subscripts in a row in a mathematical formula—something like `x_{2}_{3}`, which makes no sense. To produce $x_{2_3}$, type `x_{2_{3}}`.

`!  Double superscript.`
There are two superscripts in a row in a mathematical formula—something like
x^{2}^{3}, which makes no sense. To produce $x^{2^3}$, type x^{2^{3}}.

`!  Extra alignment tab has been changed to \cr.`
There are too many separate items (column entries) in a single row of an **array**
or **tabular** environment. In other words, there were too many &'s before the
end of the row. You probably forgot the \\ at the end of the preceding row.

`!  Extra }, or forgotten $.`
The braces or math mode delimiters don't match properly. You probably forgot
a {, \[, \(, or $.

`!  I can't find file '...'.`
You probably ran LATEX on a nonexistent file. This error can also occur if you
omitted the braces around an \input command.

`!  Illegal parameter number in definition of ... .`
This is probably caused by a \newcommand, \renewcommand, \providecommand,
\newenvironment, or \renewenvironment command in which a # is used in-
correctly. A # character, except as part of the command name \#, can be used
only to indicate an argument parameter, as in #2, which denotes the second
argument. This error is also caused by nesting one of the five commands listed
above inside another, or by putting a parameter like #2 in the last argument of
a \newenvironment or \renewenvironment command.

`!  Illegal unit of measure (pt inserted).`
If you just got a

> `! Missing number, treated as zero.`

error, then this is part of the same problem. If not, it means that LATEX was
expecting a length as an argument and found a number instead. The most
common cause of this error is writing 0 instead of something like 0in for a length
of zero, in which case typing *return* should result in correct output. However,
the error can also be caused by omitting a command argument.

`!  Misplaced alignment tab character &.`
The special character &, which should be used only to separate items in an
**array** or **tabular** environment, appeared in ordinary text. You probably meant
to type \&, in which case typing I\& followed by *return* in response to the error
message should produce the correct output.

**! Missing control sequence inserted.**
This is probably caused by a \newcommand, \renewcommand, \newlength, or \newsavebox command whose first argument is not a command name.

**! Missing number, treated as zero.**
This is usually caused by a LaTeX command expecting but not finding either a number or a length as an argument. You may have omitted an argument, or a square bracket in the text may have been mistaken for the beginning of an optional argument. This error is also caused by putting \protect in front of either a length command or a command such as \value that produces a number.

**! Missing { inserted.**
**! Missing } inserted.**
TeX has become confused. The position indicated by the error locator is probably beyond the point where the incorrect input is.

**! Missing $ inserted.**
TeX probably found a command that can be used only in math mode when it wasn't in math mode. Remember that unless stated otherwise, all the commands of Section 3.3 can be used only in math mode. TeX is not in math mode when it begins processing the argument of a box-making command, even if that command is inside a math environment. This error also occurs if TeX encounters a blank line when it is in math mode.

**! Not a letter.**
Something appears in the argument of a \hyphenation command that doesn't belong there.

**! Paragraph ended before ... was complete.**
A blank line occurred in a command argument that shouldn't contain one. You probably forgot the right brace at the end of an argument.

**! TeX capacity exceeded, sorry [...].**
TeX has just run out of space and aborted its execution. Before you panic, remember that the least likely cause of this error is TeX not having the capacity to process your document. It was probably an error in your input file that caused TeX to run out of room. For example, the following command makes a circular definition, defining \gnu in terms of itself:

```
\newcommand{\gnu}{a \gnu} % This is wrong!
```

When TeX encounters this \gnu command, it will keep chasing its tail trying to figure out what \gnu should produce, and eventually run out of space. LaTeX seldom runs out of space on a short input file, so if running it on the last few pages before the error indicator's position still produces the error, then there's almost certainly something wrong in the input file. An error that causes TEX to run out of space can be hard to find; you may have to use the divide and conquer method described in Section 8.1 to locate it.

Today's computers have enough memory to provide TEX with all the space it needs to process almost any document. However, any particular version of TEX uses only a fixed amount of space, and the version on your computer may not be big enough to process your document. In this case, you should try to get a bigger version. Meanwhile, by understanding why TEX ran out of space, you can reduce the space it needs for your document. The end of the error indicator tells what kind of space TEX ran out of. The kinds of space you are most likely to run out of are listed below, with an explanation of what uses them up.

`buffer size` Can be caused by too long a piece of text as the argument of a sectioning, `\caption`, `\addcontentsline`, or `\addtocontents` command. This error will probably occur when the `\end{document}` is being processed, but it could happen when a `\tableofcontents`, `\listoffigures`, or `\listoftables` command is executed. To solve this problem, use a shorter optional argument. Even if you're producing a table of contents or a list of figures or tables, such a long entry won't help the reader.

`exception dictionary` You have used `\hyphenation` commands to give TEX more hyphenation information than it has room for. Remove some of the less frequently used words from the `\hyphenation` commands and insert `\-` commands instead.

`hash size` Your input file defines too many command names and/or uses too many cross-referencing labels.

`main memory size` This is one kind of space that TEX can run out of when processing a short file. There are three ways you can run TEX out of main memory space: (1) defining a lot of very long, complicated commands, (2) making an index or glossary and having too many `\index` or `\glossary` commands on a single page, and (3) creating so complicated a page of output that TEX can't hold all the information needed to generate it.

The solution to the first two problems is obvious: define fewer commands or use fewer `\index` and `\glossary` commands. The third problem is nastier. It can be caused by large `tabbing`, `tabular`, `array`, and `picture` environments. (In particular, `\qbezier` commands can use a lot of main memory.) TEX's space may also be filled up with figures and tables waiting for a place to go.

To find out if you've really exceeded TEX's capacity in this way, put a `\clearpage` command in your input file right before the place where TEX ran out of room and try running it again. If it doesn't run out of room with the \clearpage command there, then you did exceed TEX's capacity. If it still runs out of room, then there's probably an error in your file.

If TEX is really out of room, you must give it some help. Remember that TEX processes a complete paragraph before deciding whether to cut the page. Inserting a \newpage command in the middle of the paragraph, where TEX should break the page, may save the day by letting TEX write out the current page before processing the rest of the paragraph. (A \pagebreak command won't help.) If the problem is caused by accumulated figures and tables, you can try to prevent them from accumulating—either by moving them further towards the end of the document or by trying to get them to come out sooner. (See Section C.9.1 for more details.) If you are still writing the document, simply add a \clearpage command and forget about the problem until you're ready to produce the final version. Changes to the input file are likely to make the problem go away.

pool size You probably used too many cross-referencing labels and/or defined too many new command names. More precisely, the labels and command names that you define have too many characters, so this problem can be solved by using shorter names. However, the error can also be caused by omitting the right brace that ends the argument of either a counter command such as \setcounter, or a \newenvironment or \newtheorem command.

save size This occurs when commands, environments, and the scopes of declarations are nested too deeply—for example, by having the argument of a \multiput command contain a picture environment that in turn has a \footnotesize declaration whose scope contains a \multiput command containing a . . .

! Text line contains an invalid character.
The input file contains some strange nonprinting character (sometimes called a control character) that it shouldn't. Instead of using a simple text editor, you may have created the file with a program that does its own formatting. Such programs usually insert strange characters into a file unless you save it as a text (or ASCII) file.

! Undefined control sequence.
TEX encountered an unknown command name. You probably misspelled the name, in which case typing I followed by the desired command name and a *return* will produce correct output. However, you still must change the input file later. If this message occurs when a LATEX command is being processed, the command is probably in the wrong place. The error can also be caused by a missing \documentclass or \usepackage command.

`! Use of ... doesn't match its definition.`
If the "..." is a LATEX command, then it's probably one of the picture-drawing commands described in Section 7.1, and you have used the wrong syntax for specifying an argument. If it's `\@array` that doesn't match its definition, then there is something wrong in an @-expression in the argument of an `array` or `tabular` environment—perhaps a fragile command that is not `\protect`'ed. The error can also be caused by an un`\protect`'ed command with an optional argument appearing in a moving argument. (The "..." may or may not be the name of the command.)

`! You can't use 'macro parameter character #' in ... mode.`
The special character `#` has appeared in ordinary text. You probably meant to type `\#`, in which case you can respond to the error message by typing `I\#` followed by *return* to produce the correct output.

## 8.4  LATEX Warnings

LATEX's warning messages begin with "LaTeX Warning:". (Some begin with an indication of the class of warning—for example, "LaTeX Font Warning:".) The most common messages are described below. Certain classes of warnings cause LATEX to print an additional message at the end to indicate that a warning of that class occurred.

`Citation '...' on page ... undefined.`
The citation key in a `\cite` command was not defined by a `\bibitem` command. See Section 4.3.

`Command ... invalid in math mode.`
The indicated command is not permitted in math mode but was used there. Remember that `\boldmath`, `\unboldmath`, and size-changing commands may not be used in math mode.

`Float too large for page by ...`
A figure or table is too tall, by the indicated length, to fit on a page. It is printed by itself on an oversize page. The length is given in points.

`Font shape '...' in size ... not available.`
You specified a font that is not available on your computer. The next line of the message describes what font LATEX is using in its place. As explained in Section 3.3.8, this message can be caused by a `\boldmath` declaration even if the font is never used.

```
h float specifier changed to ht
!h float specifier changed to !ht
```
A `figure` or `table` environment has an optional argument `h` or `!h`, but the figure or table would not fit on the current page, so it is being put on the top of a subsequent page.

```
Label '...' multiply defined.
```
Two `\label` or `\bibitem` commands have the same arguments. More precisely, they had the same arguments the preceding time that LaTeX processed the input.

```
Label(s) may have changed.  Rerun to get cross-references right.
```
Issued after processing the entire input if the numbers printed by `\cite`, `\ref`, or `\pageref` commands may be wrong because the correct values have changed since the last time LaTeX processed the input.

```
Marginpar on page ... moved.
```
A marginal note was moved down on the page to avoid printing it on top of a previous marginal note. It will therefore not be aligned with the line of text where the `\marginpar` command appeared.

```
No \author given.
```
A `\maketitle` command is not preceded by an `\author` command.

```
Optional argument of \twocolumn too tall on page ...
```
The optional argument of a `\twocolumn` command produced a box too large to fit on a page.

```
Oval too small.
```
An `\oval` command specified an oval so small that LaTeX could not draw small enough quarter-circles to put in its corners. What LaTeX did draw does not look very good.

```
Reference '...' on page ... undefined.
```
The argument of a `\ref` or `\pageref` command was not defined by a `\label` command. See Section 4.2.

```
Some font shapes were not available, defaults substituted.
```
Issued after processing the entire input if any unavailable font was specified.

```
There were multiply-defined labels.
```
Issued after processing the entire input if any label was defined by two different `\label` commands.

`There were undefined references or citations.`
Issued after processing the entire input if a `\ref` or `\cite` was found that had
no corresponding `\label` or bibliography entry.

`Unused global option(s):  [...].`
The listed options were given to the `\documentclass` command but were not
known to it or to any packages that were loaded.

`You have requested release '...' of LaTeX, but only release`
`'...' is available.`
You are using a document class or package that requires a later release of LaTeX
than the one you are running. You should get the latest release of LaTeX.

## 8.5  TEX Warnings

You can identify a TEX warning message because it is not an error message, so
no ? is printed, and it does not begin with "LaTeX Warning:". Below is a list of
some of TEX's warnings.

`Overfull \hbox ...`
See Section 6.2.1.

`Overfull \vbox ...`
Because it couldn't find a good place for a page break, TEX put more on the page
than it should. See Section 6.2.2 for how to deal with page-breaking problems.

`Underfull \hbox ...`
Check your output for extra vertical space. If you find some, it was probably
caused by a problem with a `\\` or `\newline` command—for example, two `\\` commands in succession. This warning can also be caused by using the `sloppypar`
environment or `\sloppy` declaration, or by inserting a `\linebreak` command.

`Underfull \vbox ...`
TEX could not find a good place to break the page, so it produced a page without
enough text on it. See Section 6.2.2 for how to handle page-breaking problems.

# APPENDIX A
# Using *MakeIndex*

## A.1   How to Use *MakeIndex*

*MakeIndex* is a program for making an index from information generated by `\index` commands in your document. Section A.2 below explains what `\index` commands to use to produce the index entries you want. To use *MakeIndex*, you must also put the following commands in your document:

- `\usepackage{makeidx}` in the preamble (between the `\documentclass` and `\begin{document}` commands).

- `\makeindex` in the preamble.

- `\printindex` where you want the index to appear—usually right before the `\end{document}` command.

Let's suppose that the root file (Section 4.4) of your document is `myfile.tex`. You first run LATEX on your entire document, which causes it to generate the file `myfile.idx` containing the information from your `\index` commands. You next run *MakeIndex* by typing something like

```
makeindex myfile
```

*MakeIndex* reads `myfile.idx` and produces the file `myfile.ind`. *MakeIndex* will reject an entry or issue a warning when it finds an error. If it doesn't find any, you can rerun LATEX on your document; LATEX will use `myfile.ind` to produce the index. If *MakeIndex* does find errors, see Section A.3 below.

By reading the index, you may discover additional mistakes. These should be corrected by changing the appropriate `\index` commands in the document and regenerating the `ind` file. If there are problems that cannot be corrected in this way, you can always edit the `ind` file directly. However, such editing is to be avoided because it must be repeated every time you generate a new version of the index.

*MakeIndex* can be customized in a variety of ways to make glossaries and other kinds of indexes. See the LATEX *Companion* for details.

## A.2   How to Generate Index Entries

### A.2.1   When, Why, What, and How to Index

The index is there to help the reader find things in your document. It should make this as easy as possible. Many authors index words, listing all the pages on which a word appears. A good writer indexes concepts—ideas, facts, people, etc. Here is an entry from a word index and the corresponding entry from a concept index. Imagine using each of them to find out if there are gnus in Tasmania. (Page 150 tells you that there aren't.)

gnu, 17, 25, 54, 62, 64, 74, 101,          gnu,
    103, 104, 121, 124, 125,             caged, 104, 121, 125
    150, 167, 202, 250                         distribution of, 25, 54, 150, 167
                               gnat and, 62, 64, 103, 124, 202
                               indexing, 74, 150, 250
                             size of, 17, 25, 101, 167

With the word index, you have to look at twelve pages before reaching the right one; with the concept index, you have to look at only two.

To make an index, you must first decide what concepts should appear in it. You must then figure out under what words a reader might look to find each concept. Try to understand who your readers are and how they think about the concept. Don't just list the words that you used to describe it.

You may be tempted to generate the index as you write the document. Resist the temptation. It is virtually impossible to make a good index that way. Add \index commands as you write to remind yourself of what you want to index, but be prepared to modify those commands when you produce the index.

A computer can't generate the index for you, but it can help. You have to decide whether gnus are central enough to your topic to appear in the index, and if so, where to direct the reader who wants to learn about them. The computer can help by finding all occurrences of "gnu". A good way to start writing an index is by making an alphabetized list of all the distinct words that appear in your document. Consult your *Local Guide* to see if your computer has a program to generate such a list.

Most books have indexes; most technical reports don't. They should. Any nonfiction work of more than twenty or so pages that is worth reading deserves an index. With LaTeX and *MakeIndex* doing the tedious work for you, there is no good reason not to make one.

## A.2.2   The Basics

The following example shows some simple \index commands and the index entries that they produce using *MakeIndex*. The page number refers to the page containing the text where the \index command appears.

Alpha, ii                    Page ii:        \index{Alpha}
alpha, viii, ix, 22          Page viii:      \index{alpha}
alpha bet, 24                Page ix:        \index{alpha}
Alphabet, ix                                 \index{Alphabet}
alphabet, 23                 Page 22:        \index{alpha}
alphas, 22                                   \index{alphas}
                                 Page 23:        \index{alphabet}
                                                     \index{alphabet}
                                 Page 24:        \index{alpha bet}

The duplicate \index{alphabet} commands on page 23 produce only one "23" in the index.

To produce a subentry, the argument of the \index command should contain both the main entry and the subentry, separated by a ! character.

| | |
|---|---|
| gnat, 32 | Page 7:   \index{gnat!size of} |
|   anatomy, 35 | Page 32:   \index{gnat} |
|   size of, 7 | Page 35:   \index{gnat!anatomy} |
| gnus | \index{gnus!good} |
|   bad, 38 | Page 38:   \index{gnus!bad} |
|   good, 35 | |

You can also have subsubentries.

| | |
|---|---|
| bites | Page 8:   \index{bites!animal!gnats} |
|   animal | Page 10:   \index{bites!animal!gnus} |
|     gnats, 8 | Page 12 :   \index{bites!vegetable} |
|     gnus, 10 | |
|   vegetable, 12 | |

LaTeX and *MakeIndex* support only three levels of indexing; you can't have subsubsubentries.

To specify a page range, put an \index{...|(} command at the beginning of the range and an \index{...|)} command at the end of the range. The two "..."s must be identical.

| | |
|---|---|
| gnat, vi–x, 22 | Page vi:   \index{gnat|(} |
| gnus | Page x:   \index{gnat|)} |
|   bad, 22 | Page 22:   \index{gnat} |
|   good, 28–32 | \index{gnus!bad|(} |
| | \index{gnus!bad|)} |
| | Page 28:   \index{gnus!good|(} |
| | Page 30:   \index{gnus!good} |
| | Page 32:   \index{gnus!good|)} |

As the example shows, *MakeIndex* does the right thing when both ends of the range fall on the same page, and when there is an identical entry within the range.

You can add a cross-reference to another entry as follows:

| | |
|---|---|
| at, 2 | Page 2:   \index{at} |
|   bat, *see* bat, at | Page 2:   \index{at!bat|see{bat, at}} |

Since the "see" entry does not print a page number, it doesn't matter where the \index{...|see{...}} goes, but it must come after the \begin{document} command. You might want to put all such cross-referencing commands in one place.

If you specify an entry or subentry of the form $str_1@str_2$, the string $str_1$ determines the alphabetical position of the entry, while the string $str_2$ produces the text of the entry.

| | |
|---|---|
| twenty, 44 | Page 44:  `\index{twenty}` |
| xx, 55 | Page 46:  `\index{twenty-one}` |
| twenty-one, 46 | Page 55:  `\index{twenty@xx}` |

This feature is useful because the argument of the `\index` command provides the actual input string that LaTeX uses to generate the index entry.

| | |
|---|---|
| alpha, 13 | Page 12:  `\index{alphas}` |
| $\alpha$, 14 | Page 13:  `\index{alpha}` |
| alphas, 12 | Page 14:  `\index{alpha@$\alpha$}` |
| **alps**, 33 | Page 33:  `\index{alps@\textbf{alps}}` |

The command `\index{$\alpha$}` will also produce an $\alpha$ entry in the index, but that entry will be alphabetized as `$\alpha$`.

In some indexes, certain page numbers are specially formatted—for example, an italic page number may indicate the primary reference, and an $n$ after a page number may denote that the item appears in a footnote. *MakeIndex* makes it easy to format an individual page number any way you want. For any string of characters $str$, the command `\index{...|`$str$`}` produces a page number of the form `\`$str${$n$}. Similarly, the command `\index{...|(`$str$`)` produces a page number of the form `\`$str${$n$-$m$}, or of the form `\`$str${$n$} if the specified range includes only a single page.

| | |
|---|---|
| gnat, *3*, 4n | Preamble:  `\newcommand{\nn}[1]{#1n}` |
| gnu, 5, *44-46* | Page 3:  `\index{gnat|emph}` |
| | Page 4:  `\index{gnat|nn}` |
| | Page 5:  `\index{gnu}` |
| | Page 44:  `\index{gnu|(emph}` |
| | Page 46:  `\index{gnu|)}` |

The "see" option is a special case of this facility, where the `\see` command is predefined by the `makeidx` package.

## A.2.3  The Fine Print

The argument of an `\index` command must always have matching braces, where the brace in a `\{` or `\}` command counts. Special characters like `\` may appear in the argument only if the `\index` command is not itself contained in the argument of another command. This is most likely to be a problem when indexing items in a footnote. Even in this case, robust commands can be placed in the "@" part of an entry, as in `\index{alp@\textit{alp}}`, and fragile commands can be used if protected with the `\protect` command.

*MakeIndex* works as expected when all page numbers are either arabic or lowercase roman numerals; pages numbered with roman numerals are assumed to precede those numbered with arabic numerals. *MakeIndex* can also handle other types of page numbers; consult its documentation for details.

To put a !, @, or | character in an index entry, *quote* it by preceding the character with a ". More precisely, a character is said to be quoted if it follows an unquoted " that is not part of a \" command. A quoted !, @, or | character is treated like an ordinary character rather than having its usual meaning. The " preceding a quoted character is deleted before the entries are alphabetized.

| | |
|---|---|
| exclaim (!), 2 | Page 2:  `\index{exclaim ("!)}` |
|    loudly, 3 | Page 3:  `\index{exclaim ("!)!loudly}` |
| für, 4 | Page 4:  `\index{fur@f\"{u}r}` |
| quote ("), 5 | Page 5:  `\index{quote (\verb+""+)}` |

*MakeIndex* regards spaces as ordinary characters when alphabetizing the entries and deciding whether two entries are the same. Thus, the commands `\index{gnu}`, `\index{␣gnu}`, and `\index{gnu␣}` produce three separate entries, the first appearing near the beginning of the index, since ␣ (space) comes before any letter in *MakeIndex*'s "alphabetical" order. All three entries look the same when printed, since LaTeX ignores extra spaces in the input. However, since LaTeX regards multiple spaces as a single space, `\index{a␣space}` and `\index{a␣␣space}` produce identical output on the `idx` file, so they produce a single index entry. Since % is treated as an ordinary character in the argument of an `\index` command, there is no way to split the argument across lines without inserting a space into the entry.

## A.3   Error Messages

*MakeIndex* prints out the number of lines read and written and how many errors were found. Messages to identify the errors are written on a file with extension `ilg`. There are two phases in which *MakeIndex* can produce error messages: when it is reading the `idx` file, and when it is writing the `ind` file. Each error message prints the nature of the error followed by a line number, identifying where in the file the error occurs. In the reading phase, the line number refers to the `idx` file; in the writing phase, it refers to the `ind` file. The error messages should enable you to figure out what you did wrong.

# APPENDIX B
# The Bibliography Database

As explained in Section 4.3.1, the \bibliography command specifies one or more bib files—bibliographic database files whose names have the extension bib. BibTeX uses the bib file(s) to generate a bbl file that is read by \bibliography to make the bibliography. This appendix explains how to create bib files.

Once you learn to use BibTeX, you will find it easier to let BibTeX make your reference list than to do it yourself. Moreover, you will quickly compile a bibliographic database that eliminates almost all the work of making a bibliography. Other people may have bib files that you can copy, or there may be a common database that you can use. Ask your friends or check the *Local Guide* to find out what is available. However, remember that you are responsible for the accuracy of the references in your document. Even published references are notoriously unreliable; don't rely on any bibliography information that has not been carefully checked by someone you trust.

# B.1   The Format of the bib File

## B.1.1   The Entry Format

A bib file contains a series of entries like the following:

```
@BOOK{kn:gnus,
    AUTHOR = "Donald E. Knudson",
    TITLE  = "1966 World Gnus Almanac",
    PUBLISHER = {Permafrost Press},
    ADDRESS = {Novosibirsk}                    }
```

The @BOOK states that this is an entry of type *book*. Various entry types are described below. The kn:gnus is the *key*, as it appears in the argument of a \cite command referring to the entry.

This entry has four *fields*, named AUTHOR, TITLE, PUBLISHER, and ADDRESS. The meanings of these and other fields are described below. A field consists of the name, followed by an "=" character with optional space around it, followed by its text. The text of a field is a string of characters, with no unmatched braces, surrounded by either a pair of braces or a pair of " characters. (Unlike in LaTeX input, \{ and \} are considered to be braces with respect to brace matching.) Entry fields are separated from one another, and from the key, by commas. A comma may have optional space around it.

The outermost braces that surround the entire entry may be replaced by parentheses. As in LaTeX input files, an end-of-line character counts as a space and one space is equivalent to one hundred. Unlike LaTeX, BibTeX ignores the case of letters in the entry type, key, and field names, so the entry above could have been typed as follows:

```
@Book(KN:Gnus, author={Donald E. Knudson} ,
            TiTlE  =      "1966 World
                          Gnus  Almanac",   ...    )
```

However, the case of letters does matter to LaTeX, so the key should appear exactly the same in all \cite commands in the LaTeX input file.

The quotes or braces can be omitted around text consisting entirely of numerals. The following two fields are equivalent:

```
Volume = "27"         Volume = 27
```

## B.1.2    The Text of a Field

The text of the field is enclosed in braces or double quote characters ("). A part of the text is said to be *enclosed in braces* if it lies inside a matching pair of braces other than the ones enclosing the entire field.

### Names

The text of an author or editor field represents a list of names. The bibliography style determines the format in which a name is printed—whether the first name or last name appears first, if the full first name or just the first initial is used, etc. The bib file entry simply tells BIBTeX what the name is. You should type an author's complete name, exactly as it appears in the cited work, and let the bibliography style decide what to abbreviate.

Most names can be entered in the obvious way, either with or without a comma, as in the following examples.

```
"John Paul Jones"          "Jones, John Paul"
"Ludwig van Beethoven"     "van Beethoven, Ludwig"
```

Only the second form, with a comma, should be used for people who have last names with multiple parts that are capitalized. For example, Per Brinch Hansen's last name is Brinch Hansen, so his name should be typed with a comma:

```
"Brinch Hansen, Per"
```

If you type "Per Brinch Hansen", BIBTeX will think that "Brinch" is his middle name. "van Beethoven" or "de la Madrid" pose no problem because "van" and "de la" are not capitalized.

"Juniors" present a special problem. People with "Jr." in their name generally precede it with a comma. Such a name should be entered as follows:

```
"Ford, Jr., Henry"
```

BIBTEX is sometimes confused by characters that are produced by LATEX commands—for example, accented characters and characters produced by the commands of Section 3.2.2. It will do the right thing if you put curly braces immediately around a command that produces a character:

```
"Kurt G{\"{o}}del"    "V. S{\o}rensen"    "J. Mart{\'{\i}}"
```

If there are multiple authors or editors, their names are separated by the word **and**. A paper written by Alpher, Bethe, and Gamow has the following entry:

```
AUTHOR = "Ralph Alpher and Bethe, Hans and George Gamow"
```

An **and** separates authors' names only if it is not enclosed in braces. If an **author** or **editor** field has more names than you want to type, just end the list of names with **and others**; the standard styles convert this to the conventional "et al."

### Titles

The bibliography style determines whether or not a title is capitalized; the titles of books usually are, the titles of articles usually are not. You type a title the way it should appear if it is capitalized.

```
TITLE  =  "The Agony and the Ecstasy"
```

You should capitalize the first word of the title, the first word after a colon, and all other words except articles and unstressed conjunctions and prepositions. BIBTEX will change uppercase letters to lowercase if appropriate. Uppercase letters that should not be changed are enclosed in braces. The following two titles are equivalent; the *A* of *Africa* will not be made lowercase.

```
"The Gnats and Gnus of {Africa}"
"The Gnats and Gnus of {A}frica"
```

## B.1.3   Abbreviations

Instead of an ordinary text string, the text of a field can be replaced by an *abbreviation* for it. An abbreviation is a string of characters that starts with a letter and does not contain a space or any of the following ten characters:

```
"   #   %   '   (   )   ,   =   {   }
```

The abbreviation is typed in place of the text field, with no braces or quotation marks. If **jgg1** is an abbreviation for

```
Journal of Gnats and Gnus, Series~1
```

then the following are equivalent:

```
Journal = jgg1
Journal = "Journal of Gnats and Gnus, Series~1"
```

Some abbreviations are predefined by the bibliography style. These always include the usual three-letter abbreviations for the month: `jan`, `feb`, `mar`, etc. Bibliography styles may contain abbreviations for the names of commonly referenced journals. Consult your *Local Guide* for a list of the predefined abbreviations for the bibliography styles available on your computer.

You can define your own abbreviations by putting a `@string` command in the `bib` file. The command

```
@string{jgg1 = "Journal of Gnats and Gnus, Series~1"}
```

defines `jgg1` to be the abbreviation assumed in the previous example. Parentheses can be used in place of the outermost braces in the `@string` command, and braces can be used instead of the quotation marks. The text must have matching braces.

The case of letters is ignored in an abbreviation as well as in the command name `@string`, so the command above is equivalent to

```
@STRING{JgG1 = "Journal of Gnats and Gnus, Series~1"}
```

A `@string` command can appear anywhere before or between entries in a `bib` file. However, it must come before any use of the abbreviation, so a sensible place for `@string` commands is at the beginning of the file. You can also put your abbreviations in a separate `bib` file, say `abbrev.bib`, and use the command

```
\bibliography{abbrev,...}
```

in your document. A `@string` command in a `bib` file takes precedence over a definition made by the bibliography style, so it can be used to change the definition of an abbreviation such as `Feb`.

## B.1.4   Cross-References

Several cited sources may be part of a larger work—for example, different papers in the same conference proceedings. You can make a single entry for the conference proceedings, and refer to that entry in the entries for the individual papers. Fields that appear in the proceedings' entry need not be duplicated in the papers' entries. However, every required field for a paper must be either in its entry or in the referenced entry.

```
@INPROCEEDINGS(beestly-gnats,
   AUTHOR   = "Will D. Beest",
   TITLE    = "Gnats in the Gnus",
   PAGES    = "47--59",
   CROSSREF = "ope:6cpb")
...
@PROCEEDINGS(ope:6cpb,
   TITLE     = "Sixth Conference on Parasites in Bovidae",
   BOOKTITLE = "Sixth Conference on Parasites in Bovidae",
   EDITOR    = "Ann T. L. Ope",
   YEAR      = 1975)
```

The apparently redundant BOOKTITLE field in the proceedings entry is needed to provide the field of that name for the entry of each paper that cross-references it. As explained below, the TITLE field is required to produce a reference-list entry for the proceedings; BiBTeX ignores the BOOKTITLE field when producing such an entry. The reference list made by BiBTeX may have an entry for the proceedings that is cited by the entries for the individual papers, even if the proceedings are not explicitly cited in the original document.

A cross-referenced entry like ope:6cpb in the example must come after any entries that refer to it.

## B.2   The Entries

### B.2.1   Entry Types

When entering a reference in the database, the first thing to decide is what type of entry it is. No fixed classification scheme can be complete, but BiBTeX provides enough entry types to handle almost any reference reasonably well.

References to different types of publications contain different information; a reference to a journal article might include the volume and number of the journal, which is usually not meaningful for a book. Therefore, database entries of different types have different fields. For each entry type, the fields are divided into three classes:

**required**  Omitting the field will produce an error message and will occasionally result in a badly formatted bibliography entry. If the required information is not meaningful, you are using the wrong entry type. If the required information is meaningful but not needed—for example, because it is included in some other field—simply ignore the warning that BiBTeX generates.

**optional**  The field's information will be used if present, but can be omitted without causing any formatting problems. A reference should contain any information that might help the reader, so you should include the optional field if it is applicable. (A nonstandard bibliography style might ignore an optional field when creating the reference-list entry.)

**ignored**  The field is ignored. BibTeX ignores a field that is not required or optional, so you can include any fields you want in a `bib` file entry. It's a good idea to put all relevant information about a reference in its `bib` file entry—even information that may never appear in the bibliography. For example, if you want to keep an abstract of a paper in a computer file, put it in an `abstract` field in the paper's `bib` file entry. The `bib` file is likely to be as good a place as any for the abstract, and it is possible to design a bibliography style for printing selected abstracts.

Misspelling its name will cause a field to be ignored, so check the database entry if relevant information that you think is there does not appear in the reference-list entry.

The following are all the entry types, along with their required and optional fields, that are used by the standard bibliography styles. The meanings of the individual fields are explained in the next section. A particular bibliography style may ignore some optional fields in creating the reference. Remember that, when used in the `bib` file, the entry-type name is preceded by an `@` character.

**article**  An article from a journal or magazine. Required fields: `author`, `title`, `journal`, `year`. Optional fields: `volume`, `number`, `pages`, `month`, `note`.

**book**  A book with an explicit publisher. Required fields: `author` or `editor`, `title`, `publisher`, `year`. Optional fields: `volume` or `number`, `series`, `address`, `edition`, `month`, `note`.

**booklet**  A work that is printed and bound, but without a named publisher or sponsoring institution. Required field: `title`. Optional fields: `author`, `howpublished`, `address`, `month`, `year`, `note`.

**conference**  The same as **inproceedings**, included for compatibility with older versions.

**inbook**  A part of a book, usually untitled; it may be a chapter (or other sectional unit) and/or a range of pages. Required fields: `author` or `editor`, `title`, `chapter` and/or `pages`, `publisher`, `year`. Optional fields: `volume` or `number`, `series`, `type`, `address`, `edition`, `month`, `note`.

**incollection**  A part of a book with its own title. Required fields: `author`, `title`, `booktitle`, `publisher`, `year`. Optional fields: `editor`, `volume` or `number`, `series`, `type`, `chapter`, `pages`, `address`, `edition`, `month`, `note`.

**inproceedings**  An article in a conference proceedings. Required fields: `author`, `title`, `booktitle`, `year`. Optional fields: `editor`, `volume` or `number`, `series`, `pages`, `address`, `month`, `organization`, `publisher`, `note`.

**manual** Technical documentation. Required field: `title`. Optional fields: `author`, `organization`, `address`, `edition`, `month`, `year`, `note`.

**mastersthesis** A master's thesis. Required fields: `author`, `title`, `school`, `year`. Optional fields: `type`, `address`, `month`, `note`.

**misc** Use this type when nothing else fits. Required fields: none. Optional fields: `author`, `title`, `howpublished`, `month`, `year`, `note`.

**phdthesis** A Ph.D. thesis. Required fields: `author`, `title`, `school`, `year`. Optional fields: `type`, `address`, `month`, `note`.

**proceedings** The proceedings of a conference. Required fields: `title`, `year`. Optional fields: `editor`, `volume` or `number`, `series`, `address`, `month`, `organization`, `publisher`, `note`.

**techreport** A report published by a school or other institution, usually numbered within a series. Required fields: `author`, `title`, `institution`, `year`. Optional fields: `type`, `number`, `address`, `month`, `note`.

**unpublished** A document with an author and title, but not formally published. Required fields: `author`, `title`, `note`. Optional fields: `month`, `year`.

In addition to the fields listed above, each entry type also has an optional `key` field, used in some styles for alphabetizing and forming a \bibitem label. You should include a `key` field for any entry with no `author` or author substitute. (Depending on the entry type, an `editor` or an `organization` can substitute for an author.) Do not confuse the `key` field with the key that appears in the \cite command and at the beginning of the whole entry, after the entry type.

## B.2.2  Fields

Below is a description of all the fields recognized by the standard bibliography styles. An entry can also contain other fields that are ignored by those styles.

**address** Usually the address of the `publisher` or `institution`. For major publishing houses, omit it entirely or just give the city. For small publishers, you can help the reader by giving the complete address.

**annote** An annotation. It is not used by the standard bibliography styles, but may be used by other styles that produce an annotated bibliography.

**author** The name(s) of the author(s), in the format described above.

**booktitle** The title of a book, a titled part of which is being cited. It is used only for the `incollection` and `inproceedings` entry types; use the `title` field for `book` entries. How to type titles is explained above.

**chapter** A chapter (or other sectional unit) number.

**crossref** The database key of the entry being cross-referenced.

**edition** The edition of a book—for example, "Second". (The style will convert this to "second" if appropriate.)

**editor** The name(s) of editor(s), typed as indicated above. If there is also an `author` field, then the `editor` field gives the editor of the book or collection in which the reference appears.

**howpublished** How something strange was published.

**institution** The sponsoring institution of a technical report.

**journal** A journal name. Abbreviations may exist; see the *Local Guide*.

**key** Used for alphabetizing and creating a label when the `author` and `editor` fields are missing. This field should not be confused with the key that appears in the `\cite` command and at the beginning of the entry.

**month** The month in which the work was published or, for an unpublished work, in which it was written. Use the standard three-letter abbreviations described above.

**note** Any additional information that can help the reader. The first word should be capitalized.

**number** The number of a journal, magazine, technical report, or work in a series. An issue of a journal or magazine is usually identified by its volume and number; the organization that issues a technical report usually gives it a number; books in a named series are sometimes numbered.

**organization** The organization that sponsors a conference or that publishes a manual.

**pages** One or more page numbers or ranges of numbers, such as 42--111 or 7,41,73--97.

**publisher** The publisher's name.

**school** The name of the school where a thesis was written.

**series** The name of a series or set of books. When citing an entire book, the `title` field gives its title and the optional `series` field gives the name of a series or multivolume set in which the book was published.

**title** The work's title, typed as explained above.

**type** The type of a technical report—for example, "Research Note". It is also used to specify a type of sectional unit in an `inbook` or `incollection` entry and a different type of thesis in a `mastersthesis` or `phdthesis` entry.

**volume** The volume of a journal or multivolume book.

**year** The year of publication or, for an unpublished work, the year it was written. It usually consists only of numerals, such as 1984, but it could also be something like `circa 1066`.

# APPENDIX C

# Reference Manual

This appendix describes all LaTeX commands and environments, including some features, anomalies, and special cases not mentioned earlier. You should look here when a command or environment does something surprising, or when you encounter a formatting problem not discussed in earlier chapters.

Command and environment descriptions are concise; material explained in an earlier chapter is sketched very briefly. The syntax of commands and environments is indicated by a *command form* such as:

\parbox[*pos*]{*wdth*}{*text*}

Everything in typewriter style, such as the \parbox[, represents material that appears in the input file exactly as shown. The italicized parts *pos*, *wdth*, and *text* represent items that vary; the command's description explains their function. Arguments enclosed in square brackets [ ] are optional; they (and the brackets) may be omitted, so \parbox can also have the form

\parbox{*wdth*}{*text*}

The case in which an optional argument is missing is called the *default*. If a command form has two optional arguments that come one right after the other, when only one is present it is assumed to be the first one.

A number of *style parameters* are listed in this appendix. Except where stated otherwise, these parameters are length commands. A length is rigid unless it is explicitly said to be a rubber length (Section 6.4.1).

# C.1   Commands and Environments

## C.1.1   Command Names and Arguments

The six commands # $ & ~ _ ^ are the only ones with single-character names. The character %, while not a command, causes LaTeX to ignore all characters following it on the input line—including the space character that ends the line—and all space characters at the beginning of the next line. A % can be used to begin a comment and to start a new line without producing space in the output. However, a command name cannot be split across lines.

About two dozen commands have two-character names composed of \ followed by a single nonletter. All other command names consist of \ followed by one or more letters. Command names containing an @ character can be used only in the sty files that implement packages (Section 6.1.4). Upper- and lowercase letters are considered to be different, so \gamma and \Gamma are different commands. Spaces are ignored after a command name of this form, except that a blank line following the command still denotes the end of a paragraph.

Commands may have mandatory and/or optional arguments. A mandatory argument is enclosed by curly braces { and } and an optional argument is enclosed by square brackets [ and ]. Space between arguments is ignored.

The following commands take an optional last argument:

```
\\        \linebreak   \nolinebreak   \newcounter   \twocolumn
\item     \pagebreak   \nopagebreak    \newtheorem   \suppressfloats
```

If that argument is missing and the next nonspace character in the text is a
[, then LaTeX will mistake this [ for the beginning of an optional argument.
Enclosing the [ in braces prevents this mistake.

Enclosing text in braces can seldom cause trouble.

- [This is an aside.] This is the rest of the item.

```
... \begin{itemize}
\item {[This is an aside.]} This is ...
```

A ] within the optional argument of an \item command must be enclosed in
braces to prevent its being mistaken for the ] that marks the end of the argument.

[**gnu**] A large animal, found mainly in dictionar-
ies.

[**gnat**] A small animal, found mainly in tents.

```
\begin{description}
  \item [{[gnu]}] A large animal...
  \item [{[gnat]}] A small animal...
\end{description}
```

Some commands, including \\, have a *-form that is obtained by typing a *
right after the command name. If a * is the first nonspace character following
a command like \\, then it should be enclosed in braces; otherwise, LaTeX will
mistake the \\ and * for a \\* command.

## C.1.2   Environments

An environment is begun with a \begin command having the environment's
name as the first argument. Any arguments of the environment are typed as
additional arguments to the \begin. The environment is ended with an \end
command having the environment's name as its only argument. If an environment has a *-form, the * is part of the environment's name, appearing in the
argument of the \begin and \end commands.

## C.1.3   Fragile Commands

Commands are classified as either *robust* or *fragile*. Type-style-changing commands such as \textbf and \em are robust, as are most of the math-mode
commands of Section 3.3. Any command with an optional argument is fragile.

Certain command arguments are called *moving* arguments. A fragile command that appears in a moving argument must be preceded by a \protect
command. A \protect applies only to the command it precedes; fragile commands appearing in its argument(s) require their own \protect commands. The
following are all the commands and environments with moving arguments:

- Commands with an argument that may be put into a table of contents, list of figures, or list of tables: \addcontentsline, \addtocontents, \caption, and the sectioning commands. If an optional argument is used with a sectioning or \caption command, then it is this argument that is the moving one.

- Commands to print on the terminal: \typeout and \typein. The optional argument of \typein is not a moving argument.

- Commands to generate page headings: \markboth (both arguments) and \markright. (The sectioning commands, already listed, fall under this category too.)

- The letter environment (defined in the letter document class).

- The \thanks command.

- The optional argument of \bibitem.

- An @ in an array or tabular environment. (Although @ is not a command, fragile commands in an @-expression must be \protect'ed as if they were in a moving argument.)

All length commands are robust and must not be preceded by \protect. A \protect command should not be used in an argument of a \setcounter or \addtocounter command.

## C.1.4  Declarations

A declaration is a command that changes the value or meaning of some command or parameter. The *scope* of a declaration begins with the declaration itself and ends with the first } or \end whose matching { or \begin occurs before the declaration. The commands \], \), and $ that end a math-mode environment and the } or ] that end the argument of a LaTeX command also delimit the scope of a declaration; but the } or ] ending the argument of a command defined with \newcommand, or \renewcommand, or \providecommand does *not* delimit its scope. A declaration is in effect throughout its scope, except within the scope of a subsequent countermanding declaration.

The following declarations are *global*; their scope is not delimited by braces or environments.

| | | | |
|---|---|---|---|
| \newcounter | \pagenumbering | \newlength | \hyphenation |
| \setcounter | \thispagestyle | \newsavebox | |
| \addtocounter | \pagecolor | \newtheorem | |

## C.1.5   Invisible Commands and Environments

A number of commands and environments are "invisible", meaning that they do not produce any text at the point where they appear. TEX regards an invisible command or environment in the middle of a paragraph as an invisible "word". Putting spaces or an end-of-line character both before and after an invisible word can generate two separate interword spaces, one on either side of this word, producing extra space in the output. Moreover, if the invisible word occurs at the end of a paragraph, not attached to a real word, it could appear on a line by itself, producing a blank line in the output. Invisible words caused by a command with no argument are seldom a problem, since spaces are ignored when they follow a command name that ends in a letter. Also, the following invisible commands and environments usually eliminate this extra space:[1]

| | | | |
|---|---|---|---|
| \pagebreak | \nolinebreak | \vspace | \color |
| \nopagebreak | \label | \glossary | figure |
| \linebreak | \index | \marginpar | table |

Any other invisible command with an argument that appears inside a paragraph should be attached to an adjacent word, as should the commands and environments listed above in certain unusual situations where they can produce extra space in the output.

## C.1.6   The \\ Command

\\ [*len*]
\\*[*len*]

These commands start a new line and add an extra vertical space of length *len* above it. The default is to add no extra space. The *-form inhibits a page break before the new line. They may be used in paragraph mode and within the following commands and environments:

| | | |
|---|---|---|
| array | eqnarray | \shortstack |
| tabular | tabbing | \author |

LATEX is in paragraph mode, so a \\ can be used, in the following environments (among others):

| | | | |
|---|---|---|---|
| verse | center | flushleft | flushright |

and when processing the argument of a \title, \date, or sectioning command. Do not use two \\ commands in a row in paragraph mode; instead, use an optional argument to add extra vertical space.

In the **array** and **tabular** environments, the spacing between rows is obtained by putting a strut (Section 6.4.3) on each line; a positive value of *len*

---

[1] More precisely, spaces that follow these commands and environments are ignored if there is space in the output before the invisible word that they generate.

increases the depth of this strut. This can fail to add the expected amount of extra space if an object in the row extends further below the line than the default strut.

The \\ and \\* commands are fragile.

## C.2   The Structure of the Document

A document consists of the following parts.

**prepended files**
> A possibly empty sequence of `filecontents` environments (Section 4.7).

**preamble**
> Begins with a \documentclass command. It may contain \usepackage commands, declarations that apply to the entire document, and command and environment definitions.

\begin{document}

**text of the document**

\end{document}

## C.3   Sentences and Paragraphs

### C.3.1   Making Sentences

The following commands and characters are for use mainly in paragraph and LR mode. They are robust.

**quotes**
> '   Apostrophe.     '*text*'  Single quotes.     ''*text*''  Double quotes.

**dashes**
> -   Intra-word.          --  Number-range.           ---  Punctuation.

**spacing**
> \,  Produces a small space; use it between a double and a single quote.
>
> \␣  Produces an interword space.
>
> ~   Produces an interword space where no line break can occur.
>
> \@  Causes an "end-of-sentence" space after punctuation when typed before the punctuation character. Needed only if the character preceding the punctuation character is not a lowercase letter or a number.

\frenchspacing Suppresses extra space after punctuation, even when \@
   is used. Fragile.

\nonfrenchspacing Reverses the effect of \frenchspacing. Fragile.

**special characters**

| | | | | | | | | |
|---|---|---|---|---|---|---|---|---|
| $ | \$ | % | \% | { | \{ | – | \_ | |
| & | \& | # | \# | } | \} | | | |

(These commands can be used in math mode.) See Sections 3.2 and 3.3.2
for commands to make other symbols.

**logos**

\LaTeX   Produces LaTeX logo.          \TeX   Produces TeX logo.

\today Generates the current date, in the following format: October 14, 1996.

\emph{*text*} Emphasizes *text*, usually by printing it in italic type.

\mbox{*text*} Typesets *text* in LR mode inside a box, which prevents it from
   being broken across lines. It can be used in math mode. (See Section 6.4.3.)

## C.3.2   Making Paragraphs

A paragraph is ended by one or more completely blank lines—lines not containing even a %. A blank line should not appear where a new paragraph cannot be
started, such as in math mode or in the argument of a sectioning command.

\noindent When used at the beginning of the paragraph, it suppresses the
   paragraph indentation. It has no effect when used in the middle of a
   paragraph. Robust.

\indent Produces a horizontal space whose width equals the width of the paragraph indentation. It is used to add a paragraph indentation where one
   would otherwise be suppressed. Robust.

\par Equivalent to a blank line, often used to make command and environment
   definitions easier to read. Robust.

**Style Parameters**

\textwidth Normal width of text on the page. Should be changed only in the
   preamble.

\columnwidth Normal width of a column; equals \textwidth for single-column
   styles. It should not be changed with the length-setting commands.

\linewidth Width of lines in the current environment; equals \columnwidth
   except when inside a displayed-paragraph environment such as quote or
   itemize. It should not be changed with the length-setting commands.

\parindent Width of the indentation at the beginning of a paragraph. Its value is set to zero in a parbox. Its value may be changed anywhere.

\baselineskip The minimum space from the bottom of one line to the bottom of the next line in a paragraph. (The space between individual lines may be greater if they contain tall objects.) Its value is set by a type-size-changing command (Section 6.7.1). The value used for the entire paragraph unit (Section 6.2.1) is the one in effect at the blank line or command that ends the paragraph unit. Its value may be changed anywhere.

\baselinestretch A decimal number (such as 2 or 1.5). Its default value is 1 and is changed with \renewcommand. The value of \baselineskip is set by \begin{document} and by each type-size-changing command to its default value times \baselinestretch. You can produce a "double-spaced" version of the document for copy editing by setting \baselinestretch to 2, but it will be ugly and hard to read. Any other changes to the interline spacing should be part of the complete document design, best done by a competent typographic designer.

\parskip The extra vertical space inserted before a paragraph. It is a rubber length that usually has a natural length of zero. Its value may be changed anywhere, but should be a stretchable length when a \flushbottom declaration (Section 6.1.2) is in effect.

## C.3.3   Footnotes

\footnote[*num*]{*text*}

Produces a footnote with *text* as its text and *num* as its number. The *num* argument is a positive integer, even when footnotes are "numbered" with letters or other symbols; if it is missing, then the footnote counter is stepped and its value used as the footnote number. This command may be used only in paragraph mode to produce ordinary footnotes. It should not be used inside a box except within a minipage environment, in which case it may be used in LR or math mode as well as paragraph mode and the footnote appears at the bottom of the box ended by the next \end{minipage}. This may be the wrong place for it if there are nested minipage environments. Fragile.

\footnotemark[*num*]

Used in conjunction with \footnotetext to footnote text where a \footnote command cannot be used. It produces a footnote mark (the footnote number that appears in the running text), but it does not produce a footnote. See Figure C.1 for an example of its use. It steps the footnote counter if the optional argument is missing. It may be used in any mode. Fragile.

It was $\boxed{\text{Gnats}^{12} \text{ and Gnus}^{13}}$ as we trekked through Africa in the blazing noontime heat.

⋮

————————
[12]Small insects.
[10]Large mammals.

```
It was \fbox{Gnats\footnotemark\ and
                Gnus\footnotemark}%
\addtocounter{footnote}{-1}\footnotetext
{Small insects.}\addtocounter{footnote}{1}%
\footnotetext{Large mammals.} as we ...
```

Figure C.1: Making footnotes without the \footnote command.

\footnotetext[*num*]{*text*}

Used in conjunction with \footnotemark to footnote text where the \footnote command cannot be used. See Figure C.1 for an example. It produces a footnote, just like the corresponding \footnote command, except that no footnote mark is generated and the footnote counter is not stepped. Fragile.

**Style Parameters**

\footnotesep  The height of a strut placed at the beginning of every footnote to produce the vertical space between footnotes. It may be changed anywhere; the value used is the one in effect when the \footnote or \footnotetext command is processed.

\footnoterule  A command that draws the line separating the footnotes from the main text. It is used by LaTeX in paragraph mode, between paragraphs (in TeX's inner vertical mode). The output it generates must take zero vertical space, so negative space should be used to compensate for the space occupied by the rule. It can be redefined anywhere with \renewcommand; the definition used is the one in effect when TeX produces the page of output.

## C.3.4   Accents and Special Symbols

Commands for making accents in normal text are listed in Table 3.1 on page 38, commands for making accents in math formulas are listed in Table 3.11 on page 50. See Section C.10.1 for commands used in a tabbing environment to produce the accents normally made with \=, \', and \`.

Non-English symbols are made with commands listed in Table 3.2 on page 39. The following commands for making additional special symbols can also be used in any mode:

| † | \dag | § | \S | © | \copyright |
|---|------|---|-----|---|-----------|
| ‡ | \ddag | ¶ | \P | £ | \pounds |

Section 3.3.2 gives many commands for generating symbols in mathematical formulas.

## C.4    Sectioning and Table of Contents

The use of the following commands for producing section headings and table of contents entries is illustrated in Figure C.2.

### C.4.1    Sectioning Commands

*sec_cmd* [*toc_entry*] {*heading*}
*sec_cmd* * {*heading*}

Commands to begin a sectional unit. The *-form suppresses the section number, does not increment the counter, does not affect the running head, and produces no table of contents entry. The `secnumdepth` counter, described below, determines which sectional units are numbered.

*sec_cmd* One of the following:

> \part          \section        \subsubsection      \subparagraph
> \chapter        \subsection      \paragraph

Each sectional unit should be contained in the next higher-level unit, except that \part is optional. The `article` document class does not have a \chapter command.

*toc_entry* Produces the table of contents entry and may be used for the running head (Section 6.1.2). It is a moving argument. If it is missing, the *heading* argument is used for these purposes.

*heading* Produces the section heading. If the *toc_entry* argument is missing, then it is a moving argument that provides the table of contents entry and may be used for the running head (Section 6.1.2).

---

**Gnats and Gnus Forever**

From insects embedded in amber and fossils...

In the table of contents:

Gnats . . . . . . . . . . . . . . . . . . . . 37

⇵ 2 ex

2.2x   Gnus . . . . . . . . . . . . . . . . 37
2.3     Gnats and Gnus on Gneiss . . . . . 37

In the text (on page 37):
**2.3  Insects and Ungulates on** ...

```
\subsection*{Gnats and Gnus Forever}
 From insects embedded in amber and ...
```

---

```
\addcontentsline{toc}{subsection}{Gnats}
\addtocontents{toc}{\protect\vspace
    {2ex}}
\addcontentsline{toc}{subsection}{\protect
   \numberline{2.2x}{Gnus}}
\subsection[Gnats and Gnus on Gneiss]%
{Insects and Ungulates on Metamorphic Rock}
```

Figure C.2: Sectioning and table of contents commands.

## C.4.2   The Appendix

`\appendix`

A declaration that changes the way sectional units are numbered. In the standard `article` document class, appendix sections are numbered "A", "B", etc. In the `report` and `book` classes, appendix chapters are numbered "A", "B", etc., and the chapter number is printed in the heading as "Appendix A", "Appendix B", etc. The `\appendix` command generates no text and does not affect the numbering of parts.

## C.4.3   Table of Contents

`\tableofcontents`
`\listoffigures`
`\listoftables`

Generate a table of contents, list of figures, and list of tables, respectively. These commands cause LaTeX to write the necessary information on a file having the same first name as the root file and the following extension:

| command: | \tableofcontents | \listoffigures | \listoftables |
|---|---|---|---|
| extension: | toc | lof | lot |

A table of contents or a list of figures or tables compiled from the information on the current version of this file is printed at the point where the command appears.

Table of contents entries are produced by the sectioning commands, and list of figures or tables entries are produced by a `\caption` command in a `figure` or `table` environment (Section 3.5.1). The two commands described below also produce entries.

`\addcontentsline{`*file*`}{`*sec_unit*`}{`*entry*`}`

Adds an entry to the specified list or table.

*file* The extension of the file on which information is to be written: `toc` (table of contents), `lof` (list of figures), or `lot` (list of tables).

*sec_unit* Controls the formatting of the entry. It should be one of the following, depending upon the value of the *file* argument:

toc: the name of the sectional unit, such as `part` or `subsection`

lof: `figure`

lot: `table`

There is no \ in this argument.

*entry* The text of the entry. It is a moving argument. To produce a line with a sectional-unit or figure or table number, *entry* should be of the form

$$\verb|\protect\numberline{|sec\_num\verb|}{|heading\verb|}|$$

where *sec_num* is the number and *heading* is the heading.

`\addtocontents{`*file*`}{`*text*`}`

Adds text (or formatting commands) directly to the file that generates the table of contents or list of figures or tables.

*file* The extension of the file on which information is to be written: `toc` (table of contents), `lof` (list of figures), or `lot` (list of tables).

*text* The information to be written. It is a moving argument.

### C.4.4   Style Parameters

Parameters control which sectional units are numbered and which are listed in the table of contents. Each sectional unit has a *level number*. In all document classes, sections have level number 1, subsections have level number 2, etc. In the `article` document class, parts have level number 0; in the `report` and `book` classes, chapters have level number 0 and parts have level number −1.

The following two counters (Section 6.3) are provided; they can be set in the preamble.

`secnumdepth` The level number of the least significant sectional unit with numbered headings. A value of 2 means that subsections are numbered but subsubsections are not.

`tocdepth` The level number of the least significant sectional unit listed in the table of contents.

## C.5   Classes, Packages, and Page Styles

### C.5.1   Document Class

`\documentclass[`*options*`]{`*class*`}`

Specifies the document class and options.

*class* The document class. The standard classes are: `article`, `report`, `book`, `letter` (for letters), and `slides` (for slides).

*options* A list of one or more options, separated by commas—with no spaces. The options recognized by the standard document classes are listed below. Alternatives, at most one of which should appear, are separated by the symbol "|".

10pt | 11pt | 12pt  Chooses the normal (default) type size of the document. The default is 10pt, which selects ten-point type. (These options are not recognized by the slides class.)

letterpaper | legalpaper | executivepaper | a4paper | a5paper | b5paper  Causes the output to be formatted for the appropriate paper size.

| letter | 8.5in × 11in | A4 | 210mm × 297mm |
| legal | 8.5in × 14in | A5 | 148mm × 210mm |
| executive | 7.25in × 10.5in | B5 | 176mm × 250mm |

The default is letterpaper.

landscape  Causes the output to be formatted for landscape (sideways) printing on the selected paper size. This option effectively interchanges the width and height dimensions of the paper size.

final | draft  If TeX has trouble finding good places to break lines, it can produce lines that extend past the right margin ("overfull hboxes"). The draft option causes such lines to be marked by black boxes in the output. The final option, which does not mark these lines, is the default.

oneside | twoside  Formats the output for printing on one side or both sides of a page. The default is oneside, except that it is twoside for the book class. (The twoside option cannot be used with the slides document class.)

openright | openany  Specifies that chapters must begin on a right-hand page (openright) or may begin on any page (openany). These options apply only to the report class (whose default is openany) and the book class (whose default is openright).

onecolumn | twocolumn  Specifies one-column or two-column pages. The default is onecolumn. (The twocolumn option cannot be used with the letter or slides class.)

notitlepage | titlepage  The titlepage option causes the \maketitle command to make a separate title page and the abstract environment to put the abstract on a separate page. The default is titlepage for all classes except article, for which it is notitlepage. (These options are not recognized by the letter class.)

openbib  Causes the bibliography (Section 4.3) to be formatted in open style. (This option is not recognized by the letter and slides classes.)

leqno  Puts formula numbers on the left side in equation and eqnarray environments.

fleqn  Left-aligns displayed formulas.

Putting an option in the \documentclass command effectively adds that option to any package (loaded with a \usepackage command) that recognizes it. LaTeX issues a warning message if a document-class option is recognized neither by the document class nor by any loaded package.

### Style Parameters

\bibindent Width of the extra indentation of succeeding lines in a bibliography block with the openbib style option.

\columnsep The width of the space between columns of text in twocolumn style.

\columnseprule The width of a vertical line placed between columns of text in twocolumn style. Its default value is zero, producing an invisible line.

\mathindent The amount that formulas are indented from the left margin in the fleqn document-class option.

## C.5.2   Packages

\usepackage[*options*]{*pkgs*}

*pkgs* A list of packages to be loaded. The standard packages include:

alltt Defines the alltt environment; see Section C.6.4.

amstex Defines many commands for mathematical formulas. It is described in the LaTeX *Companion*.

babel For documents in one or more languages other than English; see the LaTeX *Companion*.

color For producing colors, using special device-driver support. A device driver is specified as an option; the *Local Guide* should list the default driver for your computer. See Section 7.3.

graphics For geometrical transformations of text and including graphics prepared by other programs. It requires special device-driver support. A device driver is specified as an option; the *Local Guide* should list the default driver for your computer. See Section 7.2.

graphpap Defines the \graphpaper command for use in the picture environment (Section 7.1.4).

ifthen Defines simple programming-language constructs (Section C.8.5).

latexsym Defines some special mathematical symbols; see Section 3.3.2.

makeidx Defines commands for use with *MakeIndex* (Appendix A).

pict2e Defines enhanced versions of the `picture` environment commands that remove restrictions on line slope, circle radius, and line thickness.

showidx Causes `\index` command arguments to be printed on the page where they occur; see Section 4.5.1.

*options* A list of options, which are provided to all the specified packages. They must be legal options for all the packages.

## C.5.3 Page Styles

An output page consists of a *head*, a *body*, and a *foot*. Style parameters determine their dimensions; the page style specifies the contents of the head and foot. Left-hand and right-hand pages have different parameters. In two-sided style, even-numbered pages are left-hand and odd-numbered pages are right-hand; in one-sided style, all pages are right-hand. All commands described in this section are fragile.

`\pagestyle{`*style*`}`

A declaration, with normal scoping rules, that specifies the current page style. The style used for a page is the one in effect when TeX "cuts the scroll" (page 135). Standard *style* options are:

plain The head is empty, the foot has only a page number. It is the default page style.

empty The head and foot are both empty.

headings The head contains information determined by the document class (usually a sectional-unit heading) and the page number; the foot is empty.

myheadings Same as `headings`, except head information (but not the page number) is specified by `\markboth` and `\markright` commands, described below.

`\thispagestyle`

Same as `\pagestyle` except it applies only to the current page (the next one to be "cut from the scroll"). It is a global declaration (Section C.1.4).

`\markright{`*right_head*`}`
`\markboth{`*left_head*`}{`*right_head*`}`

These commands specify the following heading information for the `headings` and `myheadings` page styles:

**left-hand page** Specified by *left_head* argument of the last \markboth before the end of the page.

**right-hand page** Specified by *right_head* argument of the first \markright or \markboth on the page, or if there is none, by the last one before the beginning of the page.

Both *right_head* and *left_head* are moving arguments. In the headings page style, sectioning commands set the page headings with the \markboth and \markright commands as follows:

| Printing Style | Command | Document Class | |
| | | book, report | article |
| --- | --- | --- | --- |
| two-sided | \markboth[a] | \chapter | \section |
| | \markright | \section | \subsection |
| one-sided | \markright | \chapter | \section |

[a]Specifies an empty right head.

To override a heading on a right-hand page (any page for one-sided printing), put a \markright after the sectioning command and in its mandatory argument, and add an optional argument without the \markright. To change the heading on a left-hand page, put a \markboth command immediately after the sectioning command.

The right head information is always null for the first page of a document. If this is a problem, generate a blank first page with the titlepage environment.

### \pagenumbering{*num_style*}

Specifies the style of page numbers and sets the value of the page counter to 1. It is a global declaration (Section C.1.4). Possible values of *num_style* are:

**arabic**  Arabic numerals.

**roman**  Lowercase roman numerals.

**Roman**  Uppercase roman numerals.

**alph**  Lowercase letters.

**Alph**  Uppercase letters.

The \pagenumbering command redefines \thepage to be \*num_style*{page}.

### \twocolumn[*text*]

Starts a new page by executing \clearpage (Section 6.2.2) and begins typesetting in two-column format. If the *text* argument is present, it is typeset in a double-column-wide parbox at the top of the new page. Fragile.

`\onecolumn`

Starts a new page by executing `\clearpage` (Section 6.2.2) and begins typesetting in single-column format. Fragile.

**Style Parameters**

Most of the parameters controlling the page style are shown in Figure C.3, where the outer rectangle represents the physical page. These parameters are all rigid lengths. They are normally changed only in the preamble. Anomalies may occur if they are changed in the middle of the document. Odd-numbered pages use `\oddsidemargin` and even-numbered pages use `\evensidemargin`. Not shown in the figure is the parameter `\topskip`, the minimum distance from the top of the body to the reference point of the first line of text. It acts like `\baselineskip` for the first line of a page.

## C.5.4    The Title Page and Abstract

`\maketitle`

Generates a title. With the `notitlepage` document-class option (the default for the `article` class), it puts the title at the top of a new page and issues a `\thispagestyle{plain}` command. With the `titlepage` option (the default for other classes), it puts the title on a separate page, using the `titlepage` environment. Information used to produce the title is obtained from the following declarations; an example of their use is given in Figure C.4. It's best to put these declarations in the preamble.

> `\title{`*text*`}` Declares *text* to be the title. You may want to use `\\` to tell LaTeX where to start a new line in a long title.

> `\author{`*names*`}` Declares the author(s), where *names* is a list of authors separated by `\and` commands. Use `\\` to separate lines within a single author's entry—for example, to give the author's institution or address.

> `\date{`*text*`}` Declares *text* to be the document's date. With no `\date` command, the current date is used.

The arguments of these three commands may include the following command:

> `\thanks{`*text*`}` Produces a footnote to the title. The *text* is a moving argument. Can be used for an acknowledgment of support, an author's address, etc. The footnote marker is regarded as having zero width, which is appropriate when it comes at the end of a line; if the marker comes in the middle of a line, add extra space with `\␣` after the `\thanks` command.

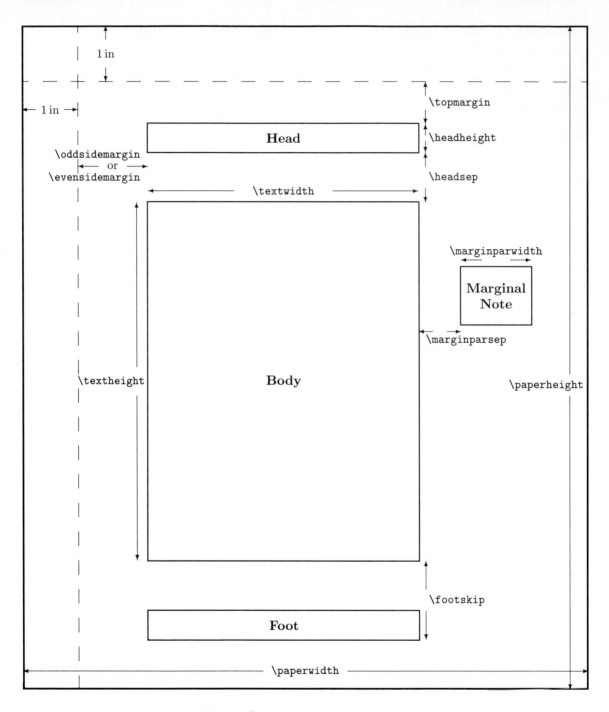

Figure C.3: Page style parameters.

Gnu Veldt Cuisine

G. Picking[*]
Acme Kitchen Products
R. Dillo
Cordon Puce School[†]
24 July 1984
Revised 5 January 1985

⋮

---

[*]Supported by a grant from the GSF.
[†]On leave during 1985.

```
\title{Gnu Veldt Cuisine}

\author{G. Picking\thanks{Supported
            by a grant from the GSF.} \\
    Acme Kitchen Products
\and
    R. Dillo \\ Cordon Puce
    School\thanks{On leave during 1985.}}

\date{24 July 1984 \\
        Revised 5 January 1985}

...

\maketitle
```

Figure C.4: An example title.

**\begin{abstract}**   *text*   **\end{abstract}**

Generates an abstract, with *text* as its contents, right where the environment occurs. The abstract is placed on a page by itself when the `titlepage` document-class option (the default for the `report` class; see Section 6.1.1) is in effect. This environment is not defined in the `book` document class.

**\begin{titlepage}**   *text*   **\end{titlepage}**

Produces a title page with the `empty` page style and resets the number of the following page to one. You are completely responsible for formatting the contents of this page.

## C.6   Displayed Paragraphs

The output produced by a displayed-paragraph environment starts on a new line, as does the output produced by the text following it. In addition to the environments described in this section, the `tabbing`, `center`, `flushleft`, and `flushright` environments and the environments defined by `\newtheorem` (Section 3.4.3) are also displayed-paragraph environments.

The text following a displayed-paragraph environment begins a new paragraph if there is a blank line after the `\end` command. However, even with no blank line, the following text may have a paragraph indentation if a right brace or `\end` command comes between it and the environment's `\end` command. This anomalous indentation is eliminated with a `\noindent` command (Section C.3.2).

Anomalous extra vertical space may be added after a displayed-paragraph environment that ends with a displayed equation (one made with the `displaymath`, equation, or eqnarray environment). This space can be removed by adding a negative vertical space with a \vspace command (Section 6.4.2). You can determine how much space to remove by trial and error.

All displayed-paragraph environments are implemented with the list or trivlist environment. These environments and the relevant formatting parameters are described in Section C.6.3 below.

## C.6.1   Quotations and Verse

\begin{quote}    *text*   \end{quote}

For a short quotation or a sequence of short quotations separated by blank lines.

\begin{quotation}    *text*   \end{quotation}

For a multiparagraph quotation.

\begin{verse}    *text*   \end{verse}

For poetry. Lines within a stanza are separated by \\ commands and stanzas are separated by one or more blank lines.

## C.6.2   List-Making Environments

\begin{itemize}       *item_list*   \end{itemize}
\begin{enumerate}     *item_list*   \end{enumerate}
\begin{description}   *item_list*   \end{description}

The *item_list* consists of a sequence of items, each one begun with an \item command (see below). Numbering in an enumerate environment is controlled by the counter enumi, enumii, enumiii, or enumiv, depending upon its nesting level within other enumerate environments. The printed value of this counter is declared to be the current \ref value (Section C.11.2).

The default labels of an itemize environment are produced by the command \labelitemi, \labelitemii, \labelitemiii, or \labelitemiv, depending upon its nesting level within other itemize environments. The "tick marks" produced by the itemize environment may be changed by redefining these commands with \renewcommand.

If an item of a description environment begins with a displayed-paragraph environment, the item label may overprint the first line of that environment. If this happens, the item should begin with an \mbox{} command to cause the environment to start on a new line.

\item[*label*]

Starts a new item and produces its label. The item label is generated by the *label* argument if present; otherwise the default label is used. In itemize and enumerate, the label is typeset flush right a fixed distance from the item's left margin. In enumerate, the optional argument suppresses the incrementing of the enumeration counter. The default label is null in the description environment. The \item command is fragile.

## C.6.3   The list and trivlist Environments

\begin{list}{*default_label*}{*decls*}   *item_list*   \end{list}

Produces a list of labeled items.

*item_list*  The text of the items. Each item is begun with an \item command (Section C.6.2).

*default_label*  The label generated by an \item command with no optional argument.

*decls*  A sequence of declarations that can be used to change any of the following parameters that control formatting in the list environment. (See also Figure 6.3 on page 113.)

\topsep  The amount of extra vertical space (in addition to \parskip) inserted between the preceding text and the first list item, and between the last item and the following text. It is a rubber length.

\partopsep  The extra vertical space (in addition to \topsep + \parskip) inserted, if the environment is preceded by a blank line, between the preceding text and the first list item and between the last item and the following text. It is a rubber length.

\itemsep  The amount of extra vertical space (in addition to \parsep) inserted between successive list items. It is a rubber length.

\parsep  The amount of vertical space between paragraphs within an item. It is the value to which \parskip is set within the list. It is a rubber length.

\leftmargin  The horizontal distance between the left margin of the enclosing environment and the left margin of the list. It must be nonnegative. In the standard document classes, it is set to \leftmargini, \leftmarginii, ... or \leftmarginvi, depending on the nesting level of the list environment.

\rightmargin  The horizontal distance between the right margin of the enclosing environment and the right margin of the list. It must be nonnegative. Its default value is zero in the standard document classes.

\listparindent  The amount of extra indentation added to the first line of every paragraph except the first one of an item. Its default value is zero in the standard document classes. It may have a negative value.

\itemindent The indentation of the first line of an item. Its default value is zero in the standard document classes. It may have a negative value.

\labelsep The space between the end of the box containing the label and the text of the first line of the item. It may be set to a negative length.

\labelwidth The normal width of the box that contains the label. It must be nonnegative. In the standard document styles, its default value is \leftmargin... − \labelsep, so the left edge of the label box is flush with the left margin of the enclosing environment. If the natural width of the label is greater than \labelwidth, then the label is typeset in a box with its natural width, so the label extends further to the right than "normal".

\makelabel{*label*} A command that generates the label printed by the \item command from the *label* argument. Its default definition positions the label flush right against the right edge of its box. It may be redefined with \renewcommand.

In addition to declarations that set these parameters, the following declaration may appear in *decls*:

\usecounter{*ctr*} Enables the counter *ctr* (Section 6.3) to be used for numbering list items. It causes *ctr* to be initialized to zero and incremented by \refstepcounter when executing an \item command that has no optional argument, causing its value to become the current \ref value (Section C.11.2). It is a fragile command.

\begin{trivlist}   *item_list*   \end{trivlist}

Acts like a list environment using the current values of the list-making parameters, except with \parsep set to the current value of \parskip and the following set to zero: \leftmargin, \labelwidth, and \itemindent. The trivlist environment is normally used to define an environment consisting of a single list item, with an \item command appearing as part of the environment's definition.

## C.6.4   Verbatim

\begin{verbatim}     *literal_text*     \end{verbatim}
\begin{verbatim*}    *literal_text*     \end{verbatim*}

Typesets *literal_text* exactly as typed, including special characters, spaces, and line breaks, using a typewriter type style. The only text following the \begin command that is not treated literally is the \end command. The *-form differs only in that spaces are printed as ␣ symbols.

If there is no nonspace character on the line following the \begin command, then *literal_text* effectively begins on the next line. There can be no space between the \end and the {verbatim} or {verbatim*}.

A verbatim or verbatim* environment may not appear in the argument of any command.

\verb*char*        *literal_text*      *char*
\verb**char*       *literal_text*      *char*

Typesets *literal_text* exactly as typed, including special characters and spaces, using a typewriter type style. There may be no space between \verb or \verb* and *char*. The *-form differs only in that spaces are printed as ␣ symbols.

*char*  Any nonspace character, except it may not be a * for \verb.

*literal_text*  Any sequence of characters not containing an end-of-line character or *char*.

A \verb or \verb* command may not appear in the argument of any other command.

\begin{alltt}   *literal_text*   \end{alltt}

Like the verbatim environment, except the three characters \, {, and } have their usual meanings. Thus, you can use commands like \input in the environment. This command is defined by the alltt package.

# C.7   Mathematical Formulas

Unless otherwise noted, all commands described in this section can be used only in math mode. See Section 3.3.8 for an explanation of the display and text math styles.

## C.7.1   Math Mode Environments

$                  *formula*      $
\(                 *formula*      \)
\begin{math}       *formula*      \end{math}

These equivalent forms produce an in-text formula by typesetting *formula* in math mode using text style. They may be used in paragraph or LR mode. The \( and \) commands are fragile; $ is robust.

\ensuremath{*formula*}

Equivalent to \(*formula*\) when used in paragraph or LR mode; equivalent to *formula* when used in math mode.

```
\[              formula    \]
\begin{displaymath}  formula    \end{displaymath}
```

These equivalent forms produce a displayed formula by typesetting *formula* in math mode using display style. They may be used only in paragraph mode. The displayed formula is centered unless the `fleqn` document-class option is used (Section 6.1.1). The commands `\[` and `\]` are fragile.

```
\begin{equation}    formula    \end{equation}
```

The same as `displaymath` except that an equation number is generated using the `equation` counter. The equation number is positioned flush with the right margin, unless the `leqno` document-class option is used (Section 6.1.1).

```
\begin{eqnarray}    eqns    \end{eqnarray}
\begin{eqnarray*}   eqns    \end{eqnarray*}
```

Produces a sequence of displayed formulas aligned in three columns. The *eqns* text is like the body of an `array` environment (Section 3.3.3) with argument `rcl`; it consists of a sequence of rows separated by `\\` commands, each row consisting of three columns separated by `&` characters. (However, a `\multicolumn` command may not be used.) The first and third columns are typeset in display style, the second in text style. These environments may be used only in paragraph mode.

The `eqnarray` environment produces an equation number for each row, generated from the `equation` counter and positioned as in the `equation` environment. A `\label` command anywhere within the row refers to that row's number. A `\nonumber` command suppresses the equation number for the row in which it appears. The `eqnarray*` environment produces no equation numbers.

The command `\lefteqn{`*formula*`}` prints *formula* in display math style (Section 3.3.8), but pretends that it has zero width. It is used within an `eqnarray` or `eqnarray*` environment for splitting long formulas across lines.

An overfull `\hbox` warning occurs if a formula extends beyond the prevailing margins. However, if the formula does lie within the margins, no warning is generated even if it extends far enough to overprint the equation number.

### Style Parameters

`\jot` The amount of extra vertical space added between rows in an `eqnarray` or `eqnarray*` environment.

`\mathindent` The indentation from the left margin of displayed formulas in the `fleqn` document-class option.

`\abovedisplayskip` The amount of extra space left above a long displayed formula—except in the `fleqn` document-class option, where `\topsep` is used. A long formula is one that lies closer to the left margin than does the end of the preceding line. It is a rubber length.

\belowdisplayskip The amount of extra space left below a long displayed formula—except in the fleqn document-class option, where \topsep is used. It is a rubber length.

\abovedisplayshortskip The amount of extra space left above a short displayed formula—except in the fleqn document-class option, which uses \topsep. A short formula is one that starts to the right of where the preceding line ends. It is a rubber length.

\belowdisplayshortskip The amount of extra space left below a short displayed formula—except in the fleqn document-class option, which uses \topsep. It is a rubber length.

## C.7.2   Common Structures

_{*sub*} Typesets *sub* as a subscript. Robust.

^{*sup*} Typesets *sup* as a superscript. Robust.

' Produces a prime symbol ($'$). Robust.

\frac{*numer*}{*denom*} Generates a fraction with numerator *numer* and denominator *denom*. Robust.

\sqrt[*n*]{*arg*} Generates the notation for the $n^{\text{th}}$ root of *arg*. With no optional argument, it produces the square root (no indicated root). Fragile.

**ellipsis** The following commands produce an ellipsis (three dots) arranged as indicated. They are all robust.

   \ldots Horizontally at the bottom of the line (    ). It may be used in paragraph and LR mode as well as math mode.

   \cdots Horizontally at the center of the line ($\cdots$).

   \vdots Vertically ($\vdots$).

   \ddots Diagonally ($\ddots$).

## C.7.3   Mathematical Symbols

See Tables 3.3 through 3.8 on pages 41–44. The symbols in Table 3.8 are printed differently in display and text styles; in display style, subscripts and superscripts may be positioned directly above and below the symbol. All the commands listed in those tables are robust.

Log-like functions, which are set in roman type, are listed in Table 3.9 on page 44. Subscripts appear directly below the symbol in display style for \det, \gcd, \inf, \lim, \liminf, \limsup, \max, \min, \Pr, and \sup. All log-like commands are robust. The following commands also create symbols:

\bmod  Produces a binary *mod* symbol. Robust.

\pmod{*arg*}  Produces "(mod *arg*)". Robust.

## C.7.4  Arrays

See Section C.10.2.

## C.7.5  Delimiters

\left*delim*   *formula*   \right*delim*

Typesets *formula* and puts large delimiters around it, where *delim* is one of the delimiters in Table 3.10 on page 47 or a '.' character to signify an invisible delimiter. The \left and \right commands are robust.

## C.7.6  Putting One Thing Above Another

\overline{*formula*}

Typesets *formula* with a horizontal line above it. Robust.

\underline{*formula*}

Typesets *formula* with a horizontal line below it. May be used in paragraph or LR mode as well as math mode. Fragile.

**accents**

Table 3.11 on page 50 lists math-mode accent-making commands. They are robust, as are the following additional accenting commands:

\widehat  Wide version of \hat.

\widetilde  Wide version of \tilde.

\imath  Dotless $i$ for use with accents.

\jmath  Dotless $j$ for use with accents.

`\stackrel{`*top*`}{`*bot*`}`

Typesets *top* immediately above *bot*, using the same math style for *top* as if it were a superscript.

## C.7.7    Spacing

The following commands produce horizontal space in math mode. They are all robust. The `\,` command may also be used in paragraph and LR mode.

|  |  |  |  |
|---|---|---|---|
| `\,` | thin space | `\:` | medium space |
| `\!` | negative thin space | `\;` | thick space |

## C.7.8    Changing Style

### Type Style

The following commands cause letters, numbers, and uppercase Greek letters in their argument *arg* to be typeset in the indicated style. The commands may be used only in math mode. They are robust.

| | | | |
|---|---|---|---|
| `\mathrm{`*text*`}` | Roman | `\mathsf{`*text*`}` | Sans Serif |
| `\mathit{`*text*`}` | *Italic* | `\mathtt{`*text*`}` | Typewriter |
| `\mathbf{`*text*`}` | **Boldface** | `\mathcal{`*text*`}` | $\mathcal{CALLIGRAPHIC}$ |

The argument of `\mathcal` may contain only uppercase letters.

The following two commands affect all characters in a formula. They may be used only in paragraph or LR mode. They are robust.

`\boldmath` Causes math formulas to be typeset in a bold style. It causes LaTeX to generate a warning if a formula could use a bold-series font that is not available, even if the font is not actually used.

`\unboldmath` Causes math formulas to be typeset in a normal (nonbold) style.

### Math Style

The following declarations can appear only in math mode. They choose the type size and certain formatting parameters, including ones that control the placement of subscripts and superscripts. All are robust commands.

`\displaystyle` Default style for displayed formulas.

`\textstyle` Default style for in-text formulas and for the items in an `array` environment.

`\scriptstyle` Default style for first-level subscripts and superscripts.

`\scriptscriptstyle` Default style for higher-level subscripts and superscripts.

## C.8    Definitions, Numbering, and Programming

### C.8.1    Defining Commands

```
\newcommand      {cmd}[args][opt]{def}
\renewcommand    {cmd}[args][opt]{def}
\providecommand{cmd}[args][opt]{def}
```

These commands define or redefine a command. They are all fragile.

*cmd* A command name beginning with \ and followed by either a sequence of letters or a single nonletter. For \newcommand it must not be already defined and must not begin with \end; for \renewcommand it must already be defined. The command \providecommand acts like \newcommand unless *cmd* is already defined, in which case it does nothing and the old definition is retained.

*args* An integer from 1 to 9 denoting the number of arguments of the command being defined. The default is for the command to have no arguments.

*opt* If this argument is present, then the first of the *args* arguments of *cmd* is optional and has a default value of *opt*. If this argument is absent, then all arguments of *cmd* are mandatory.

*def* The text to be substituted for every occurrence of *cmd*; a parameter of the form #n in *def* is replaced by the text of the $n^{\text{th}}$ argument when this substitution takes place. It may contain command- and environment-defining commands only if all commands and environments they define have no arguments.

The argument-enclosing braces of a command defined or redefined with any of these three commands do not delimit the scope of a declaration in that argument. (However, the scope may be delimited by braces that appear within *def*.) The defined command is fragile if it has an optional argument or if *def* includes a fragile command; otherwise it is robust.

### C.8.2    Defining Environments

```
\newenvironment   {nam}[args][opt]{begdef}{enddef}
\renewenvironment{nam}[args][opt]{begdef}{enddef}
```

These commands define or redefine an environment. They are both fragile.

*nam* The name of the environment; it can be any sequence of letters, numbers, and the character * that does not begin with end. For \newenvironment, neither an environment by that name nor the command \\*nam* may already be defined. For \renewenvironment, the environment must already be defined.

*args*  An integer from 1 to 9 denoting the number of arguments of the newly
defined environment. The default is no arguments.

*opt*  If this argument is present, then the first of the *args* arguments of the
environment is optional and has a default value of *opt*. If this argument is
absent, then all arguments of the environment are mandatory.

*begdef*  The text substituted for every occurrence of \begin{*nam*}; a parameter
of the form #*n* in *begdef* is replaced by the text of the $n^{\text{th}}$ argument of
\begin{*nam*} when this substitution takes place.

*enddef*  The text substituted for every occurrence of \end{*nam*}. It may not
contain any argument parameters.

The *begdef* and *enddef* arguments may contain command- and environment-
defining commands only if all commands and environments they define have no
arguments. The argument-enclosing braces of an environment that was defined
with \newenvironment or \renewenvironment do not delimit the scope of a
declaration contained in the argument.

## C.8.3  Theorem-like Environments

\newtheorem {*env_name*}{*caption*}[*within*]
\newtheorem {*env_name*}[*numbered_like*]{*caption*}

This command defines a theorem-like environment. It is a global declaration
(Section C.1.4) and is fragile.

*env_name*  The name of the environment—a string of letters. It must not be the
name of an existing environment or counter.

*caption*  The text printed at the beginning of the environment, right before the
number.

*within*  The name of an already defined counter, usually of a sectional unit. If
this argument is present, the command \the*env_name* is defined to be

$$\text{\textbackslash the} \textit{within} . \text{\textbackslash arabic} \{ \textit{env\_name} \}$$

and the *env_name* counter will be reset by a \stepcounter{*within*} or
\refstepcounter{*within*} command (Section C.8.4). If the *within* argument is missing, \the*env_name* is defined to be \arabic{*env_name*}.

*numbered_like*  The name of an already defined theorem-like environment. If this
argument is present, the *env_name* environment will be numbered in the
same sequence (using the same counter) as the *numbered_like* environment
and will declare the current \ref value (Section C.11.2) to be the text
generated by \the*numbered_like*.

Unless the *numbered_like* argument is present, this command creates a counter named *env_name*, and the environment declares the current \ref value (Section C.11.2) to be the text generated by \the*env_name*.

The \newtheorem command may have at most one optional argument. See Section C.1.1 if a \newtheorem without a final optional argument is followed by a [ character.

## C.8.4   Numbering

The following commands manipulate counters. There are packages that provide additional commands for performing arithmetic calculations; check the LaTeX *Companion*.

\newcounter{*newctr*}[*within*]

Defines a new counter named *newctr* that is initialized to zero, with \the*newctr* defined to be \arabic{*newctr*}. It is a global declaration. The \newcounter command may not be used in an \include'd file (Section 4.4). Fragile.

*newctr*  A string of letters that is not the name of an existing counter.

*within*  The name of an already defined counter. If this argument is present, the *newctr* counter is reset to zero whenever the *within* counter is stepped by \stepcounter or \refstepcounter (see below).

\setcounter{*ctr*}{*num*}

Sets the value of counter *ctr* to *num*. It is a global declaration (Section C.1.4). Fragile.

\addtocounter{*ctr*}{*num*}

Increments the value of counter *ctr* by *num*. It is a global declaration (Section C.1.4). Fragile.

\value{*ctr*}

Produces the value of counter *ctr*. It is used mainly in the *num* argument of a \setcounter or \addtocounter command—for example, the command \setcounter{bean}{\value{page}} sets counter bean equal to the current value of the page counter. However, it can be used anywhere that LaTeX expects a number. The \value command is robust, and must never be preceded by a \protect command.

**numbering commands**

The following commands print the value of counter *ctr* in the indicated format. They are all robust.

\arabic{*ctr*}  Arabic numerals.

\roman{*ctr*}  Lowercase roman numerals.

\Roman{*ctr*}  Uppercase roman numerals.

\alph{*ctr*}  Lowercase letters. The value of *ctr* must be less than 27.

\Alph{*ctr*}  Uppercase letters. The value of *ctr* must be less than 27.

\fnsymbol{*ctr*}  Produces one of the nine "footnote symbols" from the following sequence: $* \ \dagger \ \ddagger \ \S \ \P \ \| \ ** \ \dagger\dagger \ \ddagger\ddagger$. It may be used only in math mode. The value of *ctr* must be less than 10.

\the*ctr*

A command used to print the value associated with counter *ctr*. Robust.

\stepcounter    {*ctr*}
\refstepcounter{*ctr*}

Increment the value of counter *ctr* by one and reset the value of any counter numbered directly "within" it. For example, the subsection counter is numbered within the section counter, which, in the report or book class, is numbered within the chapter counter. The \refstepcounter command also declares the current \ref value (Section C.11.2) to be the text generated by \the*ctr*.

## C.8.5   The ifthen Package

The ifthen package provides commands for writing simple programs with tests and loops. The use of these commands is illustrated in Figure C.5. This section may not make much sense unless you have already done some programming.

\ifthenelse{*test*}{*then_txt*}{*else_txt*}

If *test* is true, then *then_txt* is processed, if *test* is false, then *else_txt* is processed. The *then_txt* and *else_txt* arguments can be any LaTeX input. The *test* argument must be an expression that LaTeX evaluates to *true* or *false*. It can be any of the following:

   *num₁* *op* *num₂*  A numerical relation, where *op* is one of the following three characters: $>  =  <$, and *num₁* and *num₁* are numbers. For example, \value{page} > 17 evaluates to *true* if and only if the current value of the page counter is greater than 17.

   \equal{*str₁*}{*str₂*}  Evaluates to *true* if and only if TeX regards *str₁* and *str₂* as equal. TeX may think the two arguments are different even if they print the same—for example, \today and May␣1,␣2001 are not equal, even on

The gcd (greatest common divisor) of $m$ and $n$ is printed by the following algorithm, which successively subtracts the smaller value from the larger until the two are equal.

$a := m$ ;   $b := n$ ;
**while** $a \neq b$
   **do if** $a > b$ **then** $a := a - b$
               **else**  $b := b - a$ ;
$print(a)$

For example: $\text{Gcd}(54,30) = \gcd(24,30) = \gcd(24,6)$ $= \gcd(18,6) = \gcd(12,6) = \gcd(6,6) = 6$.

```
\newcounter{ca} \newcounter{cb}
\newcommand{\printgcd}[2]{%
  \setcounter{ca}{#1}\setcounter{cb}{#2}%
  Gcd(#1,#2) =
  \whiledo{\not\(\value{ca}=\value{cb}\)}%
    {\ifthenelse{\value{ca}>\value{cb}}%
     {\addtocounter{ca}{-\value{cb}}}%
     {\addtocounter{cb}{-\value{ca}}}}%
  gcd(\arabic{ca},\arabic{cb}) = }%
\arabic{ca}.}

... For example: \printgcd{54}{30}
```

Figure C.5: Writing programs with the `ifthen` package's commands.

May 1, 2001. TeX will think $str_1$ and $str_2$ are equal if replacing every command by its definition makes them identical. For example, `no␣\g{x}` and `no␣x-gnu-x` are equal if `\g` is defined by

```
\newcommand{\g}[1]{#1-gnu-#1}
```

If you're not sure exactly what equals what, try some experiments.

`\lengthtest{`*len₁ op len₂*`}` A length relation, where *op* is one of the following three characters: > = <, and *len₁* and *len₂* are lengths. For example, `\lengthtest{\parindent < 1cm}` evaluates to *true* if and only if the current value of `\parindent` is less than 1 centimeter. In evaluating the relation, a rubber length is replaced by its natural length (Section 6.4.1).

`\isodd{`*num*`}` Evaluates to *true* if and only if the number *num* is odd. It is used to produce different text for left- and right-hand pages. However, the obvious `\isodd{\value{page}}` doesn't work, because the current value of the **page** counter could be 42 even though the text now being processed will wind up on page 43 (see Section 8.1). Instead, use `\label{`*key*`}` and `\isodd{\pageref{`*key*`}}` (Section C.11.2). The **page** counter does have the expected value when processing the page's head or foot.

`\boolean{`*nam*`}` Evaluates to the current value of the boolean register *nam*, where *nam* can be any sequence of letters. This register must be defined with the command `\newboolean{`*name*`}`. Its value is set by the command `\setboolean{`*nam*`}{`*bool*`}`, where *bool* is either **true** or **false**.

**complex expressions** A *test* can be built up from simpler expressions in the customary fashion using the boolean operators `\and`, `\or`, and `\not`, with `\(` and `\)` serving as parentheses.

`\whiledo{`*test*`}{`*body*`}`

Repeatedly processes *body* until *test* becomes false, where *test* is the same as for `\ifthenelse`. (Does nothing if *test* is initially false.)

## C.9    Figures and Other Floating Bodies

### C.9.1    Figures and Tables

| | | |
|---|---|---|
| `\begin{figure}[`*loc*`]` | *body* | `\end{figure}` |
| `\begin{figure*}[`*loc*`]` | *body* | `\end{figure*}` |
| `\begin{table}[`*loc*`]` | *body* | `\end{table}` |
| `\begin{table*}[`*loc*`]` | *body* | `\end{table*}` |

These environments produce floating figures and tables. In two-column format, the ordinary forms produce single-column figures and tables and the *-forms produce double-column ones. The two forms are equivalent in single-column format.

The *body* is typeset in a parbox of width `\textwidth` or `\columnwidth`. It may contain one or more `\caption` commands (see below). The *loc* argument contains a sequence of one to four letters, each one specifying a location where the figure or table may be placed, as follows:

h  *Here*: at the position in the text where the environment appears. (Not possible for double-column figures and tables in two-column format.)

t  *Top*: at the top of a text page.

b  *Bottom*: at the bottom of a text page. (Not possible for double-column figures or tables in two-column format.)

p  *Page of floats*: on a separate page containing no text, only figures and tables.

If the *loc* argument is missing, the default specifier is `tbp`, so the figure or table may be placed at the top or bottom of a text page or on a separate page consisting only of figures and/or tables.

The *loc* argument can also contain the character !, which directs LaTeX to try harder to place the figure or table at the earliest possible place in the document allowed by the rest of the argument. What "trying harder" means is explained below.

You may find that LaTeX puts a figure or table where you don't want it. If the figure or table is printed too soon, you can either move it later in the input or use the `\suppressfloats` command described below. If it is printed too late, you can move it earlier in the input or use an optional argument with a ! character. Occasionally, you will find that nothing seems to work. You may then think you have discovered a bug in LaTeX. You almost certainly haven't. No computer program can deduce exactly where you want your figures to go. LaTeX's figure-placement algorithm was carefully designed to do the best it could. To solve your problem, you will have to understand why LaTeX puts the figure or table where it does. LaTeX follows the rules listed below. You will have to read these rules slowly and carefully to understand what LaTeX is doing. The last rule, which mentions the formatting parameters, is likely to be the key. You will have to read the descriptions of these parameters carefully to understand the rule. There are fifteen parameters, but one of the first seven is probably responsible for your problem.

Here are the rules that determine where a figure or table is put:

- It is printed at the earliest place that does not violate subsequent rules, except that an h (here) position takes precedence over a t (top) position.

- It will not be printed on an earlier page than the place in the text where the figure or table environment appears.

- A figure will not be printed before an earlier figure, and a table will not be printed before an earlier table.[2]

- It may appear only at a position allowed by the *loc* argument, or, if that argument is missing, by the default tbp specifier.

- Placement of the figure or table cannot produce an overfull page.

- The page constraints determined by the formatting parameters described below are not violated. However, if a ! appears in the optional argument, then the constraints for text pages are ignored, and only the ones for float pages (expressed by \floatpagefraction and \dblfloatpagefraction) apply.

The last three rules are suspended when a \clearpage, \cleardoublepage, or \end{document} command occurs, all unprocessed figures and tables being allowed a p option and printed at that point.

When giving an optional *loc* argument, include enough options so these rules allow the figure or table to go somewhere, otherwise it and all subsequent figures or tables will be saved until the end of the chapter or document, probably causing TeX to run out of space.

\caption[*lst_entry*]{*heading*}

Produces a numbered caption.

---

[2]However, in a two-column page style, a single-column figure can come before an earlier double-column figure, and vice versa.

*lst entry* Generates the entry in the list of figures or tables. Such an entry should not contain more than a few hundred characters. If this argument is missing, the *heading* argument is used. It is a moving argument.

*heading* The text of the caption. It produces the list of figures or tables entry if the *lst_entry* argument is missing, in which case it is a moving argument. If this argument contains more than a few hundred characters, a shorter *lst_entry* argument should be used—even if no list of figures or tables is being produced.

A \label command that refers to the caption's number must go in *heading* or after the \caption command in the *body* of the figure or table environment. The \caption command can be used only in paragraph mode, but can be placed in a parbox made with a \parbox command or minipage environment (Section 6.4.3). It is fragile.

\suppressfloats[*loc*]

Prevents additional figures and tables from appearing on the current page. There are two possible *loc* arguments:

   t No more figures or tables at the top of the current page.

   b No more figures or tables at the bottom of the current page.

With no optional argument, additional figures and tables are suppressed from both the top and bottom of the current page. A ! in the optional argument of a figure or table environment counteracts the effect of a \suppressfloats command for that particular figure or table.

**Style Parameters**

Changes made to the following parameters in the preamble apply from the first page on. Changes made afterwards take effect on the next page, not the current one. A *float* denotes either a figure or a table, and a *float page* is a page containing only floats and no text. Parameters that apply to all floats in a one-column page style apply to single-column floats in a two-column style.

topnumber A counter whose value is the maximum number of floats allowed at the top of a text page.

\topfraction The maximum fraction of the page that can be occupied by floats at the top of the page. Thus, the value .25 specifies that as much as the top quarter of the page may be devoted to floats. It is changed with \renewcommand.

bottomnumber Same as topnumber except for the bottom of the page.

\bottomfraction Same as \topfraction except for the bottom of the page.

totalnumber A counter whose value is the maximum number of floats that can appear on a single text page, irrespective of their positions.

\textfraction The minimum fraction of a text page that must be devoted to text. The other $1 - $ \textfraction fraction may be occupied by floats. It is changed with \renewcommand.

\floatpagefraction The minimum fraction of a float page that must be occupied by floats, limiting the amount of blank space allowed on a float page. It is changed with \renewcommand.

dbltopnumber The analog of topnumber for double-column floats on a two-column page.

\dbltopfraction The analog of \topfraction for double-column floats on a two-column page.

\dblfloatpagefraction The analog of \floatpagefraction for a float page of double-column floats.

\floatsep The vertical space added between floats that appear at the top or bottom of a text page. It is a rubber length.

\textfloatsep The vertical space added between the floats appearing at the top or bottom of a page and the text on that page. It is a rubber length.

\intextsep The vertical space placed above and below a float that is put in the middle of the text with the h location option. It is a rubber length.

\dblfloatsep The analog of \floatsep for double-width floats on a two-column page. It is a rubber length.

\dbltextfloatsep The analog of \textfloatsep for double-width floats on a two-column page. It is a rubber length.

## C.9.2   Marginal Notes

\marginpar [*left_text*]{*right_text*}

Produces a marginal note using *right_text* if it goes in the right margin or there is no optional argument, otherwise using *left_text*. The text is typeset in a parbox.

For two-sided, single-column printing, the default placement of marginal notes is on the outside margin—left for even-numbered pages, right for odd-numbered ones. For one-sided, single-column printing, the default placement is in the right margin. These defaults may be changed by the following declarations:

\reversemarginpar  Causes marginal notes to be placed in the opposite margin from the default one.

\normalmarginpar  Causes marginal notes to be placed in the default margin.

When a marginal note appears within a paragraph, its placement is determined
by the declaration in effect at the blank line ending the paragraph. For two-
column format, marginal notes always appear in the margin next to the column
containing the note, irrespective of these declarations.

A marginal note is normally positioned so its top line is level with the line
of text containing the \marginpar command; if the command comes between
paragraphs, the note is usually level with the last line of the preceding paragraph. However, the note is moved down and a warning message printed on
the terminal if this would make it overlap a previous note. Switching back
and forth between reverse and normal positioning with \reversemarginpar and
\normalmarginpar may inhibit this movement of marginal notes, resulting in
one being overprinted on top of another.

## Style Parameters

\marginparwidth  The width of the parbox containing a marginal note.

\marginparsep  The horizontal space between the outer margin and a marginal
note.

\marginparpush  The minimum vertical space allowed between two successive
marginal notes.

# C.10   Lining It Up in Columns

## C.10.1   The tabbing Environment

\begin{tabbing}   *rows*   \end{tabbing}

This environment may be used only in paragraph mode. It produces a sequence
of lines, each processed in LR mode, with alignment in columns based upon a
sequence of tab stops. Tab stops are numbered 0, 1, 2, etc. Tab stop number $i$
is said to be *set* if it is assigned a horizontal position on the page. Tab stop 0 is
always set to the prevailing left margin (the left margin in effect at the beginning
of the environment). If tab stop $i$ is set, then all tab stops numbered 0 through
$i - 1$ are also set. Tab stop number $i - 1$ is normally positioned to the left of
tab stop number $i$.

The behavior of the tabbing commands is described in terms of the values
of two quantities called *next_tab_stop* and *left_margin_tab*. Initially, the value of
*next_tab_stop* is 1, the value of *left_margin_tab* is 0, and only tab number 0 is
set. The value of *next_tab_stop* is incremented by the \> and \= commands, and

```
Gnat:      swatted by: men                    \begin{tabbing}
                       cows                    Armadillo: \=                              \kill
                and  gnus                      Gnat:          \> swatted by: \= men \+\+  \\
           not very filling                                                    cows       \\
Armadillo: not edible                                           and \' gnus  \-           \\
(note also the: aardvark                                     not very filling   \-        \\
              albatross            eton)       Armadillo: \> not edible                   \\
Gnu:       eaten by      gnats                 \pushtabs
                                               (note also the: \= aardvark                \\
                                                              \> albatross  \' eton) \\
                                               \poptabs
                                               Gnu:          \> eaten by    \> gnats
                                               \end{tabbing}
```

Figure C.6: A `tabbing` environment example.

it is reset to the value of *left_margin_tab* by the \\ and \kill commands. The following commands, all of which are fragile, may appear in *rows*; their use is illustrated in Figure C.6.

\= If the value of *next_tab_stop* is $i$, then this command sets tab stop number $i$'s position to be the current position on the line and changes the value of *next_tab_stop* to $i + 1$.

\> If the value of *next_tab_stop* is $i$, then this command starts the following text at tab stop $i$'s position and changes the value of *next_tab_stop* to $i + 1$.

\\ Starts a new line and sets the value of *next_tab_stop* equal to the value of *left_margin_tab*. See Section C.1.6 for more details.

\kill Throws away the current line, keeping the effects of any tab-stop-setting commands, starts a new line, and sets the value of *next_tab_stop* to the value of *left_margin_tab*.

\+ Increases the value of *left_margin_tab* by one. This causes the left margin of subsequent lines to be indented one tab stop to the right, just as if a \> command were added to the beginning of subsequent lines. Multiple \+ commands have the expected cumulative effect.

\- Decreases the value of *left_margin_tab*, which must be positive, by one. This has the effect of canceling one preceding \+ command, starting with the following line.

\< Decreases the value of *next_tab_stop* by one. This command can be used only at the beginning of a line, where it acts to cancel the effect, on that line, of one previous \+ command.

\' Used to put text flush right against the right edge of a column or against the left margin. If the value of *next_tab_stop* is $i$, then it causes everything in the current column—all text from the most recent \>, \=, \', \\, or \kill command—to be positioned flush right a distance of \tabbingsep (a style parameter) from the position of tab stop number $i - 1$. Text following the \' command is placed starting at the position of tab stop number $i - 1$.

\` Moves all following text on the line flush against the prevailing right margin. There must be no \>, \=, or \' command after the \` and before the command that ends the output line.

\pushtabs Saves the current positions of all tab stops, to be restored by a subsequent \poptabs command. You can nest \pushtabs commands, but \pushtabs and \poptabs commands must come in matching pairs within a **tabbing** environment.

\poptabs See \pushtabs.

\a... The commands \=, \', and \` usually produce accents, but are redefined to tabbing commands inside the **tabbing** environment. The commands \a=, \a', and \a` produce those accents in a **tabbing** environment.

The **tabbing** environment exhibits the following anomalies:

- The scope of a declaration appearing in *rows* is ended by any of the following commands:

  | | | | | | |
  |---|---|---|---|---|---|
  | \= | \> | \+ | \' | \pushtabs | \kill |
  | \\ | \< | \- | \` | \poptabs | \end{tabbing} |

  No environment contained within the **tabbing** environment can contain any of these tabbing commands.

- The commands \=, \', \`, and \- are redefined to have special meanings inside a **tabbing** environment. The ordinary \- command would be useless in this environment; the effects of the other three are obtained with the \a... command described above. These commands revert to their ordinary meanings inside a parbox contained within the **tabbing** environment.

- One **tabbing** environment cannot be nested within another, even if the inner one is inside a parbox.

**Style Parameters**

\tabbingsep See the description of the \' command above.

## C.10.2   The `array` and `tabular` Environments

\begin{array}[*pos*]{*cols*}            *rows*    \end{array}
\begin{tabular}[*pos*]{*cols*}          *rows*    \end{tabular}
\begin{tabular*}{*wdth*}[*pos*]{*cols*}  *rows*    \end{tabular*}

These environments produce a box (Section 6.4.3) consisting of a sequence of rows of items, aligned vertically in columns. The `array` environment can be used only in math mode, while `tabular` and `tabular*` can be used in any mode. Examples illustrating most of the features of these environments appear in Figure C.7.

*wdth* Specifies the width of the `tabular*` environment. There must be rubber space between columns that can stretch to fill out the specified width; see the \extracolsep command below.

*pos* Specifies the vertical positioning; the default is alignment on the center of the environment.

    t align on top row.

    b align on bottom row.

| GG&A Hoofed Stock | | |
| --- | --- | --- |

| Year | Price | | Comments |
| --- | --- | --- | --- |
|  | low | high |  |
| 1971 | 97–245 | | Bad year. |
| 72 | 245–245 | | Light trading due to a heavy winter. |
| 73 | 245–2001 | | No gnus was very good gnus this year. |

```
\begin{tabular}{|r||r@{--}l|p{1.25in}|}
\hline
\multicolumn{4}{|c|}{GG\&A Hoofed Stock}
   \\ \hline\hline
&\multicolumn{2}{c|}{Price}& \\ \cline{2-3}
\multicolumn{1}{|c||}{Year}
& \multicolumn{1}{r@{\,\vline\,}}{low}
& high & \multicolumn{1}{c|}{Comments}
   \\ \hline
1971 & 97 & 245 & Bad year.   \\ \hline
   72 & 245 & 245  & Light trading due to a
                      heavy winter.  \\ \hline
   73 &    245 & 2001 & No gnus was very
              good gnus this year. \\ \hline
\end{tabular}
```

◄──────── 65mm ────────►
Table

| 1.234 | centaur | rite::gauche |
| --- | --- | --- |
| 56.7 | scenter | wright::rad |
| 8.99 | cent | write::sinister |

```
\begin{tabular*}{65mm}{@{}r@{.}l%
    @{\extracolsep{\fill}}cr%
    @{\extracolsep{0pt}::}l@{}}
\multicolumn{5}{c}{\underline{Table}}   \\
   1&234 & centaur & rite   & gauche  \\
   56 & 7  & scenter & wright & rad      \\
   8&99  & cent    & write  & sinister
\end{tabular*}
```

Figure C.7: Examples of the `tabular` and `tabular*` environments.

*cols* Specifies the column formatting. It consists of a sequence of the following specifiers, corresponding to the sequence of columns and intercolumn material:

l A column of left-aligned items.

r A column of right-aligned items.

c A column of centered items.

| A vertical line the full height and depth of the environment.

@{*text*} This specifier is called an @-*expression*. It inserts *text* in every row, where *text* is processed in math mode in the **array** environment and in LR mode in the **tabular** and **tabular\*** environments. The *text* is considered a moving argument, so any fragile command within it must be \protect'ed.

An @-expression suppresses the space LaTeX normally inserts between columns; any desired space between the inserted text and the adjacent items must be included in *text*. To change the space between two columns from the default to *wd*, put an @{\hspace{*wd*}} command (Section 6.4.1) between the corresponding column specifiers.

An \extracolsep{*wd*} command in an @-expression causes an extra space of width *wd* to appear to the left of all subsequent columns, until countermanded by another \extracolsep command. (However, it will not put space to the left of the first column.) Unlike ordinary intercolumn space, this extra space is not suppressed by an @-expression. An \extracolsep command can be used only in an @-expression in the *cols* argument. It is most commonly used to insert a \fill space (Section 6.4.1) in a **tabular\*** environment.

p{*wd*} Produces a column with each item typeset in a parbox of width *wd*, as if it were the argument of a \parbox[t]{*wd*} command (Section 6.4.3). However, a \\ may not appear in the item, except in the following situations: (i) inside an environment like **minipage**, **array**, or **tabular**, (ii) inside an explicit \parbox, or (iii) in the scope of a \centering, \raggedright, or \raggedleft declaration. The latter declarations must appear inside braces or an environment when used in a p-column element.

\*{*num*}{*cols*} Equivalent to *num* copies of *cols*, where *num* is any positive integer and *cols* is any list of column-specifiers, which may contain another \*-expression.

An extra space, equal to half the default intercolumn space, is put before the first column unless *cols* begins with a | or @-expression, and after the last column unless *cols* ends with a | or @-expression. This space usually causes no problem, but is easily eliminated by putting an @{} at the beginning and end of *cols*.

*rows* A sequence of rows separated by \\ commands (Section C.1.6). Each row is a sequence of items separated by & characters; it should contain the same number of items as specified by the *cols* argument. Each item is processed as if it were enclosed in braces, so the scope of any declaration in an item lies within that item. The following commands may appear in an item:

> \multicolumn{*num*}{*col*}{*item*} Makes *item* the text of a single item spanning *num* columns, positioned as specified by *col*. If *num* is 1, then the command serves simply to override the item positioning specified by the environment argument. The *col* argument must contain exactly one l, r, or c and may contain one or more @-expressions and | characters. It replaces that part of the environment's *cols* argument corresponding to the *num* spanned columns, where the part corresponding to any column except the first begins with l, r, c, or p, so the *cols* argument |c|l@{:}lr has the four parts |c|, l@{:}, l, and r. A \multicolumn command must either begin the row or else immediately follow an &. It is fragile.

> \vline When used within an l, r, or c item, it produces a vertical line extending the full height and depth of its row. An \hfill command (Section 6.4.2) can be used to move the line to the edge of the column. A \vline command can also be used in an @-expression. It is robust.

The following commands can go between rows to produce horizontal lines. They must appear either before the first row or immediately after a \\ command. A horizontal line after the last row is produced by ending the row with a \\ followed by one of these commands. (This is the only case in which a \\ command appears after the last row of an environment.) These commands are fragile.

> \hline Draws a horizontal line extending the full width of the environment. Two \hline commands in succession leave a space between the lines; vertical rules produced by | characters in the *cols* argument do not appear in this space.

> \cline{*col*$_1$-*col*$_2$} Draws a horizontal line across columns *col*$_1$ through *col*$_2$. Two or more successive \cline commands draw their lines in the same vertical position. See the \multicolumn command above for how to determine what constitutes a column.

The following properties of these environments, although mentioned above, are often forgotten:

- These environments make a box; see Section 6.5 for environments and commands that can be used to position this box.

- The box made by these commands may have blank space before the first column and after the last column; this space can be removed with an @-expression.

- Any declaration in *rows* is within an item; its scope is contained within the item.

- An @-expression in *cols* suppresses the default intercolumn space.

**Style Parameters**

The following style parameters can be changed anywhere outside an `array` or `tabular` environment. They can also be changed locally within an item, but the scope of the change should be explicitly delimited by braces or an environment.

`\arraycolsep` Half the width of the default horizontal space between columns in an `array` environment.

`\tabcolsep` Half the width of the default horizontal space between columns in a `tabular` or `tabular*` environment.

`\arrayrulewidth` The width of the line created by a | in the *cols* argument or by an `\hline`, `\cline`, or `\vline` command.

`\doublerulesep` The width of the space between lines created by two successive | characters in the *cols* argument, or by two successive `\hline` commands.

`\arraystretch` Controls the spacing between rows. The normal interrow space is multiplied by `\arraystretch`, so changing it from its default value of 1 to 1.5 makes the rows 1.5 times farther apart. Its value is changed with `\renewcommand` (Section 9.4).

# C.11   Moving Information Around

## C.11.1   Files

LaTeX creates a number of ancillary files when processing a document. They all have the same first name as the root file (Section 4.4). These files are referred to, and listed below, by their extensions. A `\nofiles` command in the preamble prevents LaTeX from writing any of them except the `dvi` and `log` files. Knowing when and under what circumstances these files are read and written can help in locating and recovering from errors.

**aux** Used for cross-referencing and in compiling the table of contents, list of figures, and list of tables. In addition to the main `aux` file, a separate `aux` file is also written for each `\include`'d file (Section 4.4), having the same first name as that file. All `aux` files are read by the `\begin{document}` command. The `\begin{document}` command also starts writing the main `aux` file; writing of an `\include`'d file's `aux` file is begun by the `\include` command and is ended when the `\include`'d file has been completely processed. A `\nofiles` command suppresses the writing of all `aux` files.

The table of contents and cross-reference information in the `aux` files can be printed by running LaTeX on the file `lablst.tex`.

**bbl** This file is written by BibTeX, not by LaTeX, using information on the aux file. It is read by the `\bibliography` command.

**dvi** This file contains LaTeX's output, in a form that is independent of any particular printer. (This printer-independence may be lost when using the `graphics`, `color`, and `pict2e` packages; see the introduction to Chapter 7.) Another program must be run to print the information on the `dvi` file. The file is always written unless LaTeX has generated no printed output.

**glo** Contains the `\glossaryentry` commands generated by `\glossary` commands. The file is written only if there is a `\makeglossary` command and no `\nofiles` command.

**idx** Contains the `\indexentry` commands generated by `\index` commands. The file is written only if there is a `\makeindex` command and no `\nofiles` command.

**ind** This file is written by *MakeIndex*, not by LaTeX, using information on the `idx` file. It is read by the `\printindex` command. See Appendix A.

**lof** Read by the `\listoffigures` command to generate a list of figures; it contains the entries generated by all `\caption` commands in `figure` environments. The `lof` file is generated by the `\end{document}` command. It is written only if there is a `\listoffigures` command and no `\nofiles` command.

**log** Contains everything printed on the terminal when LaTeX is executed, plus additional information and some extra blank lines. It is always written. In some systems, this file has an extension other than `log`.

**lot** Read by the `\listoftables` command to generate a list of tables; it contains the entries generated by all `\caption` commands in `table` environments. The `lot` file is generated by the `\end{document}` command. It is written only if there is a `\listoftables` command and no `\nofiles` command.

toc Read by the \tableofcontents command to generate a table of contents; it contains the entries generated by all sectioning commands (except the *-forms). The toc file is generated by the \end{document} command. It is written only if there is a \tableofcontents command and no \nofiles command.

## C.11.2 Cross-References

\label   {*key*}
\ref     {*key*}
\pageref{*key*}

The *key* argument is any sequence of letters, digits, and punctuation symbols; upper- and lowercase letters are regarded as different. LaTeX maintains a *current* \ref *value*, which is set with the \refstepcounter declaration (Section C.8.4). (This declaration is issued by the sectioning commands, by numbered environments like equation, and by an \item command in an enumerate environment.) The \label command writes an entry on the aux file (Section C.11.1) containing *key*, the current \ref value, and the number of the current page. When this aux file entry is read by the \begin{document} command (the next time LaTeX is run on the same input file), the \ref value and page number are associated with *key*, causing a \ref{*key*} or \pageref{*key*} command to produce the associated \ref value or page number, respectively.

The \label command is fragile, but it can be used in the argument of a sectioning or \caption command.

## C.11.3 Bibliography and Citation

\bibliography{*bib_files*}

Used in conjunction with the BibTeX program (Section 4.3.1) to produce a bibliography. The *bib_files* argument is a list of first names of bibliographic database (bib) files, separated by commas, these files must have the extension bib. The \bibliography command does two things: (i) it creates an entry on the aux file (Section C.11.1) containing *bib_files* that is read by BibTeX, and (ii) it reads the bbl file (Section C.11.1) generated by BibTeX to produce the bibliography. (The bbl file will contain a thebibliography environment.) The database files are used by BibTeX to create the bbl file.

\begin{thebibliography}{*widest_label*}   *entries*   \end{thebibliography}

Produces a bibliography or source list. In the standard article document class, this source list is labeled "References"; in the report and book class, it is labeled "Bibliography". See Section 6.1.4 for information on how to create a document-class option to change the reference list's label.

*widest_label* Text that, when printed, is approximately as wide as the widest item label produced by the \bibitem commands in *entries*. It controls the formatting.

*entries* A list of entries, each begun by the command

> \bibitem[*label*]{*cite_key*}

which generates an entry labeled by *label*. If the *label* argument is missing, a number is generated as the label, using the enumiv counter. The *cite_key* is any sequence of letters, numbers, and punctuation symbols not containing a comma. This command writes an entry on the aux file (Section C.11.1) containing *cite_key* and the item's label. When this aux file entry is read by the \begin{document} command (the next time LaTeX is run on the same input file), the item's label is associated with *cite_key*, causing a reference to *cite_key* by a \cite command to produce the associated label.

### \cite[*text*]{*key_list*}

The *key_list* argument is a list of citation keys (see \bibitem above). This command generates an in-text citation to the references associated with the keys in *key_list* by entries on the aux file read by the \begin{document} command. It also writes *key_list* on the aux file, causing BibTeX to add the associated references to the bibliography(Section 4.3.1). If present, *text* is added as a remark to the citation. Fragile.

### \nocite{*key_list*}

Produces no text, but writes *key_list*, which is a list of one or more citation keys, on the aux file. This causes BibTeX to add the associated references to the bibliography (Section 4.3.1). A \nocite{*} command causes BibTeX to add all references from the bib files. The \nocite command must appear after the \begin{document}. It is fragile.

## C.11.4   Splitting the Input

### \input{*file_name*}

Causes the indicated file to be read and processed, exactly as if its contents had been inserted in the current file at that point. The *file_name* may be a complete file name with extension or just a first name, in which case the file *file_name*.tex is used. If the file cannot be found, an error occurs and LaTeX requests another file name.

`\include{`*file*`}`
`\includeonly{`*file_list*`}`

Used for the selective inclusion of files. The *file* argument is the first name of a
file, denoting the file *file*`.tex`, and *file_list* is a possibly empty list of first names
of files separated by commas. If *file* is one of the file names in *file_list* or if there
is no `\includeonly` command, then the `\include` command is equivalent to

> `\clearpage \input{`*file*`} \clearpage`

except that if file *file*`.tex` does not exist, then a warning message rather than an
error is produced. If *file* is not in *file_list*, the `\include` command is equivalent
to `\clearpage`.

The `\includeonly` command may appear only in the preamble; an `\include`
command may not appear in the preamble or in a file read by another `\include`
command. Both commands are fragile.

`\begin{filecontents}{`*nam*`}`    *body*    `\end{filecontents}`
`\begin{filecontents*}{`*nam*`}`    *body*    `\end{filecontents*}`

If a file named *nam* does not exist, then one is created having *body* as its contents.
If file *nam* already exists, then a warning message is printed and no file is
written. The `filecontents` environment writes helpful identifying comments
at the beginning of the file. These comments can cause problems if the file is used
as input to a program that, unlike LaTeX, does not treat lines beginning with
`%` as comments. The `filecontents*` environment does not add any comments.
These environments can appear only before the `\documentclass` command.

`\listfiles`

Causes LaTeX to print on the terminal a list of all files that it reads when
processing the document, excluding ancillary files that it wrote. The command
may appear only in the preamble.

## C.11.5   Index and Glossary

Appendix A describes how to make an index using the *MakeIndex* program.

### Producing an Index

`\begin{theindex}`    *text*    `\end{theindex}`

Produces a double-column index. Each entry is begun with either an `\item`
command, a `\subitem` command, or a `\subsubitem` command.

`\printindex`

Defined by the `makeidx` package. This command just reads the `ind` file.

### Compiling the Entries

\makeindex Causes the \indexentry entries produced by \index commands
to be written on the idx file, unless a \nofiles declaration occurs. The
\makeindex command may appear only in the preamble.

\makeglossary Causes the \glossaryentry entries produced by \glossary
commands to be written on the glo file, unless a \nofiles declaration
occurs. The \makeglossary command may appear only in the preamble.

\index{*str*} If an idx file is being written, then this command writes an
\indexentry{*str*}{*pg*} entry on it, where *pg* is the page number. The
*str* argument may contain any characters, including special characters,
but it must have no unmatched braces, where the braces in \{ and \} are
included in the brace matching. The \index command may not appear
inside another command's argument unless *str* contains only letters, digits,
and punctuation characters. The command is fragile.

\glossary{*str*} If a glo file is being written, then this command writes a
\glossaryentry{*str*}{*pg*} entry on it, where *str* and *pg* are the same
as in the \index command, described above. The \glossary command
may not appear inside another command's argument unless *str* contains
only letters, digits, and punctuation characters. The command is fragile.

## C.11.6   Terminal Input and Output

\typeout{*msg*}

Prints *msg* on the terminal and in the log file. Commands in *msg* that are
defined with \newcommand or \renewcommand are replaced by their definitions
before being printed. LaTeX commands in *msg* may produce strange results.
Preceding a command name by \protect causes that command name to be
printed.

TeX's usual rules for treating multiple spaces as a single space and ignoring
spaces after a command name apply to *msg*. A \space command in *msg* causes a
single space to be printed. The \typeout command is fragile; moreover, putting
it in the argument of another LaTeX command may do strange things. The *msg*
argument is a moving argument.

\typein[*cmd*]{*msg*}

Prints *msg* on the terminal, just like \typeout{*msg*}, and causes TeX to stop
and wait for you to type a line of input, ending with *return*. If the *cmd* argument
is missing, the typed input is processed as if it had been included in the input
file in place of the \typein command. If the *cmd* argument is present, it must
be a command name. This command name is then defined or redefined to be

the typed input. Thus, if *cmd* is not already defined, then the command acts like

> `\typeout{`*msg*`}`
> `\newcommand{`*cmd*`}{`*typed input*`}`

The `\typein` command is fragile; moreover, it may produce an error if it appears in the argument of a L^AT_EX command. The *msg* argument is a moving argument.

# C.12   Line and Page Breaking

## C.12.1   Line Breaking

`\linebreak   [`*num*`]`
`\nolinebreak[`*num*`]`

The `\linebreak` command encourages and `\nolinebreak` discourages a line break, by an amount depending upon *num*, which is a digit from 0 through 4. A larger value of *num* more strongly encourages or discourages the line break; the default is equivalent to a *num* argument of 4, which either forces or completely prevents a line break. An underfull `\hbox` message is produced if a `\linebreak` command results in too much space between words on the line. Both commands are fragile.

`\\ [`*len*`]`
`\\*[`*len*`]`
`\newline`

These commands start a new line without justifying the current one, producing a ragged-right effect. The optional argument of `\\` adds an extra vertical space of length *len* above the new line. The `*`-form inhibits a page break right before the new line. The `\newline` command may be used only in paragraph mode and should appear within a paragraph; it produces an underfull `\hbox` warning and extra vertical space if used at the end of a paragraph, and an error when used between paragraphs. The `\\` command behaves the same way when used in paragraph mode. Both commands are fragile.

`\-`

Permits the line to be hyphenated (the line broken and a hyphen inserted) at that point. It inhibits hyphenation at any other point in the current word except where allowed by another `\-` command. Robust.

`\hyphenation{`*words*`}`

Declares allowed hyphenation points, where *words* is a list of words, separated by spaces, in which each hyphenation point is indicated by a `-` character. It is a global declaration (Section C.1.4) and is robust.

```
\sloppy
\fussy
```

Declarations that control line breaking. The `\fussy` declaration, which is the default, prevents too much space between words, but leaves words extending past the right-hand margin if no good line break is found. The `\sloppy` declaration almost always breaks lines at the right-hand margin, but may leave too much space between words, in which case TEX produces an underfull `\hbox` warning. Line breaking is controlled by the declaration in effect at the blank line or `\par` command that ends the paragraph.

`\begin{sloppypar}` *pars* `\end{sloppypar}`

Typesets *pars*, which must consist of one or more complete paragraphs, with the `\sloppy` declaration in effect.

## C.12.2   Page Breaking

`\pagebreak`    [*num*]
`\nopagebreak`[*num*]

The `\pagebreak` command encourages and `\nopagebreak` discourages column breaking by an amount depending upon *num*, where the entire page is a single column in a one-column page style. The *num* argument is a digit from 0 through 4, a larger value more strongly encouraging or discouraging a break; the default is equivalent to *num* having the value 4, which forces or entirely forbids a break. When used within a paragraph, these commands apply to the point immediately following the line in which they appear. When `\flushbottom` is in effect (Section 6.1.1), an underfull `\vbox` message is produced if `\pagebreak` results in too little text on the page. A `\nopagebreak` command will have no effect if another LATEX command has explicitly allowed a page break to occur at that point. These commands have no effect when used in LR mode or inside a box. Both commands are fragile.

`\enlargethispage` {*len*}
`\enlargethispage*`{*len*}

These commands increase the height of the page that LATEX is currently trying to produce by *len*, which must be a rigid length and may be negative. The *-form shrinks the vertical space on the page as much as possible, which is what you want to do when trying to squeeze a little more onto a page than TEX wants to put there. For two-sided printing, it is usually best to make facing pages the same height. These commands are fragile.

```
\newpage
\clearpage
\cleardoublepage
```

When one-column pages are being produced, these commands all end the current paragraph and the current page. Any unfilled space in the body of the page (Section 6.1.2) appears at the bottom, even with \flushbottom in effect (Section 6.1.1). The \clearpage and \cleardoublepage commands also cause all figures and tables that have so far appeared in the input to be printed, using one or more pages of only figures and/or tables if necessary. In a two-sided printing style, \cleardoublepage also makes the next page a right-hand (odd-numbered) page, producing a blank page if necessary.

When two-column text is being produced, \newpage ends the current column rather than the current page; \clearpage and \cleardoublepage end the page, producing a blank right-hand column if necessary. These commands should be used only in paragraph mode; they should not be used inside a parbox (Section 6.4.3). The \newpage and \clearpage commands are robust; \cleardoublepage is fragile.

## C.13   Lengths, Spaces, and Boxes

### C.13.1   Length

**explicit lengths** An explicit length is written as an optional sign (+ or -) followed by a decimal number (a string of digits with an optional decimal point) followed by a *dimensional unit*. The following dimensional units are recognized by TEX:

> cm Centimeters.
>
> em One em is about the width of the letter $M$ in the current font.
>
> ex One ex is about the height of the letter $x$ in the current font.
>
> in Inches.
>
> pc Picas (1pc = 12pt).
>
> pt Points (1in = 72.27pt).
>
> mm Millimeters.

\fill A rubber length (Section 6.4.1) having a natural length of zero and the ability to stretch to any arbitrary (positive) length. Robust.

\stretch{*dec_num*} A rubber length having zero natural length and *dec_num* times the stretchability of \fill, where *dec_num* is a signed decimal number (an optional sign followed by a string of digits with an optional decimal point). Robust.

\newlength{*cmd*} Declares *cmd* to be a length command, where *cmd* is the name of a command not already defined. The value of *cmd* is initialized to zero inches. Fragile.

\setlength{*cmd*}{*len*} Sets the value of the length command *cmd* equal to *len*. Robust.

\addtolength{*cmd*}{*len*} Sets the value of the length command *cmd* equal to its current value plus *len*. Robust.

\settowidth {*cmd*}{*text*}
\settoheight{*cmd*}{*text*}
\settodepth {*cmd*}{*text*} Set the value of the length command *cmd* equal to the natural width, height, and depth, respectively, of the output generated when *text* is typeset in LR mode. Robust.

## C.13.2   Space

\hspace {*len*}
\hspace*{*len*}

Produce a horizontal space of width *len*. The space produced by \hspace is removed if it falls at a line break; that produced by \hspace* is not. These commands are robust.

\vspace {*len*}
\vspace*{*len*}

Add a vertical space of height *len*. If the command appears in the middle of a paragraph, then the space is added after the line containing it. The space produced by \vspace is removed if it falls at a page break; that produced by \vspace* is not. These commands may be used only in paragraph mode; they are fragile.

\bigskip
\medskip
\smallskip

These commands are equivalent to the three commands

        \vspace{\bigskipamount}        \vspace{\smallskipamount}
        \vspace{\medskipamount}

where the three length commands \bigskipamount, \medskipamount, and \smallskipamount are style parameters. These space-producing commands can be used in the definitions of environments to provide standard amounts of vertical space. They are fragile.

`\addvspace{`*len*`}`

This command normally adds a vertical space of height *len*. However, if vertical space has already been added to the same point in the output by a previous `\addvspace` command, then this command will not add more space than needed to make the natural length of the total vertical space equal to *len*. It is used to add the extra vertical space above and below most LATEX environments that start a new paragraph. It may be used only in paragraph mode between paragraphs—that is, after a blank line or `\par` command (in TEX's vertical mode). Fragile.

`\hfill`

Equivalent to `\hspace{\fill}`.

`\vfill`

Equivalent to a blank line followed by `\vspace{\fill}`; it should be used only in paragraph mode.

## C.13.3   Boxes

A *box* is an object that is treated by TEX as a single character, so it will not be broken across lines or pages.

`\mbox{`*text*`}`
`\makebox[`*wdth*`][`*pos*`]{`*text*`}`

Typesets *text* in LR mode in a box. The box has the width of the typeset text except for a `\makebox` command with a *wdth* argument, in which case it has width *wdth*. In the latter case, the position of the text within the box is determined by the one-letter *pos* argument as follows:

   l Flush against left edge of box.

   r Flush against right edge of box.

   s Interword space in *text* is stretched or shrunk to try to fill the box exactly.

The default positioning is centered in the box. The `\mbox` command is robust; `\makebox` is fragile.

`\fbox{`*text*`}`
`\framebox[`*wdth*`][`*pos*`]{`*text*`}`

Similar to `\mbox` and `\makebox`, except that a rectangular frame is drawn around the resulting box. The `\fbox` command is robust; `\framebox` is fragile.

\newsavebox{*cmd*}

Declares *cmd*, which must be a command name that is not already defined, to be a bin for saving boxes. Fragile.

\sbox{*cmd*}{*text*}
\savebox{*cmd*}[*wdth*][*pos*]{*text*}
\begin{lrbox}{*cmd*} *text* \end{lrbox}

Typeset *text* in a box just as for \makebox. However, instead of printing the resulting box, they save it in bin *cmd*, which must have been declared with \newsavebox. In the lrbox environment, spaces are removed from the beginning and end of *text*. The \sbox command is robust; \savebox is fragile.

\usebox{*cmd*}

Prints the box most recently saved in bin *cmd*. Robust.

\parbox                [*pos*]{*wdth*}{*text*}
\begin{minipage}[*pos*]{*wdth*}   *text*   \end{minipage}

They produce a *parbox*—a box of width *wdth* formed by typesetting *text* in paragraph mode. The vertical positioning of the box is specified by the one-letter *pos* argument as follows:

b The bottom line of the box is aligned with the current line of text.

t The top line of the box is aligned with the current line of text.

The default vertical positioning is to align the center of the box with the center of the current line of text.

The list-making environments listed in Section 6.6 and the tabular environment may appear in *text* with the minipage environment, but not with the \parbox command. (If *text* consists of only a tabbing environment, then the width of the resulting box is the actual width of the longest line rather than the *wdth* argument.) A \footnote or \footnotetext command appearing in *text* in a minipage environment produces a footnote at the bottom of the parbox ended by the next \end{minipage} command, which may be the wrong place for it when there are nested minipage environments. These footnote-making commands may not be used in the *text* argument of \parbox.

A minipage environment that begins with a displayed equation or with an eqnarray or eqnarray* environment will have extra vertical space at the top (except with the fleqn document-class option). This extra space can be removed by starting *text* with a \vspace{-\abovedisplayskip} command.

The \parbox command is fragile.

\rule[*raise_len*]{*wdth*}{*hght*}

Generates a solid rectangle of width *wdth* and height *hght*, raised a distance of *raise_len* above the bottom of the line. (A negative value of *raise_len* lowers it.) The default value of *raise_len* is zero inches. Fragile.

\raisebox{*raise_len*}[*hght*][*dpth*]{*text*}

Creates a box by typesetting *text* in LR mode, raising it by *raise_len*, and pretending that the resulting box extends a distance of *hght* above the bottom of the current line and a distance of *dpth* below it. If the *dpth* argument or both optional arguments are omitted, TEX uses the actual extent of the box. Fragile.

\width
\height
\depth
\totalheight

Length commands that can be used only in the *wdth* argument of \makebox, \framebox, and \savebox, and in the *raise_len*, *hght*, and *dpth* arguments of \raisebox. They refer to the dimensions (width, height, depth, and height + depth) of the box obtained by typesetting the *text* argument.

**Style Parameters**

\fboxrule The width of the lines forming the box produced by \fbox and \framebox. However, the version of \framebox used in the picture environment (Section 7.1) employs the same width lines as other picture commands.

\fboxsep The amount of space left between the edge of the box and its contents by \fbox and \framebox. It does not apply to the version of \framebox used in the picture environment (Section 7.1).

# C.14   Pictures and Color

## C.14.1   The picture Environment

A *coordinate* is a decimal number—an optional sign followed by a string of digits with an optional decimal point. It represents a length in multiples of \unitlength. All argument names in this section that begin with $x$ or $y$ are coordinates.

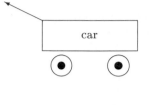

```
\newcounter{cms}
...
\setlength{\unitlength}{1mm}
\begin{picture}(50,39)
\put(0,7){\makebox(0,0)[bl]{cm}}
\multiput(10,7)(10,0){5}{\addtocounter
      {cms}{1}\makebox(0,0)[b]{\arabic{cms}}}
\put(15,20){\circle{6}}
\put(30,20){\circle{6}}
\put(15,20){\circle*{2}}
\put(30,20){\circle*{2}}
\put(10,24){\framebox(25,8){car}}
\put(10,32){\vector(-2,1){10}}
\multiput(1,0)(1,0){49}{\line(0,1){2.5}}
\multiput(5,0)(10,0){5}{\line(0,1){3.5}}
\thicklines
\put(0,0){\line(1,0){50}}
\multiput(0,0)(10,0){6}{\line(0,1){5}}
\end{picture}
```

Figure C.8: A sample `picture` environment.

`\begin{picture}`(*x_dimen*, *y_dimen*)(*x_offset*, *y_offset*)
   *pict_cmds*
`\end{picture}`

Creates a box of width *x_dimen* and height *y_dimen*, both of which must be non-negative. The (*x_offset*, *y_offset*) argument is optional. If present, it specifies the coordinates of the lower-left corner of the picture; if absent, the lower-left corner has coordinates $(0, 0)$. (Like all dimensions in the `picture` environment, the lengths specified by the arguments of the `picture` environment are given in multiples of `\unitlength`.) The `picture` environment can be used anywhere that ordinary text can, including within another `picture` environment.

The *pict_cmds* are processed in picture mode—a special form of LR mode—and may contain only declarations and the following commands:

   `\put`      `\multiput`      `\qbezier`      `\graphpaper`

Figure C.8 illustrates many of the picture-drawing commands described below.

### Picture-Mode Commands

The following are the only commands, other than declarations, that can be used in picture mode.

\put(*x_coord*,*y_coord*){*picture_object*}

Places *picture_object* in the picture with its reference point at the position specified by coordinates ($x\_coord$, $y\_coord$). The *picture_object* can be arbitrary text, which is typeset in LR mode, or else one of the special picture-object commands described below. The \put command is fragile.

\multiput(*x_coord*,*y_coord*)(*x_incr*,*y_incr*){*num*}{*picture_object*}

Places *num* copies of *picture_object*, the $i^{th}$ one positioned with its reference point having coordinates ($x\_coord + [i-1]x\_incr, y\_coord + [i-1]y\_incr$). The *picture_object* is the same as for the \put command above. It is typeset *num* times, so the copies need not be identical if it includes declarations. (See Figure C.8.) Fragile.

\qbezier[*num*](*x_coord*₁,*y_coord*₁)(*x_coord*₂,*y_coord*₂)(*x_coord*₃,*y_coord*₃)

Draws a quadratic Bezier curve whose control points are specified by the mandatory arguments (see Section 7.1.3). The *num* argument specifies the number of points plotted on the curve. If it is absent, a smooth curve is drawn, with the maximum number of points determined by the value of \qbeziermax. Use \renewcommand to change \qbeziermax:

        \renewcommand{\qbeziermax}{250}

(With the pict2e package, there is no limit to the number of points plotted.)

\graphpaper[*spcing*](*x_coord*,*y_coord*)(*x_dimen*,*y_dimen*)

Defined by the graphpap package. It draws a coordinate grid with origin at ($x\_coord$, $y\_coord$), extending *x_dimen* units to the right and *y_dimen* units up. Grid lines are spaced every *spcing* units; the default value is 10. All arguments must be integers.

## Picture Objects

\makebox  (*x_dimen*,*y_dimen*)[*pos*]{*text*}
\framebox(*x_dimen*,*y_dimen*)[*pos*]{*text*}
\dashbox {*dash_dimen*}(*x_dimen*,*y_dimen*)[*pos*]{*text*}

Produce a box having width *x_dimen* and height *y_dimen* (in multiples of \unitlength) with reference point at its lower-left corner. The *text* is typeset in LR mode, positioned in the box as specified by the one- or two-letter *pos* argument as follows:

l  Horizontally positioned flush against the left edge of the box.

r  Horizontally positioned flush against the right edge of the box.

t Vertically positioned flush against the top edge of the box.

b Vertically positioned flush against the bottom edge of the box.

The default horizontal and vertical positioning is to center *text* in the box. The \framebox command also draws a rectangle showing the edges of the box, and \dashbox draws the rectangle with dashed lines, composed of dashes and spaces of length *dash_dimen* (in multiples of \unitlength), where *dash_dimen* is a positive decimal number. For best results, *x_dimen* and *y_dimen* should be integral multiples of *dash_dimen*. The thickness of the lines drawn by \framebox and \dashbox equals the width of the lines produced by other picture commands; it is not determined by \fboxrule. All three commands are fragile.

\line    (*h_slope*, *v_slope*){*dimen*}
\vector(*h_slope*, *v_slope*){*dimen*}

Draw a line having its reference point at the beginning and its slope determined by (*h_slope*, *v_slope*), where *h_slope* and *v_slope* are positive or negative integers of magnitude at most 6 for \line and at most 4 for \vector, with no common divisors except ±1. (These restrictions are eliminated by the pict2e package.) In addition, \vector draws an arrowhead at the opposite end of the line from the reference point. The horizontal extent of the line is *dimen* (in multiples of \unitlength) unless *h_slope* is zero, in which case *dimen* is the (vertical) length of the line. However, a line that is neither horizontal nor vertical may not be drawn unless *dimen* times \unitlength is at least 10 points (1/7 inch). (This does not apply when the pict2e package is loaded.) The \vector command always draws the arrowhead. Both commands are fragile.

\shortstack[*pos*]{*col*}

The *pos* argument must be either l, r, or c, the default being equivalent to c. This command produces the same result as

        \begin{tabular}[b]{*pos*} *col* \end{tabular}

(Section 3.6.2) except that no space is left on either side of the resulting box and there is usually less interrow space. The reference point is at the left edge of the box, level with the reference point of the bottom line. Fragile.

\circle {*diam*}
\circle*{*diam*}

Draw a (hollow) circle and a disk (filled circle), respectively, with diameter as close as possible to *diam* times \unitlength and reference point in the center of the circle. The largest circle LaTeX can draw has a diameter of 40 points (about 1/2 inch) and the largest disk has a diameter of 15 points (about .2 inch). (With the pict2e package, any size circle or disk can be drawn.) Both commands are fragile.

\oval[*rad*](*x_dimen*,*y_dimen*)[*part*]

Draws an oval inscribed in a rectangle of width *x_dimen* and height *y_dimen*, its corners made with quarter circles of the largest possible radius less than or equal to *rad*. An explicit *rad* argument can be used only with the pict2e package; the default value is the radius of the largest quarter-circle LaTeX can draw without the pict2e package. The *part* argument consists of one or two of the following letters to specify a half or quarter oval: l (left), r (right), t (top), b (bottom). The default is to draw the entire oval. The reference point is the center of the (complete) oval. Fragile.

\frame{*picture_object*}

Puts a rectangular frame around *picture_object*. The reference point is the bottom left corner of the frame. No extra space is put between the frame and *picture_object*. Fragile.

## Picture Declarations

The following declarations can appear anywhere in the document, including in picture mode. They obey the normal scope rules.

\savebox{*cmd*}(*x_dimen*,*y_dimen*)[*pos*]{*text*}

Same as the corresponding \makebox command, except the resulting box is saved in the bin *cmd*, which must be defined with \newsavebox (Section 6.4.3). Fragile.

\thinlines
\thicklines

They select one of the two standard thicknesses of lines and circles in the picture environment. The default is \thinlines. Robust.

\linethickness{*len*}

Declares the thickness of lines in a picture environment to be *len*, which must be a positive length. With the pict2e package, it applies to all lines; otherwise, it applies only to horizontal and vertical lines and does not affect the thickness of slanted lines and circles, or of the quarter circles drawn by \oval to form the corners of an oval.

## C.14.2  The graphics Package

The following commands are provided by the graphics package. They are all fragile. This package requires special support from the device driver.

`\scalebox{`*h_scale*`}[`*v_scale*`]{`*text*`}`

Produces a box by typesetting *text* in LR mode and scaling it horizontally by a factor of *h_scale* and vertically by a factor of *v_scale*. The default value of *v_scale* is *h_scale*.

`\resizebox  {`*wdth*`}{`*ht*`}{`*text*`}`
`\resizebox*{`*wdth*`}{`*ht*`}{`*text*`}`

Produce a box of width *wdth* and height *ht* by typesetting *text* in LR mode and scaling it horizontally and vertically to fit. In the ∗-form, *ht* specifies the height + depth. If either argument is !, then the corresponding dimension is the one that maintains the aspect ratio of *text*.

`\rotatebox{`*ang*`}{`*text*`}`

Produces a box formed by typesetting *text* in LR mode and rotating it counterclockwise through an angle of *ang* degrees. The box is the smallest one containing the rotated box; its reference point is at the same height as that of the rotated box.

`\reflectbox{`*text*`}`

Produces a box by typesetting *text* in LR mode and reflecting it about a vertical line.

`\includegraphics  [`$x\_len_1$`,`$y\_len_1$`][`$x\_len_2$`,`$y\_len_2$`]{`*file_name*`}`
`\includegraphics*[`$x\_len_1$`,`$y\_len_1$`][`$x\_len_2$`,`$y\_len_2$`]{`*file_name*`}`

Produces a box containing the graphic material in the file named *file_name*. With no optional arguments, the reference point and size of the box are specified by the file. The optional arguments specify a box of width $x\_len_2 - x\_len_1$ and height $y\_len_2 - y\_len_1$ whose reference point is shifted a distance of $x\_len_1$ to the right and $y\_len_1$ up from the lower-left corner of the contents of the file. Specifying only one optional argument is the same as giving a first optional argument of [0pt,0pt]. The ∗-form clips the material by removing everything outside the specified box; the normal form does not.

## C.14.3  The `color` Package

The following commands are provided by the `color` package. They are all fragile. This package requires special support from the device driver.

`\definecolor{`*clr*`}{`*mdl*`}{`*val*`}`

Defines *clr*, which may be any sequence of letters and numbers, to be the name of the color specified by the color model *mdl* and color value *val*. LaTeX's standard color models are:

gray A color value is a number from 0 to 1 that specifies a shade of gray, where 0 is black.

rgb   A color value is a list of three numbers from 0 to 1, separated by commas, that describe intensities of red, green, and blue light.

cmyk A color value is a list of four numbers from 0 to 1, separated by commas, that specify amounts of cyan, magenta, yellow, and black ink.

Other color models may also be supported. The package predefines the following color names: black, white, red, green, blue, yellow, cyan, and magenta. All other color names must be defined before they are used.

\color{*clr*}

Declares *clr* to be the current text color. It obeys the normal scoping rules.

\textcolor{*clr*}{*text*}

Equivalent to {\color{*clr*} *text*}.

\colorbox{*bkgd_clr*}{*text*}

Produces a box by typesetting *text* in LR mode on a background of color *bkgd_clr*. The box includes a border of width \fboxsep.

\fcolorbox{*line_clr*}{*bkgd_clr*}{*text*}

Like \colorbox, except it also puts a line of width \fboxrule and color *line_clr* around the box.

\pagecolor{*clr*}

Declares *clr* to be the page's background color. It is a global declaration.

# C.15  Font Selection

A font is a size and style of type. A text font is selected by specifying the size and style. There are also special symbol fonts that are selected implicitly by math-mode commands. It is possible to select a font that is not available, in which case LaTeX types a warning and substitutes a similar font.

## C.15.1  Changing the Type Style

A type style is specified by three separate components: shape, series, and family. Changing one component does not affect the others. These components are changed by the following declarations, which obey the normal scope rules:

| | | | |
|---|---|---|---|
| \mdseries | Medium Series | \upshape | Upright Shape |
| \bfseries | **Boldface Series** | \itshape | *Italic Shape* |
| \rmfamily | Roman Family | \slshape | *Slanted Shape* |
| \sffamily | Sans Serif Family | \scshape | SMALL CAPS SHAPE |
| \ttfamily | Typewriter Family | \normalfont | Normal Style |

The \normalfont declaration sets series, family, and shape to that of the document's main text font. These declarations may not be used in math mode.

Each of these declarations has a corresponding command \text...{*text*} that typesets *text* in the scope of the declaration. The commands and their corresponding declarations are:

| | | | |
|---|---|---|---|
| \textmd{*text*} | \mdseries | \textup{*text*} | \upshape |
| \textbf{*text*} | \bfseries | \textit{*text*} | \itshape |
| \textrm{*text*} | \rmfamily | \textsl{*text*} | \slshape |
| \textsf{*text*} | \sffamily | \textsc{*text*} | \scshape |
| \texttt{*text*} | \ttfamily | \textnormal{*text*} | \normalfont |

When the commands are used in math mode, the *text* argument is processed in LR mode.

These commands and declarations are robust. Words typeset in typewriter style are not hyphenated except where permitted by \- commands.

## C.15.2    Changing the Type Size

The following declarations select a type size, but leave the type style unaffected. They are listed in nondecreasing size; in some document-class options, two different size declarations may have the same effect.

| | | | |
|---|---|---|---|
| \tiny | \small | \large | \huge |
| \scriptsize | \normalsize | \Large | \Huge |
| \footnotesize | | \LARGE | |

These commands may not be used in math mode; they are all fragile.

## C.15.3    Special Symbols

Special symbols can be obtained from special fonts. The LaTeX *Companion* explains how to get LaTeX to use such a font.

\symbol{*num*}

Chooses the symbol with number *num* from the current font. Octal (base 8) and hexadecimal (base 16) numbers are preceded by ' and ", respectively. Robust.

# APPENDIX D
# What's New

This appendix lists most of the differences between LaTeX 2.09, the original version of LaTeX, and the current version, LaTeX 2$_\varepsilon$.

## Document Styles and Style Options

Documents prepared for LaTeX 2$_\varepsilon$ begin with a \documentclass command (Section 2.2.2). LaTeX 2$_\varepsilon$ realizes it is processing a LaTeX 2.09 input file and enters *compatibility mode* when it encounters a LaTeX 2.09 \documentstyle command. Most LaTeX 2.09 input files will work with LaTeX 2$_\varepsilon$. However, an error may occur if LaTeX 2$_\varepsilon$ reads an auxiliary file produced by LaTeX 2.09, so it's a good idea to delete such files before running LaTeX 2$_\varepsilon$.

The document styles of LaTeX 2.09 have become document classes. SliTeX has been eliminated; slides are produced using the slides document class. Standard document-style options that controlled formatting, such as twoside, have become document-class options, and are specified as optional arguments to the \documentclass command. Other document-style options have become packages, loaded with the \usepackage command (Section 2.2.2). Most nonstandard document-style options will work as LaTeX 2$_\varepsilon$ packages.

## Type Styles and Sizes

The LaTeX 2.09 commands for changing type style, such as \tt, will still work more or less the same as before. The major difference is that \sc and \sl can no longer be used in math mode (except when LaTeX 2$_\varepsilon$ is in compatibility mode). However, instead of using these commands, you should switch to the more rational commands described in Sections 3.1 and 3.3.8 for changing type style. The new commands treat the different aspects of type style separately—for example, allowing you easily to specify bold sans serif type. The commands for changing type size are the same, but they no longer change the type style (except in compatibility mode). The \boldmath command now works better (Section 3.3.8). A few mathematical symbols now require the latexsym package—see Tables 3.4–3.7.

## Pictures and Color

The picture environment has been enhanced by the addition of the \qbezier command for drawing curves (Section 7.1.3). The pict2e package also removes many restrictions on picture environment commands, such as limitations on the slopes of lines and arrows. The graphics package allows you to insert pictures produced by other programs (Section 7.2). It also defines commands for scaling and rotating text and pictures. The color package defines commands for producing colored text (Section 7.3).

## Other New Features

You can now define a command or environment that has an optional argument. The \ensuremath command is useful for defining a command that can appear in or out of math mode. See Section 3.4.

Control of the placement of floats (figures and tables) has been enhanced with a new float-location option ! that encourages LaTeX to print the float as soon as possible, and with the \suppressfloats command to prevent additional floats on the current page.

When sending your document electronically, you can bundle other files along with your input file using the filecontents environment (Section 4.7).

Analogs of the \settowidth command have been added for determining the dimensions of text other than the width (Section 6.4.1). In the length arguments of various box-making commands, it is now possible to refer to the dimensions of the text argument using commands such as \width (Section C.13.3).

The ifthen package defines commands for writing simple programs (Section C.8.5).

The \enlargethispage command has been added to help in correcting bad page breaks (Section 6.2.2). The \samepage command still works, but is now of little use.

A few commands and options have been added to the book document class (Section 5.1).

# APPENDIX E

# Using Plain TEX Commands

LaTeX is implemented as a TeX "macro package"—a series of predefined TeX commands. Plain TeX is the standard version of TeX, consisting of "raw" TeX plus the `plain` macro package. You can use Plain TeX commands to do some things that you can't with standard LaTeX commands. However, before using Plain TeX, check the LaTeX *Companion* to see if there is a package that does what you want.

Most Plain TeX commands can be used in LaTeX, but only with care. LaTeX is designed so its commands fit together as a single system. Many compromises have been made to ensure that a command will work properly when used in any reasonable way with other LaTeX commands. A LaTeX command may not work properly when used with Plain TeX commands not described in this book.

There is no easy way to tell whether a Plain TeX command will cause trouble, except by trying it. A general rule is not to combine a LaTeX command or environment with Plain TeX commands that might modify parameters it uses. For example, don't use a Plain TeX command such as `\hangindent` that modifies TeX's paragraph-making parameters inside one of LaTeX's list-making environments.

You should not modify any parameters that are used by LaTeX's `\output` routine, except as specified in this book. In particular, you should forget about most of Chapter 15 of *The TEXbook*. However, LaTeX does obey all of TeX's conventions for the allocation of registers, so you can define your own counts, boxes, etc., with ordinary TeX commands.

Listed below are all the Plain TeX commands whose definitions have been eliminated or changed in LaTeX. Not listed are LaTeX commands that approximate the corresponding Plain TeX versions, and some "internal" commands whose names contain @ characters.

### Tabbing Commands

The following commands are made obsolete by LaTeX's `tabbing` environment:

| | | | |
|---|---|---|---|
| `\tabs` | `\tabsdone` | `\settabs` | `\+` |
| `\tabset` | `\cleartabs` | `\tabalign` | |

### Output, Footnotes, and Figures

The following commands that require Plain TeX's output routine are obsolete. They have been replaced by LaTeX's footnote-making commands and its `figure` and `table` environments.

| | | | |
|---|---|---|---|
| `\pageno` | `\nopagenumbers` | `\makeheadline` | `\topins` |
| `\headline` | `\advancepageno` | `\makefootline` | `\topinsert` |
| `\footline` | `\pagebody` | `\dosupereject` | `\midinsert` |
| `\normalbottom` | `\plainoutput` | `\footstrut` | `\pageinsert` |
| `\folio` | `\pagecontents` | `\vfootnote` | `\endinsert` |

## Font-Selecting Commands

The following Plain TEX commands are not defined in LaTeX:

| | | |
|---|---|---|
| \fivei | \fivebf | \sevensy |
| \fiverm | \seveni | \teni |
| \fivesy | \sevenbf | \oldstyle |

## Aligned Equations

The following Plain TEX commands have been made obsolete by the `eqnarray` and `eqnarray*` environments:

| | | |
|---|---|---|
| \eqalign | \eqalignno | \leqalignno |

## Miscellaneous

Plain TEX's `$$` does not work properly; it has been replaced by the LaTeX commands `\[` and `\]`. Plain TEX's `\beginsection` command has been replaced by LaTeX's sectioning commands; its `\end` and `\bye` commands have been replaced by `\end{document}`. The Plain TEX commands `\centering` and `\line` have had their names usurped by LaTeX commands, and the syntax of the `\input` command has been changed to conform to LaTeX conventions. Most functions performed by Plain TEX's `\line` command can be achieved by the `center`, `flushleft`, and `flushright` environments. The `\magnification` command of Plain TEX has no counterpart in LaTeX. Magnification of the output can often be done by the program that prints the `dvi` file.

# Bibliography

[1] Theodore M. Bernstein. *The Careful Writer: A Modern Guide to English Usage.* Atheneum, New York, 1965.

[2] *The Chicago Manual of Style.* University of Chicago Press, fourteenth edition, 1993.

[3] Michel Goossens, Frank Mittelbach, and Alexander Samarin. *The LaTeX Companion.* Addison-Wesley, Reading, Massachusetts, 1994.

[4] Donald E. Knuth. *The TeXbook.* Addison-Wesley, Reading, Massachusetts, 1994.

[5] N. E. Steenrod, P. R. Halmos, M. M. Schiffer, and J. A. Dieudonné. *How to Write Mathematics.* American Mathematical Society, London, 1983.

[6] William Strunk, Jr. and E. B. White. *The Elements of Style.* Macmillan, New York, third edition, 1979.

[7] Mary-Claire van Leunen. *A Handbook for Scholars.* Oxford University Press, New York, Oxford, revised edition, 1992.

[8] *Words Into Type.* Prentice-Hall, Englewood Cliffs, New Jersey, third edition, 1974.

# Index

␣ (space character), 13, 32
  ignored in math mode, 36, 50
  in LR mode, 36
  printing, 64
\␣ (interword space), 14, 16, 32, 33, 51,
    170
  used with \thanks, 181
# (hash mark), 12, 32, 166
  in definition, 54, 56, 192, 193
  misplaced, 141, 145
  printing, 15, 171
\# (#), 15, 39, 171
$ (dollar sign), 12, 32, 166
  delimiting formula, 18, 33, 39, 187
  delimits scope of declaration, 168
  missing, 142
  not fragile, 22
  printing, 15, 171
  unmatched, 141
\$ ($), 15, 39, 171
$$ (TeX command), 233
% (percent sign), 12, 19, 32, 166
  for ending line without adding space,
    33, 109
  in \index argument, 154
  printing, 15, 171
\% (%), 15, 39, 171
& (ampersand), 12, 32, 166
  in array or tabular environment, 45,
    206
  misplaced, 141
  printing, 15, 171
  too many in row, 141
\& (&), 15, 39, 171
~ (tilde), 12, 17, 32, 33, 166, 170
  used with \ref and \pageref, 68
\~ (~ accent), 38

_ (underscore), 12, 32, 166
  for subscript, 18, 33, 40, 189
  printing, 15, 171
\_ (_), 15, 39, 171
^ (circumflex), 12, 32, 166
  for superscript, 18, 33, 40, 189
\^ (^ accent), 38
\ (backslash), 12, 16, 32, 166
\\ (new line), 25–26, 34, 169–170, 213
  [ after, 26
  * after, 167
  after last row of array or tabular,
    62, 206
  bad use of, 147
  between paragraphs, 139
  in \address argument, 84
  in array environment, 45, 169
  in \author argument, 169
  in center environment, 111, 169
  in eqnarray environment, 47, 169
  in flushleft environment, 169
  in flushright environment, 169
  in p column of array or tabular, 205
  in paragraph mode, 96, 213
  in \shortstack argument, 169
  in \signature argument, 84
  in tabbing environment, 61, 169, 202
  in tabular environment, 62, 169
  in \title argument, 181
  in verse environment, 169, 184
  is fragile, 33
  missing, 141
  optional argument of, 167
  two in a row, 169
\\* (new line), see \\
{ (left brace), 12, 32
  enclosing argument, 33, 166

## Index Order

␣ (space)
#
$
%
&
~ (tilde)
_ (underscore)
^ (circumflex)
\ (backslash)
{
}
. (period)
: (colon)
; (semicolon)
, (comma)
?
!
' (left quote)
' (right quote)
(
)
[
]
– (dash)
/ (slash)
*
@
+
=
| (vertical line)
<
>
" (double quote)
0 ... 1
A a B ... z

237

**Index Order**

␣ (space)
#
$
%
&
~ (tilde)
_ (underscore)
^ (circumflex)
\ (backslash)
{
}
. (period)
: (colon)
; (semicolon)
, (comma)
?
!
' (left quote)
' (right quote)
(
)
[
]
– (dash)
/ (slash)
*
@
+
=
| (vertical line)
<
>
" (double quote)
0 ... 1
A a B ... z

in `bib` file, 158
in `\index` argument, 75
missing, 142
printing, 15, 171
scope delimited by, 27–28
\{ ({), 15, 39, 47, 171
in `bib` file, 156
in `\index` argument, 212
} (right brace), 12, 32
enclosing argument, 33, 166
in `bib` file, 158
in `\index` argument, 75
missing, 142
printing, 15, 171
scope delimited by, 27–28, 168
unmatched, 141
\} (}), 15, 39, 47, 171
in `bib` file, 156
in `\index` argument, 212
. (period), 12, 32, 33
invisible delimiter, 47
..., *see* ellipsis
\. (˙ accent), 38
: (colon), 12, 32
\: (medium space), 51, 191
; (semicolon), 12, 32
\; (thick space), 51, 191
, (comma), 12, 32
not allowed in citation key, 69
\, (thin space), 14, 33, 51, 170, 191
? (question mark), 12, 32, 33
in error message, 29
?' (¿), 39
¿From, 32
! (exclamation point), 12, 32, 33
in error message, 29
in `figure` or `table` argument, 197
in `\index` argument, 152
in `\resizebox` argument, 129, 224
!' (¡), 39
\! (negative thin space), 51, 191
!h float specifier changed, 146
' (left quote), 12, 13, 32, 33, 170
\' (` accent or tabbing command), 38,
    203
in parbox, 203

' (right quote), 12, 13, 32, 33, 170
in formula, 18, 189
period before, 15
specifying octal number, 226
\' (´ accent or tabbing command), 38,
    203
in parbox, 203
( (left parenthesis), 12, 32
delimiter, 47
in terminal output, 134
\( (begin formula), 18, 33, 39, 187
in `ifthen` package expression, 196
in math mode error, 136
is fragile, 22, 33
) (right parenthesis), 12, 32
delimiter, 47
in terminal output, 134
period before, 15
\) (end formula), 18, 33, 187
delimits scope of declaration, 168
in `ifthen` package expression, 196
is fragile, 22, 33
not in math mode error, 136
[ (left bracket), 12, 32, 33, 166
ambiguous, 25
delimiter, 47
printed on terminal, 135
\[ (begin displayed formula), 26, 34, 39,
    188
in math mode error, 136
is fragile, 33
] (right bracket), 12, 32, 33, 166
ambiguous, 25
delimiter, 47
delimiting optional argument, 168
in `\item` argument, 167
printed on terminal, 135
\] (end displayed formula), 26, 34, 39,
    188
delimits scope of declaration, 168
is fragile, 33
not in math mode error, 136
- (dash or minus), 12, 14, 32, 33, 170
in overfull `\hbox` message, 93
space around, 48
unary, 48
-- (number-range dash), 14, 33, 170

--- (punctuation dash), 14, 33, 170
\- (hyphenation or tabbing command),
        93, 202, 213
    error in, 140
    in parbox, 203
    in `tabbing` environment, 203
    instead of \hyphenation, 143
    needed in typewriter style, 226
/ (slash), 12, 32
    delimiter, 47
    quotient symbol, 40, 51
* (asterisk), 12, 32, 167
    acts like optional argument, 26
    after command name, 26
    argument to \nocite, 70
    in `array` or `tabular` argument, 205
    written on terminal, 30
*-expression, 205
*-form
    of command, 26, 33, 167
    of environment, 167
    of sectioning command, 174
@ (at sign), 12, 32
    command name with, 91, 166
    in \index argument, 153
    regarded as letter in `sty` file, 91
\@, 14, 33, 170
@-expression, 205
    error in, 145
    fragile command in, 168
    missing, 138
\@array, 145
\@chapter, 92
\@makechapterhead, 92
\@schapter, 92
@string, 159
+ (plus), 12, 32
    space around, 48
    unary, 48
\+ (tabbing command), 202
    error in, 140
    in Plain TeX, 232
= (equals), 12, 32
    in `bib` file, 156
    in `ifthen` package expression, 195
    in \lengthtest expression, 196

\= (¯ accent or tabbing command), 38,
        61, 201, 202
    in parbox, 203
    too many, 139
| (vertical line), 12, 32
    delimiter, 47
    in `array` or `tabular` argument, 62, 205
|| in `array` or `tabular` argument, 207
< (less than), 12, 32
    in `ifthen` package expression, 195
    in \lengthtest expression, 196
\< (tabbing command), 202
    error in, 140
> (greater than), 12, 32
    in `ifthen` package expression, 195
    in \lengthtest expression, 196
\> (tabbing command), 61, 201, 202
    error in, 140
" (double quote), 12
    in `bib` file, 156
    in index entry, 154
    specifying hexadecimal number, 226
\" (¨ accent), 38

0 (zero), 12
    incorrect use as length, 99, 141
1 (one), 12
10pt document-class option, 177
11pt document-class option, 19, 115, 177
12pt document-class option, 19, 115, 177
2.09, 2
$2\varepsilon$, 2

\a` (` accent in `tabbing` environment),
        203
\a' (´ accent in `tabbing` environment),
        203
\a= (¯ accent in `tabbing` environment),
        203
A4 paper size, 177
a4paper document-class option, 177
A5 paper size, 177
a5paper document-class option, 177
\AA (Å), 39
\aa (å), 39
abbreviation, 14
    in `bib` file, 158–159

**Index Order**

⊔   (space)
#
$
%
&
~   (tilde)
_   (underscore)
^   (circumflex)
\   (backslash)
{
}
.   (period)
:   (colon)
;   (semicolon)
,   (comma)
?
!
`   (left quote)
'   (right quote)
(
)
[
]
–   (dash)
/   (slash)
*
@
+
=
|   (vertical line)
<
>
"   (double quote)
0 ... 1
A a B ... z

**abbrv** bibliography style, 70
\abovedisplayshortskip, 189
\abovedisplayskip, 188
abstract, 90, 181–183
    not in **book** document class, 183
    on separate page, 88, 177
**abstract** environment, 90, 183
    effect of **titlepage** option, 88
accent, 38
    dotless i and j for, 38, 50, 190
    in **bib** file, 158
    in **tabbing** environment, 203
    math mode, 49–50, 190
    not available in typewriter style, 38
    wide math, 49
acknowledgment of support, 181
\acute (´ math accent), 50
\addcontentsline, 175
    argument too long, 143
    moving argument of, 168
**address** field (in **bib** file), 162
\address, 84
\addtime, 83
\addtocontents, 67, 176
    argument too long, 143
    moving argument of, 168
\addtocounter, 98, 194
    error in, 138
    \protect not used in argument of, 168
    scope of, 98, 168
\addtolength, 101, 216
\addvspace, 217
\advancepageno (TEX command), 232
\AE (Æ), 39
\ae (æ), 39
\aleph (ℵ), 43
aligning
    formulas on left, 88, 177
    in columns, 60–63, 201–207
alignment tab error, 141
**alltt** environment, 187
**alltt** package, 178, 187
\Alph, 98, 195
\alph, 98, 195
**alpha** bibliography style, 70
\alpha ($\alpha$), 41
alphabetic page numbers, 180

\amalg (⨿), 42
ambiguous [ or ], 25
American Mathematical Society, 52
ampersand, *see* &
**amstex** package, 52, 178
**and** separating names in **bib** file field, 158
\and, 21, 34, 181
    in **ifthen** package expression, 196
and others, 158
\angle (∠), 43
**annote** field (in **bib** file), 162
apostrophe, 14, 170
appendix, 22, 175
\appendix, 22, 175
\approx (≈), 43
arabic page numbers, 89, 180
\arabic, 98, 195
\arccos (arccos), 44
\arcsin (arcsin), 44
\arctan (arctan), 44
\arg (arg), 44
argument (of command), 16, 33, 166–167
    braces enclosing, 33, 55, 166
    coordinate pair as, 119
    mandatory, 166
    missing, 142
        in **thebibliography** environment, 138
    moving, *see* moving argument
    of picture command, 119
    omitted, 141
    optional, *see* optional argument
    positioning, 205, 217–218, 221–222
    processed multiple times, 110
    scope of declaration in, 27, 168
    \verb in, 140
array, 45–46
**array** environment, 45–46, 204–207
    \\ in, 45, 169
    box made by, 103
    error in, 137, 138, 141, 145
    extra space around, 205
    illegal character in argument, 137
    interrow space in, 169
    large, 143
    making symbol with, 42

scope of declaration in, 45

strut in, 169

versus **tabular**, 46, 60, 62

\arraycolsep, 207

\arrayrulewidth, 207

\arraystretch, 207

arrow

accent, *see* \vec

in formula, 53

in margin, 59

in picture, 123, 222

symbols, 43

zero-length, 123

arrowhead, 123

**article** bibliography entry type, 161

**article** document class, 19, 176

appendix in, 175

\chapter not defined in, 21, 174

default page style, 89

**thebibliography** environment in, 209

used in examples, 21

ASCII file, 144

assumption, 56

\ast (∗), 42

\asymp (≍), 43

at sign, *see* @

author, 20

**author** field (in **bib** file), 162

author's address in title, 181

\author, 20, 34, 181

\\ in argument, 169

missing, 146

authors, multiple, 21

aux file, 208

entry generated by \label, 209

entry written by \cite and \nocite,
210

error when reading, 135, 138

auxiliary file, error reading, 135, 228

axiom, 56

b (bottom)

float specifier, 197

oval-part argument, 124, 223

positioning argument, 46, 105, 121,
218, 222

\b ( ̲ accent), 38

B5 paper size, 177

b5paper document-class option, 177

babel package, 38, 94, 178

back matter (of a book), 80

\backmatter, 80

backslash, 12, 10, 32, 100

\backslash (\), 43, 47

backspace, 51, 101

bar over a symbol, 49

\bar ( ̄ math accent), 50

\baselineskip, 100, 172

\baselinestretch, 172

\batchmode, 30

bbl file, 71, 156, 208

read by \bibliography, 209

\begin, 23, 167

delimits scope of declaration, 27–28

is fragile, 22, 33

of nonexistent environment, 137

unmatched, 136

\begin{document}, 19, 170

aux file read by, 208

error while processing, 135

extra, 136

missing, 138

\beginsection (TeX command), 233

\belowdisplayshortskip, 189

\belowdisplayskip, 189

\beta (β), 41

Bezier curve, 125–126, 221

\bfseries, 37, 226

bib file, 70, 155–164

abbreviations in, 158–159

entry, 156

keeping data in, 161

specified by \bibliography, 156, 209

\bibindent, 178

\bibitem, 71, 210

moving argument of, 72, 168

bibliographic database, *see* bib file

bibliography, 69–72, 209–210

open format, 71, 177

produced by thebibliography
environment, 209

style, 70–71

\bibliography, 70, 209

bbl file read by, 208

specifies `bib` files, 156
\bibliographystyle, 70
BIBTEX, 69–71, 155–164
   `bbl` file written by, 208
   producing bibliography with, 209
big delimiter, 46
\bigcap ($\bigcap$), 44
\bigcirc ($\bigcirc$), 42
\bigcup ($\bigcup$), 44
\bigodot ($\bigodot$), 44
\bigoplus ($\bigoplus$), 44
\bigotimes ($\bigotimes$), 44
\bigskip, 216
\bigskipamount, 216
\bigsqcup ($\bigsqcup$), 44
\bigtriangledown ($\bigtriangledown$), 42
\bigtriangleup ($\bigtriangleup$), 42
\biguplus ($\biguplus$), 44
\bigvee ($\bigvee$), 44
\bigwedge ($\bigwedge$), 44
black, 132, 225
blank line, 13, 33
   above or below environment, 23
   before displayed formula, 26
   in formula, 142, 171
   in input, 166
   in sectioning command, 171
   \par equivalent to, 171
   paragraph-ending, 95, 166, 171
blank page, 97
   made by \cleardoublepage, 215
   with `titlepage` environment, 180
blob of ink, rectangular, 106
blue, 132, 225
\bmod, 44, 190
body, page, 89, 179
   height of, 100
boldface type series, 37, 226
   in math mode, 51, 191
\boldmath, 51, 191
   font warning caused by, 52, 145
book, 80
`book` bibliography entry type, 161
`book` document class, 80, 176
   appendix in, 175
   no abstract in, 183
   `thebibliography` environment in, 209

`booklet` bibliography entry type, 161
`booktitle` field (in `bib` file), 162
boolean register, 196
\boolean, 196
\bot ($\bot$), 43
bottom of line, 107
\bottomfraction, 200
`bottomnumber` counter, 199
\bowtie ($\bowtie$), 43
box, 103–108, 217
   dashed, 121, 222
   declaration local to, 103
   dimensions of, 103
   displaying, 104
   framed, 104, 217
      in `picture` environment, 222
   in formula, 103
   LR, 103–104, 107
   rule, 103, 106
   saving, 107, 127, 218
   typeset in paragraph mode, 104
   with specified width, 104
   zero-width, 121
\Box ($\Box$), 43
boxes, 217–219
   formatting with, 108–111
brace, curly, 12
   enclosing command argument, 33, 55, 166
   error caused by unbalanced, 136
   horizontal, 49
   in `bib` file, 158
   in \index argument, 75, 153
   missing, 142
   removed from first argument of \newcommand, 92
bracket, square, 12
   enclosing optional argument, 20, 166
   mistaken for optional argument, 142
   printed on terminal, 135
break, line, 93–96, 213–214
   interword space without, 17, 170
   permitting, 95
   preventing, 17, 95, 171
   with \\, 26
break, page, 96–97, 214–215
   bad, 147

in `tabbing` environment, 60
\breve (˘ math accent), 50
Brinch Hansen, Per, 157
buffer size, 143
bug, LaTeX, 139
\bullet (•), 42
Bush, George, 24
\bye (TEX command), 233

c (center) positioning argument, 45, 205
\c (˛ accent), 38
calligraphic letter, 42
calligraphic type style, 51, 191
\cap (∩), 42
capacity exceeded, 142–144
caps, small, 37, 226
caption
   cross-reference to, 68
   figure or table, 58
   multiple, 59
\caption, 58, 198
   argument too long, 143
   fragile command in, 135
   in parbox, 199
   \label in argument, 209
   list of figures or tables entry, 175, 208
   moving argument of, 58, 168
   precedes \label, 68
case of letters
   in command name, 16, 32
   in key, 68, 69
catching errors with text editor, 32
\cc, 85
\cdot (·), 42
\cdots ( ), 40, 180
`center` environment, 111
   \\ in, 111, 169
   as displayed paragraph, 183
   as list, 112
   displaying a box with, 104
   in title page, 90
   `tabular` environment in, 63
center line of formula, 46
centered
   array column, 45
   ellipsis, 40, 189
centering a figure or table, 112
\centering, 112

in p column, 205
   TEX command, 233
centimeter (cm), 99, 215
chapter, in separate file, 74
chapter counter, 97
chapter field (in bib file), 163
\chapter, 21, 174
   changes current page style, 89
   in front and back matter of a book, 80
   not in `article` document class, 174
   uses \clearpage, 97
character
   code, 116
   control, 144
   end of line, 12
   illegal, in `array` or `tabular`, 137
   input, 32
   invalid, 144
   invisible, 12, 32
   nonprinting, 144
   punctuation, 12, 32
      in key, 68
   space, *see* space character
   special, *see* special character
\check (˘ math accent), 50
`chgsam.tex` file, 9
\chi (χ), 41
\circ (○), 42
circle, 124, 222
\circle, 124, 222
\circle*, 124, 222
circular reference, 263
citation, 69–72, 209–210
   key, 69, 71, 156
   undefined, 145, 147
\cite, 69, 210
   wrong number printed by, 146
class, document, 19–20
   nonexistent, 137
`classes.dtx` file, 92
\cleardoublepage, 97, 215
   figures and tables output by, 198
\clearpage, 97, 215
   checking capacity exceeded error, 143
   figures and tables output by, 198
   used by \chapter, 97
   used by \include, 97

used by \onecolumn, 181
used by \twocolumn, 180
\cleartabs (TEX command), 232
\cline, 62, 206
clipping, 224
clock document-class option, 83
\closing, 85
cls (class) file, missing, 137
\clubsuit (♣), 43
cm (centimeter), 99, 215
cmyk color model, 132, 225
code, character, 116
colon, *see* :
color, 131–132
    background, 132
    model, 132, 224
        undefined, 140
    undefined, 140
    value, 224
color package, 131–132, 178, 224–225
\color, 131, 225
\colorbox, 132, 225
column
    aligning text in, 60–63, 201–207
    of text in picture, 123
\columnsep, 178
\columnseprule, 178
\columnwidth, 171
comma (,), 12, 32
    not allowed in citation key, 69
command, 32–33, 166–170
    *-form of, 26, 33, 167
    adding to table of contents, etc., 176
    argument, *see* argument
    definition, 7, 53–55, 192
        # in, 54
        in preamble, 55
        space character in, 54
        with optional argument, 192
        with \typein, 212
    environment made from, 108
    form, 166
    fragile, 22, 25, 26, 33, 167–168
        in @-expression, 168
    invisible, 169
    length, 99
        defining, 101

not preceded by \protect, 168
name, 16, 32, 166–167
    * after, 26
    already used error, 137
    beginning with \end, 55
    case of letters in, 16, 32
    correcting misspelled, 144
    ending with space or end of line, 16
    misspelled, 31
    one-character, 166
    with @, 91, 166
names, too many, 143, 144
nested too deeply, 144
nesting, 16
parameter, 54, 192
picture, argument of, 119
Plain TEX, 231–233
preloaded, 91
printing on terminal, 212
redefining, 55
robust, 22, 167
sectioning, *see* sectioning command
spacing, 170
text-generating, 15
with two optional arguments, 166
commas, ellipsis between, 40
comment, 19, 166
    printed on terminal, 76
common errors, 31
compatibility mode, 228
compressed bibliography style, 71
Computer Modern font, 115
computer program, formatting, 60
concept index, 150
concepts versus notation, 31
\cong (≅), 43
conjecture, 56
contents, table of, 66–67, 175–176
    adding commands to, 67
control character, 144
control sequence error, 142, 144
coordinate, 118, 219
    geometry, 118
    grid, 126–127
    local, 129
    pair, 118
        as argument, 119

\coprod ($\coprod$), 44
copy editing, double-spacing for, 172
\copyright (©), 39, 173
corner, rounded, 124–125
\cos (cos), 44
\cosh (cosh), 44
\cot (cot), 44
\coth (coth), 44
counter, 97–99
  command, error in, 144
  created by \newtheorem, 97
  creating a new, 99
  for theorem-like environment, 97, 193
  list, 114
  reset by \stepcounter and
    \refstepcounter, 194
  too large, 137
  value of, 98, 194
cross-reference, 66–69, 209
  in bib file, 159–160
  in index, 152
  information, printing, 208
  labels, too many, 143, 144
  to page number, 68
  use of aux file for, 208
crossref field (in bib file), 163
\csc (csc), 44
\cup (∪), 42
curly brace, see brace, curly
curve, Bezier, 125–126, 221
customizing style, 91–93
cyan, 132, 225

\d ( accent), 38
\dag (†), 39, 173
\dagger (†), 42
dash, 14, 33, 170
  intraword, 14, 170
  number-range, 14
  punctuation, 14
\dashbox, 121, 221
dashed box, 121, 222
\dashv (⊣), 43
data, keeping in bib file, 161
database, bibliographic, see bib file
date, 20
  generating with \today, 15, 171
  in title, 20
  in title page, 90
  on letter, 86
\date, 20, 34, 181
  \\ in, 169
\dblfloatpagefraction, 200
\dblfloatsep, 200
\dbltextfloatsep, 200
\dbltopfraction, 200
dbltopnumber counter, 200
\ddag (‡), 39, 173
\ddagger (‡), 42
\ddot ( ¨math accent), 50
\ddots ( ⋰), 41, 189
declaration, 27–28, 33, 168
  color, 131, 225
  global, 168
  local to a box, 103
  picture, 223
  scope of, see scope
  type-size changing, 115
declarations, file of, 73
\def (TeX command), 92, 93
default
  argument, 166
  page style, 179
  type size, 115
\definecolor, 132, 224
defined, multiply, 146
definition
  command, see command
  environment, see environment
  recursive, 54
  use doesn't match, 145
\deg (deg), 44
delimiter, 46–47, 190
  bad, 136
  unmatched math mode, 141
\Delta (Δ), 41
\delta (δ), 41
depth
  changing apparent, 107
  of a box, 103
\depth, 219
description environment, 24–25, 34,
    184
  as list, 112

item label overprinting text in, 184
used for glossary, 76
design
  logical, 7
  typographic, 91
  visual, 7, 88
designer, typographic, 5
\det (det), 44
  subscript of, 190
determinant, 45
device driver, 118
device-independent file, *see* dvi file
diacritical mark, *see* accent
diagonal ellipsis, 40, 189
\Diamond (◇), 43
\diamond (◇), 42
\diamondsuit (◇), 43
dictionary, exception, 143
differential, 50
digit, 12, 32
\dim (dim), 44
dimen (TeX term), 100
dimensional unit, 215
disk (filled circle), 124, 222
diskette, sending document on, 77
display math style, 52, 188, 191
displayed
  formula, 26, 34, 39
    blank line before, 26
    math style for, 52, 191
    multiline, 47–49
    numbered, 39
    space above and below, 107, 183,
      188, 189, 218
  paragraph, 183–187
  quotation, 23, 34
  text, 23–26
displaying a box, 104
displaymath environment, 26, 34, 39,
  188
  anomalous vertical space after, 183
  displaying a box with, 104
  size of symbols in, 42
\displaystyle, 52, 191
distance, *see* length
\div (÷), 42

document
  class, 19–20, 176–178
    nonexistent, 137
  multilanguage, 38
  non-English, 38
  structure of, 170
  style (LaTeX 2.09), 228
document environment, 34
document-class option, 19, 88, 176
  unused, 147
document-style option (LaTeX 2.09), 228
\documentclass, 19, 34, 170, 176–178
  in \input file, 73
  missing, 144
  unused option, 147
\documentstyle (LaTeX 2.09 command),
  228
\dosupereject (TeX command), 232
\dot (˙ math accent), 50
\doteq (≐), 43
\dotfill, 102
dotless i and j, 38, 50, 190
dots, space-filling, 102
double quote, 13, 170
double spacing, 172
double sub- or superscript error, 140, 141
double-column, *see* two-column
\doublerulesep, 207
\Downarrow (⇓), 43, 47
\downarrow (↓), 43, 47
draft document-class option, 93, 177
draft package option, 131
drawing curves, 125–126
drawing pictures, 118–129
driver, device, 118
dtx file, 92
dvi (device-independent) file, 6, 208
  page written to, 135

e-mail
  sending document by, 77
  sending file by, 32
editing, copy, double-spacing for, 172
edition field (in bib file), 163
editor field (in bib file), 163
11pt document-class option, 19
eleven-point type, 19, 115

\ell (ℓ), 43
ellipsis, 15, 33, 40–41, 189
em (unit of length), 99, 215
\em, 27
\emph (emphasis), 16, 33, 171
  in slides, 81
emphasis, 16, 33, 171
empty \mbox, 97
empty page style, 89, 179
  for title page, 90
\emptyset (∅), 43
\encl, 85
end of line
  character, 12
  ending command name with, 16
  space character at, 19
end of paragraph, 13, 166, 171
end of sentence, 13
end of word, 13
\end, 23, 167
  delimits scope of declaration, 27–28, 168
  is fragile, 22, 33
  TeX command, 233
  unmatched, 136
\end{document}, 19, 170
  error while processing, 135, 143
  figures and tables output by, 198
  lof file written by, 208
  lot file written by, 208
  missing, 30
  toc file written by, 209
\end{verbatim}, no space allowed in, 64
\end..., defining, 55
\endinsert (TeX command), 232
\enlargethispage, 214
\enlargethispage*, 96, 214
\ensuremath, 53, 187
enter key, 12
entry
  bib file, 156
  field, bibliography, 156, 160–164
  index, 75
  type, bibliography, 156, 160–162
enumerate environment, 24–25, 34, 184
  as list, 112

counters, 97
  suppressing advance of, 185
cross-reference to item number, 68
enumerated list, long, 137
enumi ... enumiv counters, 97, 184
environment, 23, 33, 167
  *-form of, 167
  \begin of nonexistent, 137
  blank line above or below, 23
  defining in terms of a command, 108
  definition, 55–56, 192–193
    with optional argument, 193
  invisible, 169
  list-making, 24–25, 112–115
  made from declaration, 27, 33
  math mode, 187–189
  nested too deeply, 144
  paragraph-making, 183–187
  parameter, 56, 193
  redefining, 56
  theorem-like, 56–57, 193–194
    as displayed paragraph, 183
    cross-reference to, 68
  undefined, 137
\epsilon (ε), 41
\eqalign (TeX command), 233
\eqalignno (TeX command), 233
eqnarray environment, 47, 188
  \\ in, 169
  anomalous vertical space after, 184
  cross-reference to equation number, 68
  formula numbers in, 88
  in leqno document-class option, 177
  space between rows in, 188
  too many columns, 139
eqnarray* environment, 48, 188
\equal, 195
equation counter, 97, 188
equation environment, 26, 34, 39, 188
  anomalous vertical space after, 184
  cross-reference to number, 68
  formula numbers in, 88
  in leqno document-class option, 177
\equiv (≡), 43
error, 133–147
  catching with text editor, 32
  common, 31

finding, 134–136
    in cross-referencing file, 66
    indicator, 29, 134
    LaTeX versus TeX, 29
    locator, 29, 134, 135
    message, 29–30
        LaTeX, 136–140
        *MakeIndex*, 154
        TeX, 140–145
    outputting, 135
    TeX versus LaTeX, 29
    typographic, 91
`errsam.tex` file, 28
et al., 158
`\eta` ($\eta$), 41
`\evensidemargin`, 181, 182
`ex` (unit of length), 99, 215
exception dictionary, 143
exclamation point, *see* !
executive paper size, 177
`executivepaper` document-class option, 177
`\exists` ($\exists$), 43
`\exp` (exp), 44
extension, file, 12
`\extracolsep`, 205

face example, 108–110
`\face`, 108–110
family of type, 36, *see* type
fat, making things, 129
`\fbox`, 104, 125, 217
    width of line, 219
`\fboxrule`, 219
    not used in picture commands, 222
    used by `\fcolorbox`, 225
`\fboxsep`, 219
    used by `\colorbox`, 225
`\fcolorbox`, 132, 225
field, bibliography entry, 156, 160–164
figure, 58–59, 197–200
    centering, 112
    in two-column format, 197
    placement of, *see* float
    too tall, 145
    vertical space in, 58
`figure` counter, 97

`figure` environment, 58–59, 197
    in parbox, 138
    misplaced, 138
    parbox made by, 104
    space around, 169
    too many, 139
`figure*` environment, 197
figures, list of, 67, 175–176
    generated from `lof` file, 208
file, 207–209
    ASCII, 144
    auxiliary, error when reading, 135, 228
    bibliographic database, *see* `bib` file
    chapter in separate, 74
    cross-referencing, 66
    device-independent, *see* `dvi` file
    extension, 12
    `\include`'d, 73
    input, *see* input
    inserting, 72
    name, 12
    needs format error, 139
    nonexistent, 137, 141
    not found error, 137
    of declarations, 73
    prepended, 170
    root, 72
    sample input, 2, 8
    sending by e-mail, 32
    text, 12, 144
`filecontents` environment, 77, 170, 211
`filecontents*` environment, 211
files, listing ones used, 77
files, multiple input, 72–74
`\fill`, 100, 102, 215
    in `tabular*` environment, 205
`final` document-class option, 177
`final` package option, 131
finding an error, 134–136
first name of file, 12
first page, right head for, 180
`\fivebf` (TeX command), 233
`\fivei` (TeX command), 233
`\fiverm` (TeX command), 233
`\fivesy` (TeX command), 233
`\flat` ($\flat$), 43

`fleqn` document-class option, 88, 177, 188, 189
  indentation in, 178, 188
float, 58–59, 199
  page, 199
    made by `\clearpage`, 97
  placement of, 59, 197
  specifier, 197
  too tall, 145
`\floatpagefraction`, 200
floats, too many, 139
`\floatsep`, 200
floppy disk, *see* diskette
flush left
  array column, 45
  text, 111
flush right
  array column, 45
  text, 111
  in `tabbing` environment, 203
`\flushbottom`, 88
  bad page break with, 96
  ignored by `\newpage`, 97
  `\parskip` value for, 172
  space between paragraphs, 100
`flushleft` environment, 111
  `\\` in, 169
  as displayed paragraph, 183
  as list, 112
`flushright` environment, 111
  `\\` in, 169
  as displayed paragraph, 183
  as list, 112
`\fnsymbol`, 195
`\folio` (TeX command), 232
font, 115–116, 225–226
  Computer Modern, 115
  for slides, 81
  length dependent on, 99
  selecting in Plain TeX, 233
  shape not available, 145, 146
  special, 116
  warning caused by `\boldmath`, 52, 145
foot, page, 89, 179
`\footline` (TeX command), 232
footnote, 17, 172–173
  colors in, when split across pages, 132

  example of difficult, 173
  in `minipage` environment, 105, 218
  in parbox, 105
  line above, 173
  mark, 172
  symbols, 195
    too many, 137
  type size in, 116
`footnote` counter, 97
  for `minipage` environment, 97
`\footnote`, 17, 33, 172
  in `minipage` environment, 105, 218
  is fragile, 22, 33
`\footnotemark`, 172
  for footnote in parbox, 105
`\footnoterule`, 173
`\footnotesep`, 173
`\footnotesize`, 115, 226
`\footnotetext`, 173
  for footnote in parbox, 105
  in `minipage` environment, 218
`\footskip`, 182
`\footstrut` (TeX command), 232
`\forall` ($\forall$), 43
foreign language, *see* non-English language
forests, preserving, 6
form, command, 166
format
  open bibliography, 177
  this file needs, 139
  two-column, 20, 59, 88, 180, 197
formatting the input file, 31
formatting, visual, 64
  for slides, 81
formula, math, 18, 33, 39–53, 187–191
  aligning on left, 88, 177
  arrow in, 53
  blank line not allowed in, 142, 171
  bold subformula of, 52
  box in, 103
  center line of, 46
  changing type size in, 116
  complicated, 52
  delimiter in, 190
  displayed, *see* displayed formula

formatting with `picture` environment, 52

lines in, 53

logical structure of, 50

`\mbox` in, 38, 39

multiline, 47–49

number on left, 177

numbered, 39

overprinting of number, 188

space character in, 18, 50

space in, 50–51

splitting across lines, 188

using `graphics` package for, 53

vertical space in, 106

visual formatting of, 49, 52

`\frac`, 40, 189

fraction, 40, 189

fragile command, 22, 25, 26, 33, 167–168

in @-expression, 168

in moving argument, 135

protecting, 22

`\frame`, 125, 223

`\framebox`, 104, 125, 217

in `picture` environment, 120, 221

use of `\width`, `\height`, `\depth`, and `\totalheight` in, 219

width of line, 219

framed box, 104, 217

in `picture` environment, 222

framing, 125

`\frenchspacing`, 171

From␣, line beginning with, 32

¿From, 32

front matter (of a book), 80

`\frontmatter`, 80

`\frown` ($\frown$), 43

function, log-like, 44–45, 190

`\fussy`, 95, 214

galley, 135

`\Gamma` ($\Gamma$), 41

`\gamma` ($\gamma$), 41

`\gcd` (gcd), 44

subscript of, 190

geometric transformation, 129

geometry, coordinate, 118

`\geq` ($\geq$), 43

`\gg` ($\gg$), 43

Gilkerson, Ellen, iii, xv, 130

`glo` (glossary) file, 75, 208

suppressed by `\nofiles`, 212

written by `\makeglossary`, 212

global declaration, 168

global option, unused, 147

glossary, 74–76, 211–212

`\glossary`, 75, 212

glo file entry written by, 208

space around, 169

too many on page, 143

`\glossaryentry`, 75, 208, 212

gnomonly, 93

gnu, 37

Goossens, Michel, xv, 2

Gordon, Peter, xvi

graphic, determining size of, 137

`graphics` package, 129–131, 178, 223–224

making figures with, 58

making formulas with, 53

graphics, unknown extension, 140

`graphpap` package, 126, 178, 221

`\graphpaper`, 126–127, 221

`\grave` (` math accent), 50

`gray` color model, 132, 225

Greek letter, 41

green, 132, 225

grid, coordinate, 126–127

h float specifier, 197

changed, 146

`\H` (″ accent), 38

half oval, 124

hash size, 143

`\hat` (^ math accent), 50

`\hbar` ($\hbar$), 43

`\hbox`, overfull, 30, 93, 147

marked with `draft` option, 93

`\hbox`, underfull, 95, 147

head, of arrow, 123

head, page, 89, 179

in two-sided printing, 89

set by sectioning command, 22, 90, 174

`\headheight`, 182

heading, *see* head
**headings** page style, 89, 179, 180
\headline (TEX command), 232
\headsep, 182
\heartsuit (♡), 43
height
   changing apparent, 107
   of a box, 103
   of page body, 100, 214
\height, 219
Helvetica, *see* sans serif type family
hexadecimal character code, 116
\hfill, 102, 217
   in marginal note, 59
   positioning item label with, 114
   used with \vline, 206
\hline, 62, 206
\hom (hom), 44
\hookleftarrow (↩), 43
\hookrightarrow (↪), 43
horizontal
   brace, 49
   line
      drawn with \rule, 106
      in **array** or **tabular** environment, 62, 206
      space-filling, 102
   mode, 36
   positioning of text, 121
   space, 101
      around **array** or **tabular** environment, 205
      in formula, 51, 191
**howpublished** field (in **bib** file), 163
\hrulefill, 102
\hspace, 101, 216
   rubber length in, 102
\hspace*, 102, 216
\Huge, 115, 226
\huge, 115, 226
hyphen, 14
   inserted by TEX, 17
hyphenation, 93
   correcting error in, 94
   of non-English words, 94
   permitting with \-, 213
   suppressed in typewriter style, 226

\hyphenation, 94, 213
   \- instead of, 143
   error in, 142
   exceeding capacity with, 143
   scope of, 168

i, dotless (for accents), 38, 43, 50, 190
\i (ı), 38
**idx** (index) file, 74, 150, 208
   suppressed by \nofiles, 212
   written by \makeindex, 212
**ifthen** package, 178, 195–196
\ifthenelse, 195
ignored bibliography field, 161
ignoring input, 19
illegal
   character in array argument, 137
   parameter number, 141
   unit of measure, 141
\Im (ℑ), 43
\imath (ı), 43, 50, 190
**in** (inch), 99, 215
\in (∈), 43
in-text formula, 39
**inbook** bibliography entry type, 161
inch (**in**), 99, 215
\include, 73, 211
   cannot be nested, 137
   numbering with, 74
   of nonexistent file, 137
   sending files read by, 77
   uses \clearpage, 97
\include'd file, 73
   \newcounter in, 138
\includegraphics, 130, 224
   cannot determine size of error, 137
\includegraphics*, 224
\includeonly, 73, 211
   entered from terminal, 76
   entering arguments with \typein, 74
   misplaced, 136
**incollection** bibliography entry type, 161
**ind** file, 150, 208
   read by \printindex, 211
\indent, 171
indentation, in **fleqn** option, 178

indentation, paragraph, *see* paragraph

index, 30, 74–76, 150–154, 211–212

\index, 74, 212

    curly brace in argument, 75

    idx file entry written by, 208

    in command argument, 153

    space around, 169

    special character in argument, 75

    too many on page, 143

\indexentry, 75, 212

    on idx file, 208

\indexspace, 75

indicator, error, 29, 134

\inf (inf), 44

    subscript of, 190

infinite loop, 252

infinitely stretchable length, 100, 102, 215

information, moving, 65–77, 207–209

\infty ($\infty$), 43

ink, rectangular blob of, 106

**inproceedings** bibliography entry type, 161

input

    character, 32

    file, 12

        displaying logical structure, 53

        formatting, 31

        page of, 13

    files, multiple, 72–74

        finding error in, 134

    from terminal, 76–77, 212–213

    ignoring, 19

    processing part of, 73–74

    sample, 2, 8

\input, 72, 210

    braces missing from argument, 141

    differs from Plain TeX version, 233

    of nonexistent file, 137

    sending files read by, 77

inserting a file, 72

**institution** field (in bib file), 163

\int ($\int$), 44, 51

integral sign, space around, 51

interaction, 76–77

intercolumn space, 178

    in **array** or **tabular** environment, 205

interrow space

    in **array** or **tabular** environment, 169, 207

    in **eqnarray** environment, 188

    in \shortstack, 124

interword space, 14, 170

    before or after \hspace command, 101

    in math mode, 51

    produced by invisible command, 169

    too much with \sloppy, 214

    without line break, 17, 170

\intextsep, 200

intraword dash, 14, 170

invalid character error, 144

invisible

    character, 12, 32

    command, 169

    delimiter, 47

    environment, 169

    term made with \mbox, 48

    text, 82, 97

\iota ($\iota$), 41

\isodd, 196

italic type shape, 16, 37, 226

    in math mode, 51, 191

    used for emphasis, 171

\item, 24–25, 34, 184

    [ following, 25

    in index, 211

    in **theindex** environment, 75

    in **trivlist** environment, 115

    is fragile, 33

    lonely, 137

    missing, 138

    optional argument of, 25, 167

    outside list environment, 137

    \ref value set by, 209

item, label, 24–25, 184

    extra-wide, 114

    positioning with \hfill, 114

\itemindent, 113, 186

    in **trivlist** environment, 115

**itemize** environment, 24–25, 34, 184

    as list, 112

    default labels of, 184

\itemsep, 113, 185

\itshape, 37, 226

j, dotless (for accents), 38, 43, 50, 190
\j (ȷ), 38
\jmath (ȷ), 43, 50, 190
\Join (⋈), 43
\jot, 188
journal field (in bib file), 163
Jr., 157
justifying lines, 95, 100

\kappa (κ), 41
\ker (ker), 44
Kernighan, Brian, 7
key
    citation, 69, 71, 156
    cross-reference, 67
    enter, 12
    return, 12
key field (in bib file), 162, 163
keyboard, see terminal
keys, listing, 69
\kill, 61, 202
Knuth, Donald Ervin, xvi, 5, 115

l (left)
    oval-part argument, 124, 223
    positioning argument, 45, 217, 221
        in array or tabular argument, 205
        of \makebox, 104, 121
        of \shortstack, 124
l (letter el), 12
\L (Ł), 39
\l (ł), 39
label
    item, 24–25, 184
        extra-wide, 114
        positioning with \hfill, 114
    mailing, 86
    multiply-defined, 146
    produced by \cite, 210
    source, 69
\label, 67, 209
    in \caption argument, 209
    in eqnarray environment, 188
    in figure or table environment, 68
    missing, 146
    preceded by \caption, 68
    similar to \bibitem, 71

space around, 169
labelitemi ... labelitemiv counters,
    184
labels may have changed warning, 146
labels, cross-reference, too many, 143,
    144
\labelsep, 113, 186
\labelwidth, 113, 186
    in trivlist environment, 115
lablst.tex file, 69, 208
\Lambda (Λ), 41
\lambda (λ), 41
Lamport, Jason, 131
Lamport, Leslie, 131
landscape document-class option, 177
landscape printing, 177
\langle (⟨), 47
language, non-English, 38, 94
\LARGE, 115, 226
\Large, 115, 226
\large, 115, 226
LaTeX
    bug, 139
    distinguished from TeX, 5
    error message, 136–140
    error versus TeX error, 29
    logo, 5, 15, 33, 171
    pronunciation of, 5
    running on part of document, 31,
        73–74
    running unattended, 30
    stopping, 30, 136
    version, 2
    warning message, 135, 145–147
LaTeX Companion, The, 2
\LaTeX, 15, 33, 171
LaTeX 2.09 versus LaTeX 2ε, 2, 228–229
LaTeX 2ε, xv, 2, 118, 132
latexsym package, 42, 178
law (mathematical), 56
\lceil (⌈), 47
\ldots, 15, 33
\ldots (...), 40, 189
\leadsto (⇝), 43
leaving math mode, 36
left margin, prevailing, 201
left_margin_tab, 201

\left, 47, 190
left, flush, *see* flush
left-hand page, 179
left-to-right mode, *see* LR mode
\Leftarrow ($\Leftarrow$), 43
\leftarrow ($\leftarrow$), 43
\lefteqn, 48, 188
\lefteye, 109
\leftharpoondown ($\leftharpoondown$), 43
\leftharpoonup ($\leftharpoonup$), 43
\leftmargin, 113, 185
  in trivlist environment, 115
\leftmargini ... \leftmarginvi, 185
\Leftrightarrow ($\Leftrightarrow$), 43
\leftrightarrow ($\leftrightarrow$), 43
legal paper size, 177
legalpaper document-class option, 177
lemma, 56
length, 99–101, 215–216
  command, 99
    defining, 101
    not preceded by \protect, 168
  font-dependent, 99
  infinitely stretchable, 100, 215
  natural, 100
  of line in picture, 122
  parameter, 100
  rigid, 100
  rubber, 100
    in \hspace or \vspace, 102
    in \lengthtest expression, 196
    infinitely stretchable, 102
  unit (in picture environment), 118
  unit of, 215
  zero, 99
\lengthtest, 196
\leq ($\leq$), 43
\leqalignno (TeX command), 233
leqno document-class option, 88, 177,
    188
letter, 32
  case of, 68, 69
  for mailing, 84–86
  Greek, 41
  lowercase, 12
  not a, 142
  script, 42

uppercase, 12
letter document class, 84–86, 176
  \parskip in, 100
letter environment
  moving argument of, 168
letter environment, 85
letter paper size, 177
letterpaper document-class option, 177
level number of sectional unit, 176
\lfloor ($\lfloor$), 47
\lg (lg), 44
\lhd ($\lhd$), 42
\lim (lim), 44
  subscript of, 190
\liminf (lim inf), 44
  subscript of, 190
\limsup (lim sup), 44
  subscript of, 190
line
  blank, *see* blank line
  bottom of, 107
  break, *see* break, line
  horizontal, *see* horizontal
  in formula, 53
  in picture, 122–123
    thickness of, 118
  justifying, 95, 100
  none to end error, 139
  slanted, minimum size of, 123
  space at beginning or end of, 102
  vertical, *see* vertical
  width, *see* width
\line, 122, 222
  error in, 136
  TeX command, 233
\linebreak, 95, 213
  optional argument of, 167
  space around, 169
  warning caused by, 147
lines, distance between, 100
\linethickness, 223
\linewidth, 171
lining up, *see* aligning
list, 24–25, 34
  counter, defining, 114
  long enumerated, 137
  margins of nested, 114

of figures or tables, 67, 175–176, 208
  adding an entry, 175
  adding commands to, 67, 176
  error in, 135
  source, 70
`list` environment, 112–114, 185
  style parameters for, 185
list-making environment, 24–25, 112–115
  defining, 114
  in parbox, 105, 218
  nested too deeply, 139
  primitive, 112
`\listfiles`, 77, 211
listing keys, 69
`\listoffigures`, 67, 175–176
  error when processing, 143
  `lof` file read by, 208
`\listoftables`, 67, 175–176
  error when processing, 143
  `lot` file read by, 208
`\listparindent`, 113, 185
`\ll` (≪), 43
`\ln` (ln), 44
local coordinates, 129
Local Guide, 2, 6, 8, 12, 20, 28, 30, 69,
      71, 77, 86, 88, 91–93, 115, 116,
      118, 124, 132, 136, 139, 140, 151,
      156, 159, 163, 178
locator, error, 29, 134, 135
`lof` (list of figures) file, 67, 175, 208
  editing, 67
  error in, 135
`log` file, 28, 76, 208
`\log` (log), 44, 51
log-like function, 44, 45, 190
logical design, 7
logical structure, 6, 88
  displaying in input file, 53
  of formula, 50
  repeated, 53
logo, LaTeX, 5, 15, 33, 171
logo, TeX, 5, 15, 33, 171
lonely `\item`, 137
`\Longleftarrow` (⇐=), 43
`\longleftarrow` (⟵), 43
`\Longleftrightarrow` (⟺), 43
`\longleftrightarrow` (⟷), 43

`\longmapsto` (⟼), 43
`\Longrightarrow` (⟹), 43
`\longrightarrow` (⟶), 43
`lot` (list of tables) file, 67, 175, 208
  editing, 67
  error in, 135
low ellipsis, 40, 189
lowercase letter, 12
lowering text, 107
LR box, 103–104, 107
LR mode, 36, 39
  in `tabbing` environment, 201
  space character in, 36
  `tabular` item processed in, 62
`lrbox` environment, 108, 218

macho TeX programmer, 92
macro parameter character error, 145
magenta, 132, 225
magnification of output, 233
`\magnification` (TeX command), 233
magnifying a picture, 118
Magritte, René, 131
mailing label, 86
main matter (of a book), 80
main memory size, 143
`\mainmatter`, 80
`\makebox`, 104, 217
  in `picture` environment, 120, 221
  use of `\width`, `\height`, `\depth`, and
      `\totalheight` in, 219
`\makefootline` (TeX command), 232
`\makeglossary`, 75, 212
  `glo` file produced by, 208
`\makeheadline` (TeX command), 232
makeidx package, 150
  defines `\printindex`, 211
*MakeIndex*, 74, 150–154
  `ind` file written by, 208
`\makeindex`, 74, 150, 212
  `idx` file produced by, 208
  misplaced, 136
`\makelabel`, 186
`\makelabels`, 86
`\maketitle`, 20, 34, 90, 181
  effect of `titlepage` option, 88
  not preceded by `\author`, 146

not preceded by \title, 138
mandatory argument, 166
**manual** bibliography entry type, 162
\mapsto (↦), 43
margin
  arrow in, 59
  changing in **tabbing** environment, 202
  determined by \textwidth and
    \textheight, 100
  of nested lists, 114
  prevailing, 201, 203
marginal note, 59–60, 200–201
  \hfill in, 59
  moved, 146
  overprinting of, 201
marginpar moved warning, 59, 146
\marginpar, 59–60, 200
  incorrectly placed, 146
  space around, 169
  too many on page, 139
\marginparpush, 201
\marginparsep, 182, 201
\marginparwidth, 182, 201
mark, footnote, 172
\markboth, 89, 90, 179
  moving argument of, 90, 168
  with **myheadings** page style, 179
\markright, 89, 90, 179
  moving argument of, 90, 168
  with **myheadings** page style, 179
**mastersthesis** bibliography entry type,
  162
math
  formula, *see* formula, math
  mode, 36, 39
    accent in, *see* accent
    bad command in, 137, 145
    blank line not allowed in, 142, 171
    defining commands for use in, 53
    environment, 187–189
    leaving, 36
    space character ignored in, 36, 50
  style, 52, 191
    display, 52, 188, 191
    for sub- and superscripts, 52, 191
    of **array** environment item, 191
    text, 52, 187, 191

symbol, 41–45
  variable-sized, 42, 52
**math** environment, 18, 39, 187
\mathbf, 51, 191
\mathcal, 42, 51, 191
mathematical, *see* math
\mathindent, 178, 188
\mathit, 51, 191
\mathrm, 51, 191
\mathsf, 51, 191
\mathtt, 51, 191
matrix, 45
\max (max), 44
  subscript of, 190
\mbox, 17, 33, 104, 171, 217
  bold subformula in, 52
  empty, 97
  for changing type size in formula, 116
  how it works, 36, 103
  in formula, 38, 39
  invisible term made with, 48
\mdseries, 37, 226
medium space, 51, 191
medium type series, 37, 226
\medskip, 216
\medskipamount, 216
memory size, 143
message
  LaTeX error, 136–140
  LaTeX warning, 145–147
    page number in, 135
  *MakeIndex* error, 154
  printing on terminal, 76
  TeX error, 140–145
  TeX warning, 30, 147
\mho (℧), 43
\mid (|), 43
\midinsert (TeX command), 232
millimeter (mm), 99, 215
\min (min), 44
  subscript of, 190
**minipage** environment, 104, 105, 218
  **footnote** counter for, 97
  footnote in, 172
  in p column of **array** or **tabular**
    environment, 205
  nested, 106

tabbing environment in, 106
    versus \parbox, 105
minus sign, 14
mirror image, 130
misc bibliography entry type, 162
misplaced
    #, 141, 145
    &, 141
    alignment tab, 141
    figure environment, 138
    \includeonly, 136
    \makeindex, 136
    \marginpar, 138
    \nofiles, 136
    table environment, 138
    \usepackage, 136
missing
    $ error, 142
    \\, 141
    { error, 142
    } error, 142
    @-expression, 138
    argument, 138, 142
    \begin{document} error, 138
    brace, 142
    control sequence error, 142
    \documentclass, 144
    \end{document}, 30
    \item, 138
    \label, 146
    number error, 142
    p-arg error, 138
    \usepackage, 144
misspelled command name, 31
    correcting, 141
Mittelbach, Frank, xv, 2
mm (millimeter), 99, 215
mod, 44, 190
mode, 36
    compatibility, 228
    horizontal, 36
    left-to-right, *see* LR mode
    LR, *see* LR mode
    math, *see* math
    paragraph, *see* paragraph
    picture, 120, 220–221
    vertical, 36

model, color, 132, 224
    undefined, 140
\models ($\models$), 43
modulo, 44, 190
month field (in bib file), 163
moved marginal note, 146
moving argument, 22, 33, 167
    fragile command in, 135
    of @-expression, 205
    of \bibitem, 72
    of \caption, 58
    of letter environment, 85
    of \markboth and \markright, 90
    of \typein and \typeout, 77, 212, 213
moving information around, 65–77,
        207–209
\mp ($\mp$), 42
mpfootnote counter, 97
\mu ($\mu$), 41
\multicolumn, 62, 206
    error in, 137, 138
    not allowed in eqnarray, 188
multilanguage document, 38
multiline formula, 47–49
multiple
    authors, 21
    captions, 59
    column item, 62, 206
    input files, 72–74
        finding error in, 134
    names in bib file field, 158
multiply-defined label warning, 146
\multiput, 127–128, 221
myheadings page style, 89, 179

\nabla ($\nabla$), 43
name
    command, *see* command
    in bib file field, 157–158
    of file, 12
named theorem, 57
names, multiple, in bib file field, 158
natural length, 100
\natural ($\natural$), 43
\nearrow ($\nearrow$), 43
\neg ($\neg$), 43
negative thin space, 51, 191

\neq (≠), 43
nested
  commands, 16
  lists, margins of, 114
  minipage environments, 106
  too deeply, 139, 144
nesting depth error, 139
\newboolean, 196
\newcommand, 53, 168, 192
  braces removed from, 92
  error in, 137, 141, 142
\newcounter, 99, 194
  error in, 137, 138
  in included file, 138
  optional argument of, 167
  scope of, 168
\newenvironment, 55–56, 114, 192
  error in, 137, 141, 144
\newlength, 101, 216
  error in, 137, 142
  scope of, 168
\newline, 95, 213
  bad use of, 147
  error in, 139
\newpage, 97, 215
  in two-column format, 97
\newsavebox, 107, 218
  error in, 137, 142
  scope of, 168
newt, 68
\newtheorem, 56, 193
  counter created by, 97
  cross-reference to environment defined
    by, 68
  environment defined by, 183
  error in, 137, 138, 144
  optional argument of, 167
  scope of, 168
next_tab_stop, 201
\ni (∋), 43
Nixon, Richard, 24
no counter error, 138
\nocite, 70, 210
\nofiles, 207
  misplaced, 136
  suppresses glo file, 212
  suppresses idx file, 212

used when editing toc file, 67
\noindent, 171, 183
\nolinebreak, 95, 213
  optional argument of, 167
  space around, 169
non-English symbol, 38–39
  in bib file, 158
nonexistent
  document class, 137
  environment, 137
  file, 141
  package, 137
\nonfrenchspacing, 171
nonmath symbol, 38–39
nonprinting character, 144
\nonumber, 48, 188
\nopagebreak, 96, 214
  optional argument of, 167
  space around, 169
\nopagenumbers (TEX command), 232
\normalbottom (TEX command), 232
\normalfont, 226
\normalmarginpar, 201
\normalsize, 115, 226
\not, 42
  in ifthen package expression, 196
notation, 53
  versus concepts, 31
note environment, 83
note field (in bib file), 163
note, marginal, 59–60, 200–201
\notin (∉), 43
notitlepage document-class option, 177
\nu (ν), 41
number
  alphabetic, 195
  arabic, 195
  assigning key to, 67
  formula, 88
    printed at left, 177
    suppressing in eqnarray, 48
  illegal parameter, 141
  missing, 142
  page, see page
  roman, 195
  wrong, 146
number field (in bib file), 163

number-range dash, 14, 170

numbered displayed formula, 39

numbering, 97–99, 194–195

  commands, \the..., 98

  page, 98

  sectional units, 176

  style, 98

  with \include, 74

  within sectional unit, 57

\numberline, 176

\nwarrow (↖), 43

O (letter oh), 12

\O (Ø), 39

\o (ø), 39

object, floating, 58

object, picture, 120, 221–223

octal character code, 116

\oddsidemargin, 181, 182

\odot (⊙), 42

\OE (Œ), 39

\oe (œ), 39

\oint (∮), 44

\oldstyle (TEX command), 233

\Omega (Ω), 41

\omega (ω), 41

omicron (o), 41

\ominus (⊖), 42

omitted argument, error caused by, 141

one (1), 12

one-column format, 181

one-sided printing, marginal notes in, 59

onecolumn document-class option, 177

\onecolumn, 88, 181

oneside document-class option, 177

only in preamble error, 136

\onlynotes, 84

\onlyslides, 83

open bibliography format, 71, 177

openany document-class option, 80, 177

openbib document-class option, 71, 177

\opening, 85

openright document-class option, 80, 177

\oplus (⊕), 42

option

  clash error, 138

document-class, 176

document-style (LaTeX 2.09), 228

  unknown, 140

optional argument, 20, 166

  [ or ] in, 25

  default, 166

  defining a command with, 192

  defining an environment with, 193

  of array environment, 46

  of \item, 25

  of \marginpar, 59

  of sectioning command, 174

  of \twocolumn too tall, 146

  square bracket mistaken for, 142

  square brackets enclosing, 20, 33, 166

optional arguments, command with two, 166

optional bibliography field, 160

\or, 196

organization field (in bib file), 163

origin, 118

\oslash (⊘), 42

\otimes (⊗), 42

outerpar mode, not in, 138

output

  line, space at beginning or end of, 102

  printing, 6, 208

  routine, Plain TEX, 232

  to terminal, 76–77, 212–213

<output> printed on terminal, 135

\output routine, 232

outputting error, 135

oval, 124–125, 223

  too small, 146

\oval, 124–125, 223

oval-part argument, 124

\overbrace, 49

overfull \hbox

  marked with draft option, 93

  message, 30, 93, 147

overfull \vbox message, 147

overlay environment, 82

\overline, 49, 190

overlining, 49, 190

overprinting

  of equation number, 188

  of marginal notes, 201

overriding item position in `tabular` environment, 63

p
   float specifier, 197
   in `array` or `tabular` argument, 205
`\P` (¶), 39, 173
p-arg missing error, 138
package, 2, 20, 178–179
   creating your own, 91
   loaded twice, 138
   nonexistent, 137
page
   blank, 97
      made by `\cleardoublepage`, 215
      with `titlepage` environment, 180
   body, 89, 179
      height of, 100, 214
   break, *see* break, page
   color of, 132
   first, right head for, 180
   float, 199
      made by `\clearpage`, 97
   foot, 89, 179
   head, 89, 179
      in `twoside` option, 90
      set by sectioning command, 90, 174
   input file, 13
   last, output by `\stop`, 136
   left-hand, 179, 196
   number, 98
      alphabetic, 180
      arabic, 89, 180
      cross-reference to, 68
      in warning message, 135
      indexing different styles, 154
      printed on terminal, 135
      roman, 89, 180
      style of, 180
   one-column, 181
   positioning relative to, 111
   range, in index, 152
   right-hand, 179, 196
      starting on, 97
   space at top or bottom, 102
   squeezing extra text on, 96, 214
   starting a new, 215

   style, 89–90, 179–182
      default, 89, 179
   title, *see* title
   too many `\index` or `\glossary` commands on, 143
   too many `\marginpar` commands on, 139
   two-column, 20, 88, 180
   width of text on, 100
page counter, 97, 98
   current value of, 196
   set by `\pagenumbering`, 180
`\pagebody` (TeX command), 232
`\pagebreak`, 96, 214
   in two-column format, 97
   optional argument of, 167
   space around, 169
`\pagecolor`, 132, 225
   scope of, 168
`\pagecontents` (TeX command), 232
`\pageinsert` (TeX command), 232
`\pageno` (TeX command), 232
`\pagenumbering`, 89, 180
   scope of, 168
`\pageref`, 68, 209
   ~ used with, 68
   undefined, 146
   used with `\isodd`, 196
   wrong number printed by, 146
pages field (in `bib` file), 163
pages, how TeX makes, 135
`\pagestyle`, 89, 179
   after `\chapter`, 89
   scope of, 89
paper size, 177
`\paperheight`, 182
`\paperwidth`, 182
`\par`, 171
paragraph, 13, 171
   bad end of, 142
   beginning of, 183
   displayed, 183–187
   end of, 13, 166, 171
   in picture, 104
   in table item, 104
   indentation, 171
      anomalous, 183

removing with \noindent, 183
width of, 99, 172
mode, 36
\\ in, 96
box made in, 103
box typeset in, 104
center environment in, 111
figure or table body processed in, 58
marginal note processed in, 59
new, 33
unit, 94
paragraph counter, 97
\paragraph, 21, 174
paragraph-making environment, 105,
183–187
paragraphs
\\ between, 139
space between, 100, 172
\parallel (∥), 43
parameter
length, 100
number error, 141
of command, 54, 192
of environment, 56, 193
style, 166
parbox, 104–106, 218
\caption in, 199
figure or table environment in, 138
in array or tabular column, 205
in tabbing environment, 203
list-making environment in, 105, 218
marginal note typeset in, 200
paragraph-making environment in,
105
\parindent set to zero in, 172
positioning with \raisebox, 105
tabbing environment in, 105
tabular environment in, 218
\parbox, 104, 218
versus minipage environment, 105
parenthesis, 12, 15
\parindent, 99, 100, 172
equals zero in parbox, 105
in list environment, 114
\parsep, 113, 185
\parskip, 100, 172
in letter document class, 100

in list environment, 114, 185
part counter, 97
part of input, processing, 31, 73–74
\part, 21, 22, 174
\partial (∂), 43
\partopsep, 113, 185
when added, 114
pasting, 58
pattern, repeated, 127–128
pc (pica), 215
period, 33
space after, 14–15
\perp (⊥), 43
phdthesis bibliography entry type, 162
\Phi (Φ), 41
\phi (φ), 41
\Pi (Π), 41
\pi (π), 41
pica (pc), 215
pict2e package, 118, 179, 221–223
picture, 118–129
command, argument of, 119
declaration, 223
in float, 58
line thickness in, 118
magnifying, 118
mode, 120, 220–221
object, 120, 221–223
paragraph in, 104
reducing, 118
picture environment, 118–129, 219–223
box made by, 103
example, 220
formatting formula with, 52
large, 143
making figures with, 58
reusing, 107
zero-width box in, 121
placement
of figures and tables, 59, 197
of marginal note, 59–60
of \protect, incorrect, 142
of tabular environment, 63
plain bibliography style, 70
plain page style, 89, 179
Plain TeX, 231–233
\plainoutput (TeX command), 232

\pm ($\pm$), 42
\pmod, 44, 190
poetry, 25–26, 34, 184
point (unit of length), 93, 99, 215
point, reference, 103, 221
pool size, 144
\poptabs, 203
    unmatched, 138
position, specifying by coordinate, 118
positioning
    argument, 45–46, 104–105, 121, 124
    of item label, 114
    of parbox with \raisebox, 105
    of text, 121, 217, 219
    relative to a fixed point on page, 111
    relative to a line of text, 110
    text in picture, 121
    vertical, *see* vertical
\pounds (£), 39, 173
\Pr (Pr), 44
    subscript of, 190
preamble, 19, 34, 170
    command definition in, 55
    error in, 138
    \hyphenation command in, 94
    \makeindex in, 74
    only in error, 136
    visual design commands in, 88
\prec ($\prec$), 43
\preceq ($\preceq$), 43
preloaded command, 91
preparing input file, 12
prepended file, 170
previewer, screen, 6
prime symbol, 18, 189
\prime ($\prime$), 43
primitive list-making environment, 112
principle, 56
\printindex, 150, 211
    ind file read by, 208
printing
    aux file information, 208
    counter values, 98
    landscape, 177
    LaTeX output, 6, 208
    one-column, 181
    one-sided, marginal notes in, 59

slides and notes separately, 83
two-column, 20, 180
two-sided, 19, 177
    increasing page height in, 214
    marginal notes in, 59
proceedings bibliography entry type, 162
\prod ($\prod$), 44
program, formatting a, 60
programming in LaTeX, 195
pronunciation of LaTeX and TeX, 5
proposition, 56
\propto ($\propto$), 43
\protect, 22, 33, 167
    in @-expression, 205
    in \caption argument, 58
    in \index argument, 153
    in \typeout argument, 212
    incorrect placement of, 142
    not before length command, 100, 168
    not in \addtocounter or \setcounter argument, 168
    not used with \value, 194
protecting a fragile command, 22
\providecommand, 168, 192
    error in, 141
\ps, 86
\Psi ($\Psi$), 41
\psi ($\psi$), 41
pt (point), 99, 215
publisher field (in bib file), 163
punctuation character, 12, 32
    in key, 68, 69
punctuation dash, 14, 170
punctuation, space after, 14–15, 170, 171
\pushtabs, 203
    unmatched, 138
\put, 120, 221
    sequence replaced by \multiput, 127
    space in argument, 129

\qbezier, 125–126, 221
    TeX space used by, 143
\qbeziermax, 126, 221
quarter oval, 124
question mark (?), *see* ?

quotation environment, 24, 34, 184
  as list, 112
quotation marks, 13–14, 33, 170
quotation, displayed, 23, 34
quote
  double, 13, 170
  left ('), 12, 13, 32, 33, 170
  right ('), 12, 13, 15, 32, 33
    in formula, 18
  single, 13, 170
quote environment, 23–24, 34, 184
  as list, 112
quotient symbol (/), 51
quoting character in index entry, 154

r (right)
  oval-part argument, 124, 223
  positioning argument, 45, 217, 221
    in array or tabular argument, 205
    of \makebox, 104, 121
    of \shortstack, 124
ragged right, 111
\raggedbottom, 88
  bad page break with, 96
\raggedleft, 112
  in p column, 205
\raggedright, 112
  in p column, 205
\raisebox, 107, 219
  positioning parbox with, 105
  use of optional arguments, 109
  use of \width, \height, \depth, and
    \totalheight in, 219
raising text, 107
\rangle ()), 47
\rceil (⌉), 47
\Re (ℜ), 43
reading auxiliary file, error when, 135,
  228
reclaiming saved box's space, 127
rectangular blob of ink, 106
recursive definition, 54
red, 132, 225
redefining a command, 55, 168, 192
  with \typein, 212
redefining an environment, 56, 192
reducing a picture, 118

\ref, 67, 209
  ˜ used with, 68
  similar to \cite, 71
  undefined, 146
  value, 209
    in enumerate environment, 184
    in list environment, 186
    in theorem-like environment, 193,
     194
    set by \refstepcounter, 195
  wrong number printed by, 146
reference point, 103, 221
  of picture object, 120
reference undefined warning, 146, 147
reference, circular, 243
\reflectbox, 130, 224
reflection, 130
\refstepcounter, 195
  \ref value set by, 209
  resets counter, 194
register, boolean, 196
Reid, Brian, 7
remark in citation, 210
\renewcommand, 55, 168, 192
  error in, 141, 142
\renewenvironment, 56, 192
  error in, 141
repeated logical structure, 53
repeated pattern in picture, 127–128
report document class, 19, 176
  appendix in, 175
  default page style, 89
  thebibliography environment in, 209
  titlepage option the default, 88
report cls file, 92
required bibliography field, 160
\resizebox, 129–130, 224
\resizebox*, 224
return key, 12
reusing a picture environment, 107
\reversemarginpar, 201
\rfloor (⌋), 47
rgb color model, 132, 225
\rhd (▷), 42
\rho (ρ), 41
right head for first page, 180
right margin, prevailing, 203

\right, 47, 190
right, flush, *see* flush right
right-hand page, 179
    starting on, 97
\Rightarrow ($\Rightarrow$), 43
\rightarrow ($\rightarrow$), 43
\rightharpoondown ($\rightharpoondown$), 43
\rightharpoonup ($\rightharpoonup$), 43
\rightleftharpoons ($\rightleftharpoons$), 43
\rightmargin, 113, 185
    in trivlist environment, 115
rigid length, 100
\rmfamily, 37, 226
robust command, 22, 167
roman page numbers, 89, 180
roman type family, 37, 226
    in math mode, 51, 191
    in slides document class, 81
\Roman, 98, 195
\roman, 98, 195
Romanian, 94
root file, 72
root, square, 40, 189
    space around, 51
\rotatebox, 130, 224
\rotatebox*, 224
rotation, 130
rounded corner, 124–125
rubber length, 100
    in \hspace or \vspace, 102
    in \lengthtest expression, 196
    infinitely stretchable, 102, 215
rule (mathematical), 56
rule box, 103, 106
\rule, 106, 219
    horizontal line drawn with, 106
    vertical line drawn with, 106
running head, *see* head
running LaTeX
    on part of document, 31, 73–74
    unattended, 30

s positioning argument, 217
\S ($\S$), 39, 173
Samarin, Alexander, 2
\samepage (LaTeX 2.09 command), 229
sample input, 2, 8

sample2e.tex file, 3, 8, 19, 28, 93
sans serif type family, 37, 226
    in math mode, 51, 191
save size, 144
\savebox, 107, 218, 223
    in picture environment, 120, 127
    use of \width, \height, \depth, and
        \totalheight in, 219
saving a box, 107–108, 127, 218
saving typing, 54
\sbox, 108, 218
\scalebox, 129–130, 224
scaling, 129
school field (in bib file), 163
scope of declaration, 27–28, 168
    in argument of user-defined command
        or environment, 55, 56, 192
    in array environment, 45
    in tabbing environment, 61, 203
    nested too deeply, 144
    within command argument, 193
screen output, *see* terminal
screen previewer, 6
script letter, 42
script math style, 52, 191
scriptscript math style, 52, 191
\scriptscriptstyle, 52, 191
\scriptsize, 115, 226
\scriptstyle, 52, 191
scroll, the, 135
\scshape, 37, 226
\searrow ($\searrow$), 43
\sec (sec), 44
secnumdepth counter, 174, 176
section counter, 97
section numbering, 176
section structure, 21
\section, 21, 174
sectional unit, 21
    cross-reference to, 67
    in different document classes, 21, 22
    level number of, 176
    numbering of, 174
    numbering within, 57
sectioning command, 21–22, 174–176
    \\ in, 169
    *-form of, 174

argument too long, 143

blank line not allowed in, 171

examples, 174

fragile command in, 135

in front and back matter of a book, 80

\label in argument, 209

moving argument of, 168

optional argument of, 174

page heading set by, 90, 174

table of contents entry, 22, 174, 209

"see" index entry, 152

\see, 153

sending a document, 77

sentence, 13

series field (in bib file), 163

series of type, *see* type

\setboolean, 196

\setcounter, 98, 194

error in, 138, 144

\protect not used in argument of, 168

scope of, 98, 168

\setlength, 101, 216

\setminus (\), 42

\settabs (TeX command), 232

\settime, 83

setting tab stops, 61

\settodepth, 101, 216

\settoheight, 101, 216

\settowidth, 101, 216

\sevenbf (TeX command), 233

\seveni (TeX command), 233

\sevensy (TeX command), 233

\sffamily, 37, 226

shape of type, 36

\sharp (♯), 13

\shortstack, 123–124, 222

\\ in argument, 169

showidx package, 75, 179

\Sigma (Σ), 41

\sigma (σ), 41

sign, minus, 14

\signature, 84

\sim (∼), 43

\simeq (≃), 43

simulating typed text, 63–64

\sin (sin), 44

single quote, 12, 13, 170

single-column format, 181

\sinh (sinh), 44

size

buffer, 143

hash, 143

main memory, 143

of paper, 177

of type, *see* type

pool, 144

save, 144

skinny, making things, 129

skip (TeX term), 100

slanted line, minimum size of, 123

slanted type shape, 37, 226

slash through symbol, 42

slide environment, 81

slides, 80–84, 228

slides document class, 80–84, 176

SliTeX, 228

slope of line in picture, 122

\sloppy, 94, 214

causes underfull \hbox message, 147

sloppypar environment, 94, 214

causes underfull \hbox message, 147

\slshape, 37, 226

small caps type shape, 37, 226

\small, 115, 226

small2e.tex file, 2

\smallskip, 216

\smallskipamount, 216

\smile (⌣), 43

source list, 69, 70, 209

source, bibliographic, 69

source2e.tex file, 91

space, 216, 217

above displayed formula, 107, 188, 189

after punctuation, 14–15, 170, 171

after tabbing command, 61

around + and −, 48

around \hspace command, 101

around integral sign, 51

around square root, 51

at beginning or end of output line, 102

at top or bottom of page, 102

avoiding unwanted, 98, 109

below displayed formula, 107, 189

between paragraphs, 100, 172

character, 13
   at end of line, 19
   ignored in math mode, 36
   in command definition, 54
   in formula, 18
   in LR mode, 36
   in \put argument, 129
   in \typeout or \typein argument, 212
   multiple, 13, 154
   not allowed after \verb command, 64
   not allowed in \end{verbatim}, 64
ending command name with, 16
ending line without adding, 33
horizontal, *see* horizontal space
ignored after command name, 16
in array, 45
in formula, 50–51
intercolumn, *see* intercolumn space
interrow, *see* interrow space
interword, *see* interword space
medium, 51, 191
negative thin, 51, 191
thick, 51, 191
thin, 14, 33, 51, 170, 191
vertical, *see* vertical space
\space, 212
space-filling dots, 102
space-filling horizontal line, 102
spacing, 101–103
   command, 170
   double, 172
\spadesuit (♠), 43
special character, 12, 32, 171
   in \index argument, 75, 153
   in verbatim environment, 64
   used incorrectly, 31
special font, 116
special symbol, 38–39, 226
\sqcap (⊓), 42
\sqcup (⊔), 42
\sqrt (√ ), 40, 51, 189
\sqsubset (⊏), 43
\sqsubseteq (⊑), 43
\sqsupset (⊐), 43
\sqsupseteq (⊒), 43

square bracket, 12
   enclosing optional argument, 20, 33, 166
   mistaken for optional argument, 142
square root, 40, 189
   space around, 51
\ss (ß), 39
stack, 123–124
stacking symbols, 50
\stackrel, 50, 191
   making symbol with, 42
\star (⋆), 42
\stepcounter, 195
   resets counter, 194
\stop, 30
   last page produced by, 136
stopping LaTeX, 30, 136
storage bin, 107, 127
\stretch, 215
stretchable length, *see* rubber length
structure
   logical, 6, 88
   of document, 170
   section, 21
   theorem-like, 56–57
strut, 106
   example of use, 110
   in array and tabular environments, 169
stupidity, in Unix, 32
sty (package) file, 91, 166
   @ regarded as letter in, 91
   missing, 137
style
   bibliography, 70–71
   customizing, 91–93
   math, *see* math
   numbering, 98
   page, *see* page
   parameter, 166
   type, *see* type
subentry, index, 75
\subitem, 75, 211
subparagraph counter, 97
\subparagraph, 21, 174
subpicture, 128

subscript, 18, 33, 40, 189
  double, error, 140
  math style for, 52, 191
  of log-like function, 190
  size of type in, 52, 116
subsection counter, 97
\subsection, 21, 174
\subset ($\subset$), 43
\subseteq ($\subseteq$), 43
substituted type style, 37
subsubentry, index, 75
\subsubitem, 75, 211
subsubsection counter, 97
\subsubsection, 21, 174
\succ ($\succ$), 43
\succeq ($\succeq$), 43
\sum ($\sum$), 44
sundial, 94
\sup (sup), 44
  subscript of, 190
superscript, 18, 33, 40, 189
  double, error, 140
  math style for, 52, 191
  size of type in, 52, 116
support, acknowledgment of, 181
\suppressfloats, 199
  optional argument of, 167
\supset ($\supset$), 43
\supseteq ($\supseteq$), 43
\surd ($\surd$), 43
\swarrow ($\swarrow$), 43
symbol
  bar over, 49
  bold, 51
  footnote, 105
    too many, 137
  making with array environment, 42
  making with \stackrel, 42
  math, 41–45
  non-English, 38–39
    in bib file, 158
  nonmath, 38–39
  not in typewriter style, 38
  not provided by LaTeX, 116
  slash through, 42
  special, 38–39, 226
  stacking, 50

variable-sized, 42, 52
\symbol, 116, 226

t (top)
  float specifier, 197
  oval-part argument, 124, 223
  positioning argument, 46, 105, 121,
    218, 222
\t ($\hat{}$ accent), 38
tab overflow error, 139
tab stop, 61, 201
  too many, 139
  undefined, 140
tab, alignment, error, 141
\tabalign (TeX command), 232
tabbing command
  Plain TeX, 232
  space after, 61
tabbing environment, 60–62, 201–203
  \\ in, 169
  as displayed paragraph, 183
  example, 202
  in minipage environment, 106, 218
  in parbox, 105
  large, 143
  redefinition of commands in, 203
  scope of declaration in, 61
  used instead of verbatim, 64
  versus tabular, 60
\tabbingsep, 203
\tabcolsep, 207
table, 58–59, 197–200
  centering, 112
  in two-column format, 197
  item, paragraph in, 101
  made with tabular environment, 58
  of contents, 66–67, 175–176
    adding an entry, 175
    adding commands to, 67, 176
    depth, 176
    entry made by sectioning
      command, 22, 174
    error in, 135
    example, 174
    generated from toc file, 209
  placement of, see float
  too tall, 145

table counter, 97

table environment, 58–59, 197
  in parbox, 138
  misplaced, 138
  parbox made by, 104
  space around, 169
  too many, 139

table* environment, 197

\tableofcontents, 66, 175–176
  error when processing, 143
  toc file read by, 209

tables, list of, 67, 175–176

\tabs (TEX command), 232

\tabsdone (TEX command), 232

\tabset (TEX command), 232

tabular environment, 62–63, 204–207
  \\ in, 169
  box made by, 103
  error in, 137, 138, 141, 145
  example, 204
  extra space around, 205
  footnoting item of, 105
  illegal character in argument, 137
  in parbox, 218
  interrow space in, 169
  large, 143
  making tables with, 58
  strut in, 169
  versus array, 46, 60
  versus tabbing, 60

tabular* environment, 204–207

\tan (tan), 44

\tanh (tanh), 44

\tau (τ), 41

techreport bibliography entry type, 162

ten-point type, 19, 115

\teni (TEX command), 233

term, invisible, 48

terminal, 28
  defining command from, 76
  input, 76–77, 212–213
  message, spaces in, 212
  output, 76–77, 212–213
    written on log file, 208
  printing command on, 212

TEX, 5, 231–233
  distinguished from LATEX, 5

error message, 140–145
error versus LATEX error, 29
logo, 5, 15, 33, 171
pronunciation of, 5
warning message, 147

\TeX, 15, 33, 171

text
  editor, 12, 32
  emphasized, 16, 171
  file, 12, 144
  invisible, 82, 97
  math style, 52, 187
  positioning of, 107, 121
  typed, simulating, 63–64

text-generating command, 15

\textbf, 37, 226

\textcolor, 131, 225
  used for invisible text in slide, 82

\textfloatsep, 200

\textfraction, 200

\textheight, 100, 182

\textit, 37, 226

\textmd, 37, 226

\textnormal, 226

\textrm, 37, 226

\textsc, 37, 226

\textsf, 37, 226

\textsl, 37, 226

\textstyle, 52, 191
  used with \stackrel, 50

\texttt, 37, 226

\textup, 37, 226

\textwidth, 100, 171, 182

\thanks, 181
  moving argument of, 168

\the... numbering commands, 98, 195

thebibliography environment, 71–72, 209
  as list, 112
  missing argument in, 138

theindex environment, 75–76, 211
  \item in, 75

theorem, 56
  named, 57

theorem-like environment, 56–57, 193–194
  as displayed paragraph, 183

as list, 112
counter for, 97, 193
cross-reference to, 68
theorem-like structure, 56–57
\thepage redefined by \pagenumbering, 180
\Theta (Θ), 41
\theta (θ), 41
thick space, 51, 191
\thicklines, 119, 223
thickness, *see* width
thin space, 14, 33, 51, 170, 191
thin, making things, 129
\thinlines, 118, 223
\thispagestyle, 89–90, 179
scope of, 168
tick marks, 184
tilde (˜), 12, 17, 32
\tilde (˜ math accent), 50
time, printing on notes, 83
\times (×), 42
\tiny, 115, 226
title, 20–21
acknowledgment of support in, 181
author's address in, 181
date in, 20
example, 183
in bib file, 158
page, 20–21, 88, 90, 177, 181–183
title field (in bib file), 163
\title, 20, 34, 181
\\ in, 169
not given error, 138
titlepage document-class option, 88, 90, 177
titlepage environment, 90, 183
making blank page with, 180
toc (table of contents) file, 66, 67, 175, 209
editing, 67
error in, 135
tocdepth counter, 176
\today, 15, 33, 171
in title page, 90
redefining in letters, 86
\top (⊤), 43
\topfraction, 199

\topins (TEX command), 232
\topinsert (TEX command), 232
\topmargin, 182
topnumber counter, 199
\topsep, 113, 185
in fleqn option, 188, 189
\topskip, 181
\totalheight, 219
totalnumber counter, 200
Trahison des Images, La, 131
transformation, geometric, 129
\triangle (△), 43
\triangleleft (◁), 42
\triangleright (▷), 42
trivlist environment, 112, 115, 186
Truman, Harry, 24
\ttfamily, 37, 226
12pt document-class option, 19
twelve-point type, 19, 115
two-column format, 20, 88, 180
\cleardoublepage in, 97
\clearpage in, 97
figures and tables in, 197
marginal notes in, 59
\newpage in, 97
\pagebreak in, 97
two-sided printing, 19, 177
increasing page height in, 214
marginal notes in, 59
page heading in, 89
twocolumn document-class option, 20, 177
marginal notes in, 59
\twocolumn, 88, 180
optional argument of, 167
optional argument too tall, 146
twoside document-class option, 19, 177
default in book class, 80
evens page bottoms, 88
marginal notes in, 59
page heading in, 90
type
bibliography entry, 156, 160–162
eleven-point, 19, 115
family, 36
roman, 37, 51, 191, 226
sans serif, 37, 51, 191, 226

typewriter, 37, 51, 191, 226
font, *see* font
series, 36
  boldface, 37, 51, 191, 226
  medium, 37, 226
shape, 36
  italic, 37, 51, 191, 226
  slanted, 37, 226
  small caps, 37, 226
  upright, 37, 226
size, 226
  changing, 115–116
  default, 115
  in footnote, 116
  of sub- and superscripts, 52, 116
style, 36–37, 225–226
  calligraphic, 51, 191
  in math mode, 51–52, 191
  substituted, 37
  unavailable, 37, 116
ten-point, 19, 115
twelve-point, 19, 115
type field (in bib file), 164
typed text, simulating, 63–64
\typein, 76, 212
  moving argument of, 77, 168
  of \includeonly, 74
\typeout, 76, 212
  moving argument of, 77, 168
typesetter, 6
typewriter type family, 37, 226
  in math mode, 51, 191
  no accents or symbols in, 38
typewriter, simulating, 63–64
typing, saving, 54
typographic
  design, 91
  designer, 5
  error, 91

\u (˘ accent), 38
unary + and −, 48
unavailable type style, 37, 116
unbalanced braces, error caused by, 136
\unboldmath, 191
undefined
  citation, 145, 147

color, 140
color model, 140
control sequence error, 144
environment error, 137
\pageref, 146
\ref, 146
reference, 146, 147
tab position, 140
\underbrace, 49
underfull \hbox message, 95, 147
  caused by \\ and \newline, 213
  caused by \linebreak, 147, 213
  caused by \sloppy, 147, 214
  caused by sloppypar, 147
underfull \vbox message, 147
  caused by \pagebreak, 214
\underline, 49, 190
underlining, 49, 190
unit
  length, 118
  of length, 215
  of measure, illegal, 141
  paragraph, 94
  sectional, *see* sectional unit
\unitlength, 118, 219
  for subpictures, 129
Unix, e-mail in, 32
Unix, stupidity in, 32
unknown graphics extension, 140
unknown option, 140
\unlhd (⊴), 42
unmatched
  $ (dollar sign), 141
  }, 141
  \begin, 136
  brace, 31
  \end, 136
  math mode delimiter, 141
  \poptabs, 138
  \pushtabs, 138
unpublished bibliography entry type,
    162
\unrhd (⊵), 42
unsrt bibliography style, 70
\Uparrow (⇑), 43, 47
\uparrow (↑), 43, 47
\Updownarrow (⇕), 43, 47

\updownarrow (↕), 43, 47
\uplus (⊎), 42
uppercase letter, 12
upright type shape, 37, 226
\upshape, 37, 226
\Upsilon (Υ), 41
\upsilon (υ), 41
use doesn't match definition error, 145
\usebox, 107, 218
\usecounter, 114, 186
\usepackage, 20, 34, 170, 178–179
    misplaced, 136
    missing, 144
    option obtained from \documentclass
        command, 178
    redundant, 138
user-defined command or environment,
        scope in argument of, 55, 56, 192

\v (˘ accent), 38
value of counter, 194
\value, 194
    in ifthen package expression, 195
van Leunen, Mary-Claire, 8
\varepsilon (ε), 41
variable-sized math symbol, 42, 52
variant Greek letters, 41
\varphi (φ), 41
\varpi (ϖ), 41
\varrho (ϱ), 41
\varsigma (ς), 41
\vartheta (ϑ), 41
\vbox, overfull, 147
\vbox, underfull, 147, 214
\vdash (⊢), 43
\vdots (⋮), 41, 189
\vec (⃗math accent), 50
\vector, 123, 222
    error in, 136
\vee (∨), 42
\verb, 64, 187
    in argument of a command, 140
    text ended by end of line, 140
\verb*, 64, 187
verbatim environment, 63–64, 186
verbatim* environment, 64, 186

verse environment, 25–26, 34, 184
    \\ in, 169
    as list, 112
version, of LATEX, 2, 228–229
\Vert (‖), 43, 47
\vert (|), 47
vertical
    alignment, 46, 60–63, 201–207
    ellipsis, 40, 189
    line
        drawn with \rule, 106
        in tabular environment, 62
    mode, 36
    positioning
        of array environment, 46
        of array item, 46
        of text, 107, 121, 219
    space, 102
        above displayed formula, 188, 189,
            218
        adding, 106, 216
        at top or bottom of page, 102
        below displayed formula, 183, 189
        in math formula, 106
\vfill, 102
\vfootnote (TEX command), 232
visual design, 7, 88
    of marginal notes, 60
visual formatting, 64
    for slides, 81
    of formula, 49, 52
    with boxes, 108–111
visual property, 37
\vline, 206
volume field (in bib file), 164
\vspace, 102, 216
    in figure, 58
    removing space with, 184
    rubber length in, 102
    space around, 169
    using strut instead, 106
\vspace*, 102, 216

warning message, 30
    LATEX, 145–147
    TEX, 147
\wedge (∧), 42

\whiledo, 197
white, 132, 225
wide math accent, 49
\widehat (⌢ math accent), 49, 190
\widetilde (⌢ math accent), 49, 190
width
    box with specified, 104
    of a box, 103
    of line, 91, 171
        for \fbox and \framebox, 219
        in array or tabular environment,
            207
        in picture, 118, 223
    of paragraph indentation, 99
    of text on page, 100, 171
\width, 219
Wiles, Andrew, 57
window, 28
word, 13
    index, 150
\wp (℘), 43
\wr (≀), 42
writing, 8
wrong number printed by \cite,
        \pageref, and \ref, 146
WYSIWYG, 7

\Xi (Ξ), 41
\xi (ξ), 41

year field (in bib file), 164
yellow, 132, 225

zero (0), 12
zero length, 99
zero-length arrow, 123
zero-width box, 121
\zeta (ζ), 41